SEMIOTICS AND THE

WITH SPECIAL REFERENCE TO THE
SEMIOTICS OF CHARLES S. PEIRCE

APPROACHES TO TRANSLATION STUDIES
Founded by James S Holmes

Edited by Raymond van den Broeck
Kitty M. van Leuven-Zwart

Volume 12

SEMIOTICS AND THE PROBLEM OF TRANSLATION

WITH SPECIAL REFERENCE TO THE SEMIOTICS OF CHARLES S. PEIRCE

Dinda L. Gorlée

Rodopi

Amsterdam - Atlanta, GA 1994

ISBN: 90-5183-642-2 (CIP)

Printed in The Netherlands

00. CONTENTS

01. ACKNOWLEDGMENTS

"Truth, crushed to earth, shall rise again"
(*MS*:L75D:234,1902)

This is originally my doctoral thesis at the University of Amsterdam (Gorlée 1993), now revised and expanded into this book. Thanks are due to Professors Kitty M. van Leuven-Zwart and Raymond van den Broeck, for helpful comments and identification of faults in the text of this treatise.

I wish to express my profound indebtedness to Distinguished Professor Thomas A. Sebeok, now Emeritus, without whose encouragement and keen interest in my work I would not have been able to complete this project. Since he first invited me to be appointed as Research Associate at the Research Center for Language and Semiotic Studies, Indiana University at Bloomington, in 1988, I have during yearly stays at Indiana University immensely benefited from our stimulating conversations as well as from the vast semiotic resources Indiana University has to offer. These resources include not only the richest semiotic library worldwide, but also Charles Sanders Peirce's voluminous unpublished writings, at the Indianapolis-based Peirce Edition Project, where I have had the privilege to be Visiting Scholar in 1988 and subsequent years. I thank its Director, Professor Christian J. W. Kloesel, and its scholars, particularly Emeritus Professor Max H. Fisch and Professor Nathan Houser, for their hospitality and helpfulness.

I have also profited from the professional generosity of Professor Claus Huitfeldt, Director of the Wittgenstein Archives at the University of Bergen, where I have served as an Associate Professor.

Having access to the posthumous unpublished writings of both Peirce and Wittgenstein, whose philosophical thought is highlighted in this study, has put me in a particularly felicitous position insofar as the primary scholarly material for this study is concerned.

I have received considerable moral support, and so much more, from my friends, a geographically scattered group of scholars, to whom -- as Peirce reminded us in his essay on "Evolutionary Love" -- "we live near, not locally perhaps but in life and feeling" (*CP*:6.288). I must thank especially (in alphabetical order) Professors Maria Lucia Santaella Braga, Donald J. Cunningham, Jørgen Dines Johansen, Werner Koller, Svend Erik Larsen, Floyd Merrell, Ursula Niklas, Alois Pichler, Roland Posner, José Romera Castillo, Jean Umiker Sebeok, and Sven Storelv. My thanks to all.

My thanks to the University of Groningen, and especially to Mr. Tjalling de Vries, for helping me computer edit the manuscript of this book.

02. INTRODUCTION

"A symbol, once in being, spreads among the peoples" (*CP*:2.302,c.1895)

Introductory remarks

The goal of this study is modest and ambitious at the same time. It is a voyage into uncharted waters, in which I seek to anchor some temporary intellectual buoys. In Charles Sanders Peirce's spirit, here is where I present the trophies of my voyage of discovery to the community of scholars. The area covered is vast, including not only the disciplines which, as the title of this study suggests, have served as my beacons --translation theory, Peirce's philosophy of signs, and their interrelations--, but also selected aspects of general linguistics, logic, and language philosophy, with side excursions into game theory, geometry, law, and the history of thought.

This study is primarily concerned with problems within semiotics, translation theory, and the interface between these two disciplines, or better areas of research. It treats of a critical analysis of the concept of translation in, particularly, Peirce's doctrine of signs, and the semiotic implications of the process of translation. On the one hand it is assumed here that Peirce's semiotic theory and method is a mode of clarifying the phenomena commonly but broadly referred to as translation. Yet, conversely, understanding of the various aspects of translation also elucidates Peirce's sometimes dense "semeiotic". Therefore I hope that by showing how each acts in turn as interpretant for the other, a discussion of translation from a semiotic perspective will contribute to Peirce scholarship as well as throwing new, Peircean light upon central problems in translation theory.

In order to corroborate and diversify my argument I have drawn a series of analogies with, in particular, Ludwig Wittgenstein's philosophy of language,

Walter Benjamin's theory of language and linguistic fragmentation, and game theory. These, together with Roman Jakobson's ubiquitous three kinds of translation, are by no means arbitrary exemplifications of how the process of translation may be described and analyzed as strategic habit-taking. In short, this study affirms that translation is and may be logically assimilated to semiosis, or sign activity, in Peirce's sense of this concept.

The essays presented here are intellectual experiments, abstract thought-signs. Intended as exercises in pure translation theory, they do not pretend to solve practical problems. However, this does not mean they are experiments of interesting, even suggestive, but total impracticality. Out of this study it should be possible to extract a model that would operationalize semiotic methodology in Peirce's truly general sense, and thus be capable of providing a framework for linking diverse systems of inquiry into new unified relations. In response to those critics whose demand for practical "relevance" rejects all theoretical constructs as being of interest only to a narrow inner circle of scholars, as having no direct connection to lived experience, I would like to argue that, at least in Peirce's philosophy of signs, theory and practice are never mutually exclusive, but that the difference between them is merely a difference in relative hierarchy (Niklas 1988). For Peirce, the theoretical presupposes the practical in the same way as culture presupposes, and builds upon, nature. Both must be thought of as different stages or "forms" of thought, yet placed on a continuum with beginning nor end. Holmes, after distinguishing between descriptive, theoretical, and applied translation studies, likewise emphasized that the relation between them is not unidirectional but dialectical,

> with each of the three branches supplying materials for the other two, and making use of the findings which they in turn provide it. Translation theory, for instance, cannot do without the solid, specific data yielded by research in the descriptive and applied translation studies, while on the other hand one cannot even begin to work in one of the other two fields without having at least an intuitive theoretical hypothesis as one's starting point. (Holmes 1988:78)

These ideas lead the charge into new territory which I present here. As Holmes remarked elsewhere (albeit apropos of verse translation): "The territory remains, though it must not remain *terra incognita*" (Holmes 1988:64).

Semiotics and translation studies: generalities

Semiotics and translation theory have until recently virtually ignored each other's existence, led by the *idée fixe* that their ontological differences and the divergence of their respective researches would forbid a productive rapprochement, let alone the possibility of a systematic joint exploration of problems which translation studies and semiotics have in common. This neglect[1] is somewhat surprising because both translation studies and semiotic studies address, albeit from different methodological vantage-points, aspects of communication, and both are concerned with the use, interpretation, and manipulation of messages or texts, --that is of signs.

Semiotics studies the production, transmission, exchange, and interpretation of messages consisting in one or more signs. Its general theoretical branch has developed a sophisticated conceptual and terminological apparatus serving again as methodological tools to analyze and describe, in applied semiotics, any discrete phenomenon (visual, auditory, plastic, etc.) in the physical and mental world which is considered to be a sign. In translation, the situation is rather the reverse and translation practice has preceded and dominated translation theory. Indeed, it would seem that the empirical nature of the translational discipline has long discouraged the harmonious evolvement of a tradition of serious theoretical approaches to the phenomenon of translation.

Whereas general semiotics has been successful in developing a coherent set of concepts of its own, more often than not created *ex novo*, translation studies is marked by an eclectic attitude, displaying a syncretism of "borrowed" methods, paradigms, and models, often with a linguistic (sociolinguistic, psycholinguistic, ethnolinguistic, etc.) bias. This language-based transdisciplinarity, in addition to contributions from such disciplines as information theory and mathematics, has unfortunately not (yet) been able to put forth one unified theory of translation, or even to provide consistent answers to the fundamental questions translation-theoreticians have time and again asked themselves --such as questions concerning translatability, equivalence, and fidelity vs. infidelity.

In this study it will be extensively argued that this situation can be remedied if translation, both as a process and as a product of this process, is seen as a phenomenon which, at least on an abstract level, may be dealt with more fruitfully in the framework of a general theory of signs than with research methods --semiotic or otherwise-- which are language-based. Since the latter include sign theory in the French-European tradition --modern structuralism and poststructuralism under its different names and guises-- , my project will concentrate upon semiotics in the American tradition --that is, following the philosophical thought of Charles Sanders Peirce. As opposed to Saussure's

1 The recent monumental and momentous *Handbook of Semiotics* (Nöth 1990) testifies to this relative lack of interest from the side of semiotics. As shall be shown later in this Chapter, only a handful of titles from the enormous body of writings on translation is concerned with semiotics.

language-orientedness, which subordinates the nonverbal to the verbal, Peirce gave equal epistemological status to verbal and nonverbal signs and sign systems. Unless used metaphorically, the former, logocentric approach will be a useful method to deal with problems in translation in the narrow sense only --referring, that is, to natural language. The latter, general approach --Peirce's "method of methods" (*CP*:7.59,1882)-- will, however, enable translation theory to address adequately Jakobson's all *three* types of translation --intralingual, interlingual, and intersemiotic translation[2]-- , thereby stretching its domain beyond the exclusively linguistic.

In this study I intend to show that the old controversies on translation can be overcome if, following Peirce, linguistics is (re)defined semiotically. At a time when "translation" meant primarily translation of the Bible and/or literary translation (the latter with specific reference to the Latin and Greek classical authors), what was emphasized in the received view on translation were the virtues and shortcomings of so-called "literal" translation vs. those of "free" translation, as well as the equivalence between original and translation. Framed in a normative attitude, this discussion was destined to lead straight to a paradoxical conclusion, namely that translation in the strict sense is an impossibility. Not until the advent of modern linguistics (with Chomsky and the Massachusetts Institute of Technology) would the normative view start to yield to a descriptive approach permitting the old topics to be discussed in a new and more productive framework[3], thereby bypassing the "untranslatability" claim. Indeed, under the impulse of the generative-transformational approach to language, translation definitively lost its merely intuititive, impressionistic, and experiential character. The turning-point in this development away from behaviorism and toward a rationalization and technicalization of linguistic studies, has been the introduction, for better or worse, of automatic translation (or machine translation), which considers all translational phenomena as susceptible of being logically described, schematized, and formalized. Despite the strong stimuli which *Übersetzungswissenschaft* received from modern linguistics, no definitive breakthrough has as yet been achieved.

Linguistic semiotics is at this time still mainly based upon Saussure and, to some degree, Morris, the latter the behaviorist psychologist who was again inspired by Peirce's triadic thought. Peirce's impact on the work of semiotic linguists has mostly remained indirect. Point of departure of semiotic linguistics

---

2 See Jakobson 1959:233;1971b:261, where the three kinds of translation are still rather narrowly defined by Jakobson. Jakobson's contribution to translation studies will be the subject of Chapter 8.

3 See Koller 1992:179ff.

is the Saussure-based claim that all language is a system, a coherent semiotic structure, and that, consequently, all texts can be described and analyzed semiotically. Whereas for Saussure, the founder of linguistic semiology (or structuralism, as it is more commonly called), the basic linguistic unit was still the word, structuralist analysis after him takes as its object the text considered as a structural and significant whole. Following and expanding Saussurean thought, textual analyses have been developed at three hierarchically organized levels: sentential, trans-sentential, and textual. Methodologically, the analyses have focused on the three aspects of the sign introduced by Morris, who distinguished between the syntactic, semantic, and pragmatic aspects of a semiotic sign. The relation between signs themselves is syntactic; the relation between signs and their *denotata* is semantic; and the relation between signs and sign users is pragmatic[4].

While textual studies are concerned with texts in general[5] (in accordance with the Chomskyan notion of "competence", which corresponds *grosso modo* to Saussurean "*langue*"), translation studies addresses concrete texts (that is, "performance" or "*parole*") and their translation(s). Text linguistics considers the text as the product of a three-dimensional (syntactic, semantic, pragmatic) interactive process. This discipline is important for translation studies because, in pointed contrast to Saussurean linguistics, it deals with the mechanisms determining the genesis, components, internal structure, and communicative functioning of individual texts. Translation studies has greatly benefited from the work done by text-linguists upon text typology and upon "text grammar": the latter defines textual cohesion again in terms of Morris's three elements.

For Nida,

> Language consists of more than the meanings of the symbols and the combination of symbols; it is essentially a code in operation, or, in other words, a code functioning for a specific purpose or purposes. Thus we must analyze the transmission of a message

---

4 See Morris 1971:21-27,301-303. For the sake of clarity it must be noted here that behaviorism rejected mentalist accounts of meaning (such as Saussure's definition of the signified as a concept) as unscientific because concepts are unobservable, and hence unverifiable, entities. After the "behaviorist period" in American linguistics was declared closed by Chomsky in 1959 (see Harris 1987:89 and n.23), the study of meaning was reinstated, albeit as a purely mechanical problem, which was dealt with in as mechanistic a fashion as had been the behavioristic approach. However, modern linguistics, with developments such as cognitive semantics, has resumed the study of meaning in a mentalistic fashion (Nöth 1990:99). Jakobson (1977:1029) pointed out that "many fruitless discussions about mentalism and anti-mentalism would be avoided if one approached the notion of meaning in terms of translation", --as Peirce would have it. See also Chapter 8.

5 See, for instance, van Dijk 1978.

> in terms of a dynamic dimension. This dimension is especially important for translation, since the production of equivalent messages is a process, not merely of matching parts of utterances, but also of reproducing the total dynamic character of the communication. Without both elements the results can scarcely be regarded, in any realistic sense, as equivalent. (Nida 1964:120)

In semiotic text analysis, text linguistics aims to make this complex structure transparent and to make its internal and external "dynamic character" visible. The schematic descriptions provide "objective" criteria which translation studies may again "translate" into translational strategies. Source text and target text are semiotically equivalent only if and when their respective analyses are largely congruent with one another and, their bilinguality notwithstanding, only permit one semiosis. Intertext between two texts, the analysis is thus the *tertium comparationis* which is both the a priori blueprint for the translation and the testing clue, *a posteriori*, of the equivalence achieved between original and translated text, on all levels. Yet no justice has so far been done to the fact that Nida's approach to translation (such as manifested in the passage quoted above) points away from Saussure's static concept of text and toward Peirce; that Nida's "dynamic dimension" in which "equivalent messages" are produced refers to translation as a series of events approaching Peirce's continuous process through which a sign stands in a certain dynamic relation to the sign(s) preceding it and the sign(s) following it, thereby forming a system of signs. Translation has as yet not received such a study based upon Peircean semiotics. To fill this gap (or, at least, to embark upon this project) will be the main objective of this study.

Mention of developments within one, important subdiscipline of translation studies, literary translation studies, is in order here, because this field has certainly been unfolding beyond the limitations of a strictly normative approach, which has been the primary concern of linguistically-oriented *Übersetzungswissenschaft* and one important reason of the stagnation of the entire discipline. In more recent years Holmes[6] has been the initiator of a new approach, which deemphasizes the one-sided (that is, source-oriented) study of literary translation as it has traditionally been the rule. Since the process of translation itself occurs in a "black box", about which very little is known, its study must remain empirical. Taking as its object of investigation the source-sign and contrasting it with the translated sign, the traditional approach is largely confined to a restrictive and prescriptive program of what the translator must do (and must not do) in order to solve translational problems. Following

6 See his lucid and highly informative essay (written in 1972) on "The name and nature of translation studies" (Holmes 1988:67-80).

Holmes's timely remarks, the emphasis is now increasingly away from the (still mysterious) translation process and upon its product, which is readily available to inspection, both as an actual object in itself and as an artifact functioning within the target culture (or, since we are dealing here with literary translation, within its literary system).

The "new paradigm" for the study of literary translation has been described by one of its scholars, thus:

> . . . a view of literature as a complex and dynamic system; a conviction that there should be a continual interplay between theoretical models and practical case studies; an approach to literary translation which is descriptive, target-oriented, functional and systemic; and an interest in the norms and constraints that govern the production and reception of translations, in the relation between translation and other types of text processing, and in the place and role of translations both within a given literature and in the interaction between literatures. (Hermans 1985a:10-11)

From this short characterization it may already be clear that modern literary translation displays a Jakobsonian affinity with Eastern European semiotic (and pre-semiotic) approaches to the (literary) sign; and that the (traditional) idea of translational norms has not been rejected, but appears in a new, nonprescriptive form. Both tendencies have been developed with particular argumentational force in the work of Toury, the Israeli literary translation scholar whose work is placed within the above-mentioned semiotic tradition.

For Toury,

> . . . although the process of translating obviously precedes its product (and the cross-systemic transference --the intra-systemic employment of the transferred for communicative purposes) *in time*, it turns out that from the *semiotic* point of view, the (potential) product, and especially its (prospective) position and functions in the target system, should be assigned precedence over the process. (Toury 1986:1121)

Toury's work within a semiotically-inspired translation theory will also be discussed in the next section. Special mention must be made here of Toury's redefinition of translational norms. On Toury's (1978:89) view, "translation, especially literary translation, always involves an encounter, if not a confrontation, between two sets of norms", which correspond to the two codes involved. For Toury, norms also determine one of the most controversial concepts in translation, translation equivalence, defined by Toury as "some combination of, or compromise between, the two basic types of constraints which draw from the incompatible poles of the target system and the source text and system: acceptability and adequacy, respectively" (Toury 1986:1123). Toury places norms, as intersubjective constraints, halfway between fully subjective idiosyncrasies and relatively absolute rules. He has developed (Toury 1978) a structuration of norms in literary translation, in which each translator in each case draws up a hierarchy of preliminary/operational, primary/secondary, etc. norms, thereby determining both the varieties of the product and its varying functions in the culture into which it is "imported". Toury's view on norms is descriptive, functional, and, paradoxically, non-normative. And in this sense it may be said to approach Peirce's non-doctrinaire doctrine of signs, his logic, which, after esthetics and ethics, is the third of the "normative sciences" - the sciences, that is, which provide norms governing action as well as being governed by it. Peirce's norms are really laws of growth, which enable signs - esthetical, ethical, and logical signs - to unfold their full meaning. Without pressing the analogy too far, there is certainly a common core here, the implications of which deserve further study.

The remarks made in these paragraphs are still general. This generality is due to the fact that (general) semiotic studies and (general) translation studies have at this point not (or at least not yet) made common cause, nor for that matter been able to present one comprehensive theory in which both are unified. True, the earlier gap between both disciplines has meanwhile narrowed; yet the attempts by translation-theoreticians and semioticians at linking the two areas of research together have not yet led to definitive results. The efforts made in this direction are not unlike the fusing of the famous duck-rabbit example in Wittgenstein's *Philosophical Investigations*, which shows that we shift back and forth from seeing first a rabbit, then a duck, and then the third, new figure, a duckrabbit which has its proper reality in the union of both objects. It is neither a duck nor a rabbit but a new ideational sign (in the non-Platonic sense of mental event) constructed by the mind out of both primary signs[7]. By the same token, the confluence of two otherwise distinct "ideas", such as semiotic studies and translation studies, brings about the possibility of a third "idea", called semiotic (as opposed to semiological) translation studies.

Semiotics and translation studies: The state of the art

At present many writings that discuss translation theory and translation practice are classified, or classify themselves, as semiotic in nature[8]. Yet such a wide

---

7 See Sonesson 1989:270ff., where this scholar also points out that Wittgenstein used the duck-rabbit picture to make a different point: to demonstrate the impossibility of separating the duck as well as the rabbit from their common substratum.

8 Such a self-definition is not always justified. A case in point is Kaemmerling 1980, where no explicit semiotic method is adopted, but which nonetheless describes itself as semiotic. The fact that the object under investigation --a theatrical text-- has a multimedia (audiovisual) nature and is characterized by Kaemmerling as an interactive process, does not provide in itself grounds

use of the term tends to trivialize and obscure the singularly distinctive contribution which semiotics, as a radically general method, is able to make to theoretical and applied scholarship in translation studies as a multidisciplinary and interdisciplinary endeavor[9].

Nida (1964) is a pioneering work arguing strongly in favor of the systematic study of translation processes. In this and his subsequent work on, particularly, Bible translating, Nida, the American linguist, also uses concepts from communication theory, cybernetics, and information theory, which give his theoretical approach a pre-semiotic (or pseudosemiotic) ring. That theological research had at an early date "discovered" semiotics is also shown in Güttgemans's (1982:156-157) survey article.

All current work in this area is to a higher or lesser degree rooted in Jakobson's classical remarks on the three kinds of "interpreting a verbal sign" (1959:233;1971b:261) --intralingual translation, interlingual translation, intersemiotic translation-- , the only translation typology, as pointed out by Toury , "which has gained some currency", though, like most others, it is "afflicted with the traditional bias for *linguistic* translating" (Toury 1986:113[10]). Jakobson must be considered as the originator of the semiotic approach to translation. From a theoretical-exegetical viewpoint this has been confirmed in Waugh's (1984) account of Jakobson's concept of the linguistic sign as, first and foremost, translatable; translatability is, for Jakobson, the "intrinsic nature of the signatum" (see Waugh 1984:412-414). In his recent (1991) article "On Jakobson on translation", Sturrock throws quite novel light upon some of Jakobson's translational concepts based upon Saussure: (word-based) synonymy (which, as Sturrock argues, should be replaced by the broader notion of sentence-based equivalence), signifier/signified (which excludes the material item in reality, or referent), and code (which, in terms such as

---

to call a study semiotic. Another example is Hermans (1985a:9), where the "psychological approach" to translation is described as being "backed up by some impressive semiotic terminology"; what this translation scholar presumably means by this is the use of communication-theoretical concepts such as sender, addresser, channel, etc.

9 In Chapter 6 of Hatim and Mason's (1990) *Discourse and the Translator*, the authors intend to make a case for "semiotics-conscious translating" (Hatim and Mason 1990:104). However, to squeeze several sign-theoretical schools, and hence several approaches to translation, into a couple of printed pages, together with illustrative examples, is an impossible task, the result of which is a loosely argued, chaotic text which, plagued by factual errors and vital omissions, fails to be convincing. Nor is Hanne Martinet (1985) any more successful as an attempt at showing how semiotics is helpful when trying to deal with the problem of translation.

10 For this and other prolific translation scholars offerings of *recent* publications will be preferred here; the list of bibliographical references therein will lead one further to earlier works.

"decoding" and "recoding", only pertains to the "translation", according to unequivocal rules, of artificial languages --digital codes-- into natural languages). Unfortunately, however, Jakobson's example has not been followed in any systematic way; and the work done (by other scholars) in this area during the 1960s and earlier 1970s remained mostly rhapsodic and its semiotic component often vague and implicit[11].

The phenomenon of literary translation, and particularly Jakobson's intersemiotic translation, has been the object of thoroughgoing investigation, both theoretical and applied, in the Brazilian school of semiotics at the Catholic University of Sao Paulo. Following the extensive work by Décio Pignatari and Haroldo de Campos[12], intersemiotic translation has, under the direction of Santaella Braga, been placed into a Peircean framework and, creatively, applied to artistic signs by Plaza (see his 1981,1985,1987a,1987b)[13].

The two Slavic scholars, Jakobson and Lotman, have also inspired the *Dictionary for the Analysis of Literary Translation* (Popovic c.1975), an influential typescript. For the Czechoslovakian scholar, Popovic, the semiotic aspects of (literary) translation are essentially two: intertemporality and interspatiality. He writes: "The semiotic aspect in translation is concerned with the differences met within the process of translation which are a consequence of a different temporal and spatial realization of the translated text" (Popovic c.1975:16).

Popovic's fellow-countryman, the literary translation scholar, Levy, is the

---

11 A case in point is Quine 1960, the starting point of a long-lasting discussion (for three recent contributions, see Stanosz 1990, van Luxemburg-Albers 1990, and Johansen 1993:238-241). Here, Quine brought in his thesis of the indeterminacy of translation which, without being semiotic, shares the idea of verification with Peirce's doctrine (Føllesdal 1973). In Quine's "radical translation, i.e., translation of the language of a hitherto untouched people, . . . all help of interpreters is excluded" (Quine 1960:28) and in this theoretical situation meaning must be constructed by the observer by relying entirely on his or her own experimental observations. For lack of adequate verification, radical translation is, for Quine, not possible or, more exactly, what is a good translation and what not must remain indeterminate (see Quine 1960:78). Peirce's pragmatic empiricismism favored verification, which is implied in his pragmatic maxim (see Chapter 3). Yet its development from indeterminacy toward determinacy is rooted in evolutionary principles alien to Quine's empiricist thought on translatability.

12 Campos's theory (or rather "theory") of poetic translation, or (in this scholar's own words) "critical transcreation" is an extrapolation, in a personal vein, from his extensive work as a literary translator, and draws upon insights from Jakobson, Valéry, Hölderlin, Max Bense, Walter Benjamin, Octavio Paz, and, to some extent, Peirce. See, for instance, Campos 1970:21-38,1981:71-118,1987a,1987b. See also Chapter 7, note 1.

13 See also the appliedly-oriented study on "intersemiosis" by Anspach (1987), in which this scholar (also from Sao Paulo) analyzes the verbal-pictorial dialogue in drawings by Saul Steinberg, while drawing upon the cultural-semiotic thought of Jakobson and Lotman.

author of a structural-linguistically-inspired monograph, *Die literarische Übersetzung. Theorie einer Kunstgattung* (Levy 1969), thoroughgoing and unique in its kind, and which is conceived in terms of binary polarities (such as the literary work as autonomous entity/as functioning in the receiving literature, culture, etc., form/content, whole/part). Levy pits what he calls the illusionistic method of translation (in which a translation is produced which is meant to create in the reader the illusion that he or she is reading an original text) against its anti-illusionistic counterpart (which has no such pretense). Levy clearly favors the illusionistic method. See also his two posthumously published essays, Levy 1967 and 1970, in which this scholar provides a generative model of (literary) translation as a decision process[14].

With its roots in Russian formalism and Jakobson's semiotic thought on art and culture, a literary structuralism has since 25-plus years been developed by the scholars of the Tartu-Moscow school of semiotics, headed by Lotman from the University of Tartu, Estonia. In his latest book in English, *Universe of the Mind* (1990), Lotman has put forth his concept of "semiosphere"[15], while also emphasizing the central role played by translation in the development of culture. Indeed, on Lotman's view, cultural texts, which may be in a heterogeneity of verbal and nonverbal languages, "relate to each other along the spectrum which runs from complete translatability to just as complete mutual untranslatability" (Lotman 1990:125). The whole of culture is continuously restructured by the "foreign", "assymetrical", "peripheral" texts which are imported into a "central" culture. This makes the study of the process of their assimilation, or translation, "a universal scientific task" (Lotman 1990:269).

Lotman's cultural-semiotic ideas have had a strong impact upon the work of the literary translation scholars at The Porter Institute for Poetics and Semiotics at Tel Aviv University. Two of them, Toury and Even-Zohar, have distinguished themselves particularly in their writings on translation as intersystemic cultural communication[16]. It is assumed by them that literature has a privileged status in the "cultural world", Lotman's semiosphere; it is as

---

14 See also my discussion in Chapter 4.

15 By analogy with what Vernadsky came to call in 1926 the region of the "biosphere" (Vernadsky 1926), Lotman defines semiosphere as "the semiotic space necessary for the existence and functioning of [verbal and non-verbal] languages, not the sum total of different languages; in a sense the semiosphere has a prior existence and is in constant interaction with languages . . . The semiosphere is the result and the condition for the development of culture" (Lotman 1990:123,125).

16 Their ideas and the earlier structuralist approaches to literary translation have been further developed in Van den Broeck 1984-1985.

such, to continue Lotman's terminology, a primary modeling system[17] .

Even-Zohar's work (see, e.g., his recent 1990 work on "polysystem studies" and the bibliographical references quoted there) concentrates upon the description of the position of translated literary texts within the target literary polysystem. Toury (1980a,1986,1987), the (literary) translation-theoretician and semiotician, describes translation as cross-systemic transference inscribed in the broad general framework of a semiotics of culture. In the widest of its possible senses, translation is, Toury writes,

> . . . a series of operations, or procedures, whereby one semiotic entity, which is a [functional] constituent (element) of a certain cultural (sub)system, is transformed into another semiotic entity, which forms at least a potential element of another cultural (sub)system, providing that some informational core is retained "invariant under transformation", and on its basis a relationship known as "equivalence" is established between the resultant and initial entities . . . [N]ot only discrete signs, on the one hand, and entire messages, on the other, [can] have a semiotic value, but also, e.g., the rules and norms which govern the combination of (elementary and complex) signs into higher order, [more] complex ones, or into messages, institutionalized models for the establishment of culturally significant texts, etc.; and all these can also be transferred over and across systemic borders, with the appropriate transformations. (Toury 1986:1112-1113)

Toury develops Lotman's ideas applied to Jakobson's three kinds of translation, thus:

> [V]erbal texts . . . are not the representation of only one organizing principle, that which pertains to their basic, primary code, but also of one or more than one "secondary modeling systems" . . . , so that, when undergoing an act of translating, they may have *more* than one semiotic border to cross (e.g., when an oral story in one language becomes a literary, written one in another; when a religious text is transformed into a secular one, a literary work into a non-literary text, etc.). (Toury 1986:1113)

Unsurprisingly, considering the semiotic and translation-theoretical traditions there, early moves into the field of a semiotic approach to translation have typically come from the Slavic tradition of Saussurean linguistics. This is not limited to Jakobson, Lotman, Levy, and Popovic alone, nor is it confined to the semiotics of verbal art or, more broadly, culture. For Lotman (1992;

---

17 A primary modeling system is here the verbal text functioning as a model of how our experience of the world is organized. Subsequently, this model can be reconstructed - differently structured - through one or more secondary modeling systems, that imply a verbal infrastucture. See, e.g., Lotman 1972.

written in 1975 with a post-scriptum of 1990) culture is supra-individual (collective) intelligence; and this scholar distinguishes between reversible, symmetrical algorithmic translation --a logical procedure produced by (artificial) intelligence-- and irreversible translation --the result of creative intelligence. Only the latter is susceptible of creating new information. The Moscow scholar, Ivanov (1992) applies notions taken from information theory to poetic translation. Following the Prague School, he argues that in poetry the sound-meaning (or signifier-signified) relation is not arbitrary. The Rumanian mathematician and semiotician, Marcus's article on "Eight types of translation in the scientific language" (Marcus 1975) treats scientific language as having two components, one belonging to natural language and one to a formal (or artificial) language; he argues that these components are differently translatable, while showing how they may be combined[18]. The Bulgarian-born mathematician and specialist in machine translation, Ludskanov, is the author of the article called "A semiotic approach to the theory of translation" (Ludskanov 1975). Despite this title, Ludskanov's concern with non-natural languages seems to lead him away from a semiotic approach toward information theory. This becomes particularly clear in Ludskanov's somewhat puzzling remark, highly relevant to the topic of translation, that semiotics "does not provide the concept of *semiotic transformation*, though such transformations certainly exist" (Ludskanov 1975:6), which, oddly enough, seems to disregard altogether the existence of one of the most productive semiotic notions, namely semiosis. An instructive survey article is also Lawendowski (1978). This Polish-born scholar advocates that translation must be approached semiotically because it is a semiolinguistic process combining (anthroposemiotic) verbal signs with (originally zoosemiotic) nonverbal signs --implying, that is, Sebeok's (1975) six species of signs: signals, symptoms, icons, indexes, symbols, and names. Lawendowski uses forms of oral interlingual translation (German: *dolmetschen*) to illustrate his argument.

Petöfi (1983a), the (originally Czechoslovakian) text linguist, defines translation as the applied branch of "verbal semiotics"; the latter is characterized, rather nonspecifically, by this scholar as a theory of linguistic communication with four dimensions: co-text, context, text, and a system of beliefs/knowledge. Petöfi is not the only scholar who approaches the phenomenon of translation thus, "semiotically", through some kind of text

18 See also Saumjan 1970, who within a formal aproach to language (both natural and artificial languages) and linguistics has sought to construct a semiotic theory of generative grammar based upon *interlingua* as used in machine translation.

linguistics. The articles included in Wilss (ed.) (1980) share the same bias[19]. Despite the book's opening paragraph, on Peirce's philosophy of signs (Wilss (ed.) 1980:9), Wilss's book views the relations between translation studies and semiotics largely in terms of a translation-oriented text linguistics (that is, based upon text-grammatical research) and Morris's semiotics, while in this connection also centering on the relevance of text typology for the didactics of translation.

French structuralism and poststructuralism have made several contributions toward the study of translational phenomena (in the broad sense) from a Saussurean-linguistic perspective, often placed in a psychoanalytical framework and/or filtered through Jakobson's semiotic thought on verbal art. Greimas and Courtés have included an entry on "*Traduction*" in their *Sémiotique: Dictionnaire raisonné de la théorie du langage* (1979:397-398; translated in 1982:350-351)[20]. In Kristeva's 1974 *La révolution du langage poétique*, published shortly before this scholar abandoned her work in semiotics proper, Kristeva introduced the notion of "transposition"[21], a notion that crosses Saussure's division between signifier and signified and approaches translation taken in its broad sense. Building upon the older pair, Freud's *"Verschiebung"*, "shift, displacement", and his *"Verdichtung"*, "condensation" (from Freud's *Traumdeutung*), transposition is also germane to Jakobson's dichotomies, selection/combination, metaphor/synonymy, similarity/contiguity. As a translation-related concept, Kristeva's transposition shows the possibility of the signifying process to transform itself and be transformed: "the old system is abandoned and after a propulsive intermediary stage common to both systems, the new system is articulated as a new configuration" (Kristeva 1974:60;my trans.). That the notion of translation (which is etymologically synonymous with "metaphor" and "transference") had a central importance in Freud's own writings, is shrewdly argued in Mahony 1982[22].

The image of the psychoanalyst as a translator of sorts is also the topic of one of the (mostly applied) finely argued essays in the volume, *Difference*

---

19 An exception must be made for Toury's contribution, "Communication in translated texts: A semiotic approach" (Toury 1980b), in which (as in Toury's other work) the emphasis is upon the semiotic theories of Jakobson and Lotman.

20 The Saussurean-linguistic perspective is also incorporated (if as a marginal aspect) in Ladmiral 1979.

21 Transposition is compatible with Bachthin's dialogism and akin to the earlier concept, intertextuality, as well as to Greimas' *intersémioticité* (cf. Greimas and Courtès 1986:119-122).

22 Freud used the term *Übersetzung* (1) as the equivalent of "verbalization"; more importantly, (2) neuroses and symptoms are for him translations of unconscious material; and (3) the analyst's interpretations are also translations; thereby implicitly referring to Jakobson's third category, of intersemiotic translation (see Chapter 8), as well as implying that psychoanalytic treatment must be equated with the process of semiosis.

in Translation (Graham (ed.) 1985). In this volume translation is addressed from a pronouncedly poststructuralist, deconstructive perspective, in which references to Derrida are ubiquitous and the text of the latter's ingenious essay on "*Des Tours de Babel*" (on the function of "difference" --French *différence* vs. *différance*-- in language and translation) forms the centerpiece of the collection and its overall reference point. Not coincidentally, van den Broeck's 1987 article on "Jacques Derrida and the Tower of Babel" also addresses translation (particularly literary translation) from a deconstructive viewpoint building upon Saussure's theory of language and criticizing the arbitrary nature of language (that is, its systematic, twofold divide between the signifier and signified)[23].

Eco's *A Theory of Semiotics* forms the source of inspiration for the "model of the translation process" developed in Frawley (1984a). On Frawley's view, "translation is nothing short of an essential problem of semiosis: it is the problem of transfer of codes" (Frawley 1984a:160). Concentrating upon codes, Frawley argues that translation as recodification

> . . . is an uncertain act, and the uncertainty results from the inevitable structural mismatch of the codes. . . [T]ranslation is the bilateral accomodation of a matrix and target code. . . The translation itself, as a matter of fact, is essentially a third code which arises out of the bilateral consideration of the matrix and target codes: it is, in a sense, a subcode of each of the codes involved. (Frawley 1984a:167-168).

A new code with new information, a translation "establishes the essential *difference* necessary for semiosis" (Frawley 1984a:169); and by doing so it "may be either a *moderate innovation* or a *radical innovation*, with respect to the codes that contribute to its genesis" (Frawley 1984a:173). In his book, Frawley applies his ideas on translation to a fragment of an English translation of Pablo Neruda's *Las Alturas de Macchu Picchu*[24].

Finally, the few titles (all of them recent work, written mostly during the last decade) dealing with translation from a Peircean point of view. Not surprisingly, they also rely heavily on Jakobson's thought, while Morris's is here de-emphasized. Besides my own published articles on the theoretical implications of this subject (see Gorlée 1986,1989a,1991,1992), there are Liszka (1990) and Johansen (1993); of a mixed theoretical-applied nature are Plaza

---

23 For deconstruction and its bearing upon translation theory, see also van den Broeck 1988. The Babelic confusion of tongues as discussed by Derrida, is also central to Walter Benjamin's earlier theory of language and translation, which is the subject of Chapter 7.

24 Based on Frawley, while also drawing on insights from Nida, is Siskin's 1987 article on "A medieval semiotics of translation". In this study (which is only semiotic in an indirect way), Frawley's ideas on linguistic equivalence in translation are applied to a fourteenth-century Biblical glossary, written in Hebrew and Old French.

(1981,1985,1987a,1987b) and Deledalle-Rhodes (1991); while an earlier article, van Kesteren (1978), is wholly applied work.

"Peirce's interpretant"[25] (the title of Liszka's philosophically-oriented 1990 article) contains a finely argued account of how the concept of interpretant was developed by Peirce at an early stage as a case of triadic sign translation, or semiosis; and how subsequently the concept of interpretant was fine-tuned by Peirce in tandem with his development of pragmatism, to which it is especially pertinent. Liszka writes (1990:34) that "the interpretant is a rule of translation or inference" involving an increase of information about the object. Its semiosic character, in which translation is connected with information, inference, and interpretant, gives sign translation a truly central place in Peirce's philosophy of signs; a place which, however, only recently has received explicit recognition as such by Peirce scholarship.

Also Johansen's recent (1993) book, *Dialogic Semiosis: An Essay on Signs and Meaning*, an important contribution to modern Peirce scholarship, addresses in its pages Peirce's concept of the interpretant and questions concerning interpretation as a process of translation[26]. In the section on "Translation, synonymity, and use", Johansen writes that the only difference between "*homme*" and "man", or

> . . . between a given text and its ideal translation into another language would be that they signify they belong to two different languages, their extension and comprehension otherwise being exactly the same. For Peirce, however, synonymity (or as he preferred to call it, equivalence) between symbols is connected to their function, i.e., their being used for some purpose. (Johansen 1993:152)[27]

Later on in his book, in the section on "Code and reference" (1993:235ff.), Johansen discusses the pertinence of the concept of collateral experience (factual or imagined) to the meaning of linguistic signs, both as Peirce saw it (in terms of the concepts of universe of discourse and common ground, and the interaction of iconicity, indexicality, and symbolicity)[28], and as Jakobson restated the issue, particularly in his essay "On linguistic aspects of translation" (Jakobson 1959), much-quoted yet rather superficially touched upon by most

---

25 For details of and about Peirce's doctrine of signs, its semiotic concepts and terminology, see Chapter 3.

26 This is prefigured in Johansen 1988.

27 See note 25. That Peirce's notion of equivalence is not equal to synonymity is argued in Chapter 9. Peirce's concepts of extension and comprehension, as related to sign translation, will be addressed in Chapter 10.

28 See note 25.

translation critics[29]. As interpreted by Johansen (see 1993:237ff.), ostensive definition (the identification of the actual object or state of affairs referred to) is, for Jakobson, unable to provide sufficient grounds for establishing the meaning of a linguistic utterance, and the latter needs to be defined as the outcome of an interpretative process involving both code and reference, --that is, involving both metalinguistic (intralingual) and intersemiotic translation.

As mentioned above, Plaza's work (1981,1985,1987a,1987b) concentrates upon Jakobson's intersemiotic translation epitomized in the translation of artistic objects or texts. Stretching Jakobson's rather narrow conception of intersemiotic translation, Plaza argues that in intersemiotic translation a confrontation takes place between "the lucid and the ludic" (Plaza 1987a:209;my trans.), which serves to show the relative nature and function of the codes representing Peirce's Thirdness and Firstness[30] respectively. On this broadened view on intercode translation as intersemiotic transmutation, art can materialize and signify one message in more than one way; and by appealing to different senses, intersemiotic translation effectively bridges the gap between different "languages" --aesthetic, political, philosophical, cognitive, electronic, etc. Taking examples from painting, music, and literature, Deledalle-Rhodes (1991) likewise shows that in art translation (particularly intersemiotic translation) is the central activity.

Van Kesteren wrote in 1978:

> Over the last decade a tendency has become noticeable for the development of various fields within the humanities on the basis of semiotics: linguistics, the theory of literature, the theory of architecture, art history, musicology, and drama theory have in one way or another made use of the theory of signs. However, one particular field has hardly been "infiltrated" by semiotics: *theory of translation*. (van Kesteren 1978:48)

Following this still timely --from 1978 to date-- remark, van Kesteren's self-described attempt is "to develop a semiotic model for translation theory" (1978:48) based upon "Peirce, supplemented by certain operations introduced by two German scholars who have adapted Peirce's system, Bense and Walther" (van Kesteren 1978:48), while also using notions from Morris, Popovic, and Holmes. In his article, van Kesteren applies Peirce's three separate sign divisions and trichotomies of signs (qualisign-sinsign-legisign, icon-index-symbol, rheme-proposition-argument)[31] to Hesse's poem "September" and its English translation, thereby establishing nine kinds of equivalence between both

---

29 See note 2.

30 See note 25.

31 See note 25.

literary texts.

Peirce and translation studies

As announced above, this study chooses Peircean semiotics to serve as its sign-theoretical paradigm. This choice (or rather, this preference) is both the result of my (necessarily limited) resources and a natural consequence of the broad scope of the concept of translation used in these pages; which is in no way confined to linguistic signs but concerns itself with signs of all sorts, linguistic as well as non-linguistic.

That does not mean that my semiotic-methodological orientation here would exclude or even reject an approach from a Saussurean viewpoint; rather, that the latter is included in the former, both being different conjectural approaches to semiotics and linguistics. In contradictinction to Saussure's language-directed theory of signs, with its more direct concrete applicability, Peirce's radically general semiotics is no doubt better able to accomodate theoretical studies concerning translation in the broad sense; indeed, in the latter area semiology must be called a reductionistic method[32]. In any case, while I intend no criticism of Saussure by de-emphasizing his thought on signs here, neither do I wish to indulge in the elevation of Peirce to some kind of universal Olympian sage. This study is an exercise in neither hagiography nor demonology. It has no particular ideological axes to grind, nor does it look for methodological shortcuts or easy answers. It is as skeptical of all facile dogmatism as it is wary of all distortion or biased interpretation: it tries its best to let the source material tell its own story.

Because this study is to a large degree a textual interpretation, I must rely heavily upon the actual statements in, particularly, Peirce's writings, published as well as unpublished. This corresponds to the common practice in Peirce scholarship. According to Pharies,

> A distinguishing feature of Peirce scholarship is its almost exegetic character, as seen in the ample use of quotations from his works. This strategy is justified by the fragmented character of the writings. The Peirce scholar attempts to draw the separate parts into a coherent whole, then to show, through quotation, that Peirce himself might have connected the various aspects of his philosophy in a certain way. A second justification is that the writings continue to yield new insights, which must be documented. (Pharies 1985:9,n.6)

There are at least two ways of construing the topic of my project. One way is

---

32 See further the section on "Semiology vs. semiotics" in Chapter 3, and the very instructive article, Short 1988.

to consider how Peirce himself conceived the relevance of his general theory of signs to the study of translation. Another is to examine how Peirce's semiotics is relevant to translation-theoretical investigations, quite apart from what Peirce himself actually wrote or clearly implied about the relationship between the two disciplines. Here the topic shall be construed in both ways, though the concern will principally be with how Peirce's general theory of signs is pertinent to the more specialized theory of translation as it stands today. The argument shall be clarified by introducing "auxiliary" scholars from different areas of investigation, who in their work implicitly or explicitly bridge the gap between semiotics and translation theory. By and large the essays transcend the overall topic and enlighten not only Peirce's semiotics and translation but also adjacent subjects, some of which may at first blush seem remote. Such extended implications are, as I hope to argue, useful companions along the way of inquiry.

General point of departure is what is expressed in Peirce's much-quoted statement that the meaning of a sign is its translation into another equivalent or perhaps more developed sign (*CP*:2.228,1897). Consequently, the overall purpose of the project here is to help develop a new and comprehensive theory of translation based upon the general theory of signs elaborated by Peirce, who throughout his intellectual career used sign interpretation, or sign translation, as a systematic heuristic device in his evolutionary theory of meaning. Some of Peirce's fundamental semiotic issues --most particularly triadic sign-action, or semiosis-- will be discussed here in their manifold implications for the concept of translation, broad and narrow, logico-philosophical and empirical, lingual and non-lingual. Both semiosis and translation must be understood and approached as dynamic, goal-directed processualities occurring between a (verbal or nonverbal) sign, its object (or referent in reality, or "reality"), and what Peirce called the interpretant, or better the (infinite) series of interpretants (signs interpreting the primary sign).

Though Peirce himself was no linguist, yet he was a polyglot endowed with an unusual gift for, and insight in, language and linguistic problems. His work abounds with references to language and linguistics, which need to be the main starting point for what may be called a Peircean linguistics. This aspect of Peirce scholarship is still embryonic, so that the attempts made in this direction must necessarily remain tentative and open to further discussions. Interestingly in the context here, Peirce was also a professional translator himself, one who made remarks and commentaries, both practical and theoretical, on the subject of translation[33].

To sum up the concrete business and limits of my project as outlined

---

33 See further Chapter 6.

here: Peirce's doctrine of signs is so unfamiliar to most intellectual readers and so intimidating to many others that I feel compelled to provide an introduction to his semiotics as a "new" model in order to develop the notion of translation theory which is central to this book. Peirce's semiotics as it is presented here (in Chapter 3) and, then, interpreted and re-interpreted in the light of the overall topic, shall be complemented in subsequent Chapters with other (language-)philosophical approaches to sign translation which may be, and will be, assimilated to Peirce's thought and redefined in Peircean terms. These include relevant insights of Ludwig Wittgenstein, who included numerous references on translation in his language-philosophical writings; of Roman Jakobson, the first among linguists to apply Peirce's semiotic concepts in the field of, especially, the verbal arts of prose and poetry, as well the nonverbal art of the cinema, of whose birth and further development he was a particularly shrewd eyewitness; of the German hermeneutic of the Frankfurt School, Walter Benjamin, who put forth a spiritual, prophetic theory of language and translation which, as shall be argued, has definite and intriguing Peircean overtones; and of other theories and thinking-models which are salient to a Peircean semiotics, such as a (non-formalized) game theory according to which problem-solving and decision-making in translation is a game-like procedure; and legal theory, where a close examination of the law of contract shows that translation can be considered as having a contractual nature. All of the essays collected here deal, from different points of view, with the problem of translation as sign interpretation, --its scope, its purposes, its limits, and its constraints.

Written over a period of seven years (1985-1992), the essays reflect my own development and, hopefully, intellectual growth during this period. It must be underscored here that this is originally not conceived as a book: it is a sequence of articles now expanded and consolidated into a book. In their present form the individual Chapters may still be read in any order. Given that each individual Chapter forms a unity and may be taken separately, I can imagine at least two objections to the structure given to this study. Some might find that the following pages do not comprise a book, but rather present a collection of essays on diverse topics. Others might voice the opposite complaint: every essay in this book is the same; no matter what its putative topic, each essay finally reduces to an argument in which the central figures are Peirce, translation, semiosis, and interpretant. This second group would be right, at least to the extent that the Chapters are separate essays which revolve in concentric circles around the same topic. They inevitably include repetitions and even some partial overlappings. To unify the texts in this book and facilitate the reading, many references and cross-references as well as an index, have been added.

Concretely, this treatise takes as its starting point the substantial research which I have conducted earlier in this field, and which has resulted in a whole and coherent series of published (in international journals and proceedings volumes) articles addressing the interactions of semiotics and translation theory. Most of the papers included here are in fact rethought, revised, expanded, and in part also rewritten versions of articles. Earlier versions of most of the Chapters have been previously published, or they will appear shortly: Chapter 3, which serves as a reference point for the entire work, appeared in *Livstegn* (Gorlée 1992a) and, in a different version (in Spanish) in *Signa* (Gorlée 1992c); Chapter 4 first appeared in 1986 (Gorlée 1986); Chapter 5 appeared in the first issue of *Target* (Gorlée 1989a); Chapter 7 is forthcoming in Vienna; Chapter 8 appeared in Imatra, Finland (Gorlée 1992); Chapter 9 was published, in a totally different form, in 1991 (Gorlée 1991)and will also appear, again in a different, shorter version, in *Semio-Nordica*. Chapters 2, 6, 10, and 11 appear here for the first time. I thank the publishers of previously published Chapters and parts of Chapters, for their permission to republish copyrighted material. On behalf of the Department of Philosophy of Harvard University, Professor Hilary Putnam has graciously given permission to publish materials from Peirce's unpublished manuscripts in Houghton Library, Cambridge, Massachusetts.

From here on, page numbers are indicated in brackets after all quotations following the first mentioning of the source, e.g. (Jakobson 1971b:703). References to the writings of Peirce, Wittgenstein, and Saussure are made in the manner specified in the Bibliography (Chapter 12). Furthermore, critical and technical terms belonging to specific theories, semiotic and otherwise, which are analyzed and/or used in the course of this book, are systematically set in double quotation marks as they are first mentioned; foreign words and expresssions, and words with special emphasis are italicized.

My final introductory remark is that every reference to Peirce's writings, published as well as unpublished, is (as far as possible) dated in order to show that Peirce maintained a fairly consistent attitude toward his major contributions throughout the various chronological phases of his long and complex philosophical development.

03. FUNDAMENTALS OF THE SEMIOTICS OF CHARLES S. PEIRCE

"Do not block the way of inquiry" (*CP*:1.135,c.1899)

Introductory remarks

In this chapter I shall give a survey of the semiotic thought of the American philosopher and mathematician, Charles Sanders Peirce (1839-1914). The ideas and concepts of Peirce's contemporary, the Swiss linguist, Ferdinand de Saussure (1857-1913), which form the groundbase on which modern continental European semiology is built, are generally better-known than semiotics in the American tradition; therefore I intend in the following to briefly touch on the Saussurean-based theory of signs and pit it against a Peircean-based semiotics. Whereas the former is linguistically oriented, the latter is processual, with attention directed towards ever-evolving contexts with respect to *all* forms of communication, linguistic as well as otherwise. Contrary to the exclusive natural language model of semiology (or, as it is also called, structuralism), semiotics in the Peircean tradition embraces thus a vastly more extensive repertoire:

> The Peircean theory is so ample and general that it is capable of serving as foundation to any other theory of any type. Under that light, the Peircean system is more effective as an infra-theory than as a meta-theory. This is how semiotics can help us to analyze any special semiosis, whether vegetable, animal, human, psychic, social, cellular, neuronic or (probably) stellar. (Santaella Braga 1991:132).

My argument, in this light, involves demonstration, however superficial, considering the purpose of the discussion here, of the more limited Saussurean dyadic conception of the sign vis-à-vis Peirce's radically general triadic paradigm.

Semiology vs. semiotics[1]

Charles Sanders Peirce's philosophy of signs has recently enjoyed increasing attention among humanists in the United States, Europe, and various other parts of the world (particularly in East Asia and South America). Yet this patriarch of modern semiotics has been all too often either misinterpreted, mis-represented, or altogether ignored; and the profound differences separating his and Saussure's theories of signs have frequently been misconstrued. This has for many years unduly harmed the reputation of this semiotic pioneer. This may be illustrated by the following typical example. Hawkes, in his *Structuralism and Semiotics*, writes that

> The terms *semiology* and *semiotics* are both used to refer to [the science of signs], the only difference between them being that *semiology* is preferred by Europeans, out of deference to Saussure's coinage of the term, and *semiotics* tends to be preferred by English speakers, out of deference to the American Peirce. (Hawkes 1977:124)

On the same page Hawkes contends that the boundaries of the field of semiotics,

> . . . are coterminous with those of structuralism: the interests of the two spheres are not fundamentally separate and, in the long run, both ought properly to be included within the province of a third, embracing discipline called, simply, *communication*. (Hawkes 1977:124)

Only towards the end of his book, Hawkes touches upon Peirce's triadic concept of the sign, strangely neglecting its radical difference from Saussurean binarism. Subsequently, he returns to Saussure with the expressed purpose of illustrating the semiologist-structuralist's craft; after which Peirce's semiotics is not mentioned again.

Regarding Hawkes's (and other authors') conflation of semiotics with semiology, Sebeok's response, in his 1984 article on "Signs of life", goes as follows:

> Nothing could be a more deluded misconstrual of the facts of the matter, but the speciousness of this and associated historical deformations are due to our own inertia in having hitherto neglected the serious exploration of our true lineage. (Sebeok 1984:1)

Sebeok's critical remarks were --and still are- highly opportune. Unfortunately, however, there are scholars who continue to use "semiology", "semiotics", and "structuralism" indiscriminately, while others, most notably Eco (see his 1976 *A*

---

1 For a more detailed account of this, see also Gorlée (1992b).

Theory of Semiotics) have sought to harmonize both semiotic traditions and to integrate them into one comprehensive perspective.

Linguistic semiotics --as semiology may also be called-- is in fact one branch of semiotics, which has particularly distinguished itself in the study of verbal messages. Cultivated with particular zeal in France, it is inspired by the ingenuity and elegance which are, it would seem, characteristic of the French intellectual spirit. Semiology derives first and foremost from Saussure's *Course in General Linguistics*, but also draws eclectically on various more recent linguistic theories (Jakobson, Harris, Chomsky, Pike) as well as on language philosophy (Carnap, Wittgenstein). Major sources of inspiration are further Russian literary formalism and structural anthropology. Propp's 1958 *Morphology of the Folktale* (first published in Russian in 1928 but not "discovered" until thirty years later) and the work of Lévi-Strauss since his 1958 *Anthropologie structurale*, have both provided, and indeed themselves been, important methodological tools for the analysis of narrative structures from the structuralist point of view. Narrative structures which were found in literary (in the broadest sense of the term) texts and which were systematically couched in terms of the binary "oppositions" which --as such, or again combined in "semiotic squares"-- were soon to become structuralism's trademark.

Heirs to Saussure, Hjelmslev, as well as Jakobson, French structuralists turned to linguistics for their model. The resulting linguistic model and its conceptual apparatus are, however, not only applied to linguistic objects of study but also, indirectly and by analogy, to objects belonging to other sign systems or semiotic codes. This would permit any object of research, language-based or not, to be considered as a "text" and to be analyzed "linguistically", thereby making language the one universal interpretant. Since culture is for semiologists identical to language, any cultural phenomenon can be studied semiologically, as a meaningful sign structure. A typical example of this is Barthes's (1967) "linguistic" analysis of fashion. For the purpose of the analysis it is, however, often neglected by followers of linguistic semiotics to realize the full implications of a methodological procedure which is, and can only be, essentially metaphorical. Naturally, the linguistic-semiotic procedure favors the cognitive, system-bound dimension of non-linguistic objects, thereby neglecting, for instance, that they also convey emotions, and do so in a direct, non-cognitive (or at least pre-cognitive) fashion which is unthinkable in linguistic signs or sign systems. The metaphorical procedure seems further to take for granted that non-linguistic objects have a syntax determining their component parts and how these parts may combine. Violation of the rules determining the perpendicular axes of paradigm/syntagm and selection/combination, means that the non-linguistic object is deprived of its well-formedness, in the same way as it would make a linguistic object agrammatical. Therefore, whenever applied unreservedly to nonlinguistic objects, the linguistic-semiotic approach fails to do justice to both language and the nonlinguistic objects. What is explicitly or implicitly stressed here are their similarities and parallelisms; whereas their differences are ignored.

This "linguistic imperialism" may be appreciated in the works of Barthes and Lévi-Strauss, for example. Barthes is primarily concerned with sociocultural systems of signification, with the (linguistic) rules and codes underlying and governing different cultural phenomena. His treatment of, among others, the "garment system", the "food system", the "car system", and the "furniture system" as so many "languages" (Barthes 1986:25ff.) seems, however, to take for granted that the vestimentary, alimentary, etc. codes serve as much a communicative purpose as does verbal language. The same implication may be found in Lévi-Strauss's anthropological thought, which treats marriage rules and kinship systems as languages communicating a message. Whether this is defensible as a plausible presupposition, is, to put it mildly, doubtful. Spoken and written language is evidently produced to "tell" something to somebody; consequently, linguistic signs must be interpreted as message-bearers. But since the message contained in nonverbal signs can either be produced unwittingly or never be produced in the form in which it is interpreted, a semiotic "reading" of nonverbal signs runs the risk --even more so than a reading of verbal signs-- of becoming a *Hineininterpretierung* attributing to the object a meaning which cannot be validated and is, therefore, a reflection on the interpreter him- or herself. To deny this, and give an "objective" truth status to such an interpretation, is to stretch dangerously the concept of objectivity[2].

Essential to modern French structuralism is that it considers semiology to be subordinate to, and limited by, linguistics. Saussure did in fact acknowledge nonverbal sign systems, but he underscored the privileged status of language as "a system of signs that express ideas, and is therefore comparable to a system of writing, the alphabet of deaf-mutes, symbolic rites, polite formulas, military signals, etc." (Saussure 1966:16); to which Saussure immediately added: "But it [language] is the most important of these systems" (Saussure 1966:16). Linguistic signs are for Saussure wholly arbitrary and unmotivated, which means that a signifier has no natural or logical connection with its signified[3] This

---

2 See Ransdell's seminal article on "Semiotic objectivity" (Ransdell 1986a).

3 In the article mentioned in n.2, Ransdell argues against the customarily used term "arbitrary": "Take any word: the English word *table*, let us say. The meaning of this perceptual configuration is no doubt *arbitrary* in the sense that it has the meaning it has only because it just happened to have entered into an activity or practice of some people (just as, say, *mesa* or *Tisch* happened to have entered into similar activities or practices of other peoples). Perhaps *accidental* would be a more exact word for arbitrariness, in this sense. In any case, though, there is nothing about the configuration itself which makes it mean what it means linguistically. Only considerations of

disconnection of the linguistic sign-as-such from the concept it stands for, is nonetheless for Saussure the strength of language:

> Signs that are wholly arbitrary realize better than the others the ideal of the semiological process: that is why language, the most complex and universal of all systems of expression, is also the most characteristic; for in this sense linguistics can become the master-pattern for all branches of semiology although language is only one particular semiological system. (Saussure 1966:68)

While nonlinguistic objects of investigation were in Saussure, and hence in sign theory in the Saussurean tradition, seen and analyzed according to the linguistic "master-pattern", Saussure himself also prefigured the future moment in which both disciplines would compete for hegemony. He went as far as considering the possibility that semiology, as the study of nonlinguistic objects, would evolve so dramatically that it would emancipate itself from the domination by linguistics, and even take the leading role itself:

> Semiology would show what constitutes signs, what laws govern them. Since the science does not yet exist, no one can say what it would be; but it has a right to existence, a place staked out in advance. Linguistics is only a part of the general science of semiology; the laws discovered by semiology will be applicable to linguistics, and the latter will circumscribe a well-defined area within the mass of anthropological facts. (Saussure 1966:16)[4]

---

history and convenience, of no logical import, seem to account for its having this property" (Ransdell 1986a:246). Ransdell considers meaning in language as a property which has at some point been literally bestowed upon the word, for instance; as something agreed-upon or ruled consensually: "This seems to me to be a fairly precise statement of what is meant in saying that linguistic signs are conventional. The use of the term *convention* . . . originates in the idea of a convening of persons for the purpose of an explicit act of meaning-bestowment, a laying down of the law, as it were . . ." (Ransdell 1986a:248). This insight leads Ransdell to refer to Saussurean semiotics as "conventionalism" or "conventionalist semiotics".

4 Barthes inverted again this Saussurean proposition when he affirmed that it is not linguistics which is a part of semiology, but semiology which is a part of linguistics (1964:81). In reference to this, Barthes said (in an interview he gave in March 1967, on the occasion of the publication of *Le système de la mode*) that, on the one hand, this book on, as its translated title suggests, *The Fashion System*, "corresponds to a 'nascent' semiology", while on the other, ". . . Saussure's theories have been "completed" (indeed, contested) by a new linguistics represented principally by Chomsky, but also by certain of Jakobson's and Benveniste's analyses; this linguistics is less taxonomic because it concerns itself less with the classification and analysis of signs than with the rules of speech production. I have been following this evolution, particularly on the question of the linguistic analysis of literature. But if I maintain the Saussurean categories for 'written' clothing it's because they seem to me precisely proper for the definition and analysis of objects reified and mythicized by mass culture" (Barthes 1985:45).

The two disciplines, semiology and linguistics, are in modern French structuralism two branches of one tree; and they are different only in a hierarchical manner of speaking[5].

As far as the domains of application of semiological research are concerned, literary analysis and (anthropological) mythology can be said to be favored. This predominance is hardly surprising, considering the sources from which structuralist semiology received its initial inspiration. When narrative texts are studied and explained as syntagmatic structures in which a logical semantic content is textualized --temporarized--, as is commonly done in semiological analyses, mere structural description becomes an analysis of the way in which meaning is produced on the textual level. Meaning is here seen deductively as a model of oppositions necessarily realized in the text. The general procedure followed is that this text or text-like object is divided into different types of previously articulated logico-discursive binary oppositions. This division then precedes a program in which the oppositions are combined and made to interact meaningfully. The resulting description of the textual network is finally supposed to provide an exhaustive analysis of the research object.

Following Saussure and expanding Chomsky, structuralism concentrates on how signs combine and function in a sign system. Structuralism is therefore the study of "signifiers" (the sensory aspect of signs) and not of "signifieds" (their meaning aspect); it does not ask *what* signs mean but *how* they mean. While emphasizing on syntactics and, to some extent, pragmatics, semantics is in fact bracketed. The "object" of the sign --that is, its referent in reality-- falls outside structuralist models, and meaning is wholly an affair of intratextuality and intertextuality. This is one consequence drawn from Saussure's concept of the sign, where signifier and signified have no separate identity and both are concepts of the "real thing" which conjointly they refer to. This insight makes the "thing" itself a sign-external entity, and thus irrelevant to sign theory in the Saussurean tradition.

A study of messages which excludes the explicit study of meaning content in its relation to extralinguistic reality --the objects and the state of affairs of the real world as well as ficticious ones-- , is intrinsically unconcerned with what these messages are about. The sole emphasis on signification in the sign structure does in fact limit the scope of modern structuralist textual scholarship to a mere text-internal investigation of textualized meaning. This procedure undercuts, as it were, the very notion of communication which is for obvious reasons a crucial concept of text theory; so crucial that, on Ransdell's view, "semiotics is a movement toward a comprehensive theory of communication, construed in terms

---

5 For a full discussion of this, see Rauch 1986.

of interpretational responses to meaning-properties" (Ransdell 1986a:236). The "sense" which structuralists make of the objects of study does not deal with Ransdell's meaning-properties, but is, however cleverly deviced and executed, a sophisticated attempt at circumventing the whole meaning issue[6]

To even approach exhaustive analysis, a semiotic theory should account for the semantic content which is being communicated in the sign process; and it should do so more than just insofar as it suits divisions into *a priori* oppositions. By relying wholly on the resources of binary analysis, no technique is proposed for assessing the relative value of the binary pairs which emerge in a certain text. Binary analysis can certainly provide intellectually stimulating insights, but it is bound to remain a superior form of intellectual exercise. Detached as it remains from observable reality, it is ultimately an unverifiable practice more tailored to meet semiologists's own needs than committed to let the object under investigation speak freely in all its eloquent intricacies. The latter is what a Peircean analysis claims to do.

Peirce's life and works[7]

Charles Sanders Peirce (1839-1914) was the son of Benjamin Peirce, who was Professor of mathematics and astronomy at Harvard University, Cambridge, Massachusetts, and the only internationally well-known American mathematician of his time. His son Charles grew up in an intellectually stimulating environment, and from his earliest years he showed great promise in mathematics, logic, and the physical sciences. The fields of his encyclopedic learning would eventually include logic, philosophy, chemistry, astronomy, biology, as well as the social sciences --particularly psychology and sociology, then emerging. Though not a linguist, Peirce had a keen gift for languages, and wrote a great deal on language-related issues. One field Peirce seemed not to be particularly interested in is art. Though he did not develop any specific thoughts on artistic communication, his conceptual apparatus can be applied successfully to analyze artistic or aesthetic signs as well.

Peirce was on the whole an evolutionary thinker much influenced by Darwinism. Though attracted by Darwin's ideas upon progress and evolution, Peirce did (as convincingly argued by Pencak 1991 and Brent 1993:60) by no means identify himself with them. Peirce's notion of evolution did not hinge upon

6 In Gardin's words, this "is in fact only the sense the observer gives to the object in virtue of more or less experimental criteria; more exactly, it is only *one* sense which the observer has chosen among other possible interpretations because of its usefulness to construct an efficient theory" (Gardin 1974:74; my trans.)

7 See also the recent important Brent 1993, which came to my attention after completion of the essays here.

smooth continuity and harmonious evolvement from the past into the present towards the future, as was stressed by Darwinism in its more conservative variety. Instead came Peirce's deep and longstanding conviction that new ideas only emerge by the violent breaking up of habits previously built up, by bold leaps and educated guesses in reasoning which apparently come from nowhere but which alone form the basis of major scientific discoveries, and hence of progress.

Despite the wide scope of his learning, Peirce was never able to secure an academic career that presumably would have provided institutional support for his work. He lectured for some years at Harvard University and at Johns Hopkins University, but was not offered a tenured position and, as a matter of fact, he was dismissed there. Instead, he earned his livelihood for nearly thirty years as a scientist employed by the United States Coast and Geodetic Service. In 1887, after having inherited some money, he retired to Milford, Pennsylvania, where he lived in relative isolation and continued his philosophical work on his own. To ease his financial stringencies, he wrote book reviews (particularly for *The Nation*) and dictionary entries (for *The Century Dictionary*). Seen from today's perspective, Peirce was at that moment perhaps the greatest philosopher in the world; but since he worked in almost complete isolation, his work became more and more speculative and obscure. This is hardly surprising, considering he had few colleagues and no students to respond to his ideas. In 1914, Peirce died, at the age of 74, in poverty and without recognition.

Although Peirce's published writings as per today total more than 10,000 pages, and several collections have appeared since his death, the bulk of his work remains as yet unpublished, and therefore little-known. The eight volumes of the misnamed *Collected Papers of Charles Sanders Peirce* (*CP*), published from the 1930s onward, do not represent the amazing depth and breath of Peirce's thought and work. It is a relatively small but good (that is, a representative) selection of until then unpublished material arranged more or less topically. The *Collected Papers* form, however, a collage of widely heterogeneous texts from widely different moments and periods, put together by the editors with scissors and gluepot, as it were. A *bricolage*, in Lévi-Strauss's terminology, but a very useful one, also for the serious student of Peirce's thought, semiotic and otherwise[8].

In progress is now, since 1982, the ambitious project of *The Writings of Charles S. Peirce: A Chronological Edition* (*W*), in which much of Peirce's monumental *oeuvre* will appear. So far researchers have tracked down more than

---

8 Other important collections of Peirce's writings include Hardwick's *Semiotic and Significs: The Correspondence between Charles S. Peirce and Victoria Lady Welby* (*PW*) and Eysele's *The New Elements of Mathematics* (*NEM*). See also the following useful selections: Buchler's *Philosophical Writings of Peirce* (Peirce 1955) and Wiener's *Charles S. Peirce: Selected Writings* (*SW*).

90,000 scattered and unpublished manuscript pages --enough material for some 65 (!) volumes. Since this would, for practical reasons, be an unrealistic project, the *Chronological Edition* is scheduled to eventually include approximately 30 volumes, of which vol. 4 (covering until 1884, when Peirce was 45 years old) was published in the Fall of 1989. This means that much of Peirce's most important sign-theoretical work from his mature period (1902 onward) will have to remain inaccessible to a wider public until the beginning of the next century. Needless to say this is a great pity for Peirce scholarship.

Peirce's thought

Peirce's overall concern as a philosopher was expanding the thought of Immanuel Kant (1724-1804), by which he was much influenced and from which he had acquired the architectonic theory of philosophy. Kant was concerned with how the synthesis of appearances proceeds in accordance with necessary laws. For him, synthetic judgments must operate not just with empirical data but with rules ensuring objective knowledge. As Peirce wrote early in his intellectual career:

> . . . Immanuel Kant asked himself the question, "How are synthetical judgments *a priori* possible?" By synthetical judgments he meant such as assert positive fact and are not mere affairs of arrangement; in short, judgments of the kind which synthetical reasoning produces, and which analytic reasoning cannot yield. By *a priori* judgments he meant such as that all outward objects are in space, every event has a cause, etc., propositions which according to him can never be inferred from experience. . . . But before asking *that* question he ought to have asked the more general one, "How are any synthetical judgments at all possible?" How is it that a man can observe one fact and straightaway pronounce judgment concerning another different fact not involved in the first? Such reasoning . . . has . . . no definite probability. (*CP*:2.690;*W*3:303-304,1878)

The fundamental question over which Peirce mused has been paraphrased by Savan as follows:

> How does mathematics grow, so that from accepted principles the mathematician passes to new and surprising discoveries? How do the natural sciences grow, so that from past observations and theories the scientist may venture more or less assured predictions of as yet unobserved events? How does rational thought in whatever form --religion, science, technology, art, and philosophy-- grow to broader and deeper power over human action, imagination, and life? (Savan 1987-1988:1)

These are the fundamental questions Peirce, as many other philosophers before and after him, asked himself. Peirce shifted the Kantian problem to the process of synthetic inference and to scientific inquiry. He believed that the answer was to be found in the theory of the "categories" as it was developed through his doctrine of signs, his "semeiotic". And Peirce thought that his most important contribution to philosophy was precisely his theory of these three categories, or fundamental modes of reality.

Peirce wrote to his English correspondent, Victoria Lady Welby --who was the first woman semiotician-- on December 23, 1908:

> . . . it has never been in my power to study anything --mathematics, ethics, metaphysics, gravitation, thermodynamics, optics, chemistry, comparative anatomy, astronomy, psychology, phonetics, economic, the history of science, whist, men and women, metrology, except as a study of semeiotic. (*PW*:85-86)

Maybe he wrote this half-jokingly, but at the same time there must have been some truth in his remark. Peirce's earliest publications (1867-1868) already advance a broadly comprehensive semiotic theory, and much of his later work is a development --radical and innovative, as the spirit of Peirce's doctrines itself-- of this early theory of signs. Peirce's semiotics, more than any other aspect of his work, is based upon his universal categories, "Firstness", "Secondness", and "Thirdness", roughly corresponding to the modes of being: possibility, actual fact, and law (*CP*:1.23,1903). This theory --which he later called "phenomenology" or "phaneroscopy"-- is closely linked to his study of Kant and of logic. Peirce argued convincingly that all thought is in signs. Yet, while he first viewed logic as a branch of semiotics, in his later period he came to consider it in a broadened sense as identical with it. Before expounding his semiotic thought, I need therefore to sketch his early theory of logic and, prior to it, present a summary of his theory of the three categories, in which all of his logic (and therefore, his semiotics) is rooted.

The categories

Peirce had at an early date identified thought and reasoning with his three ways of dealing with reality, the experiential modes or categories, and hence with signs[9]. The categories --Firstness, Secondness, and Thirdness--, which constitute the foundation of Peirce's work and thought, will be referred to throughout this study, from the different viewpoints required by discussion of aspects of Peirce's work. Suffice it to advance here, for those unfamiliar with Peirce's triadic thought, my earlier, brief description of, *seriatim*, Firstness, Secondness, and Thirdness:

> Of the three ways of perceiving facts, Firstness is the hardest to understand, in spite of the fact that it represents "pristine simplicity" (*CP*:7.551) and "*naïveté*" (*CP*:8.329). Firstness means unanalyzed, instantaneous, immediate feeling: direct "suchness" dependent on nothing else beyond itself for its comprehension. For example, Firstness is experienced

9 See his "On a new list of categories" (*CP*:1.545-1.549;*W2*:49,1867).

in [Peirce's examples] the feeling of acute pain, an electric shock, a thrill of physical delight, the sensation of redness or blackness, the piercing sound of a train whistle, a penetrating odor, or any other impression which is forced upon the mind and compels its total attention. Peirce himself also included in his list of Firsts "the quality of the emotion upon contemplating a fine mathematical demonstration, the quality of falling in love" (*CP*:1.304). Firstness is thus the idea of the timeless present instant experienced as "pure emotion of the *tout ensemble*" (*CP*:1.311) prior to any thought. One cannot "think" a First. (Gorlée 1987:46)
Whereas Firstness means undivided and undividable oneness, Secondness involves the dynamic idea of "otherness", of two-sided consciousness, the experience of action and reaction, stimulus and response, change and resistance to change. The idea of hitting and getting hit is a true Second, since it contains the elements of polarity, interaction, comparison, and struggle. While a First is a potentiality, a possibility, "merely something that *might* be realized", a Second is a hard fact, "an occurrence . . . something that *actually* takes place" (*CP*:7.538). According to Peirce, "the real is that which insists upon forcing its way to recognition as something *other* than the mind's creation" (*CP*:1.325). Therefore, it is through Secondness that we face [and deal with] reality [around us] and in the process acquire experience. All knowledge of the factual world and the more practical aspects of human life --such as opening a door, making a phone call, and kicking a football-- are Seconds. Secondness is involved whenever we make an effort, a decision, or a discovery; orientate ourselves in time and space; or experience surprise (*CP*:5.52-5.58). Secondness differs from Firstness in always occurring *hic et nunc*; yet it must also be based upon the past and the lessons we draw from it. Peirce states that "we may say that the bulk of what is actually done consists of Secondness --or better, Secondness is the predominant character of what *has been done*" (*CP*:1.343). (Gorlée 1987:46)
Beyond the vague generality of Firstness, "a mere idea unrealized", and the definite nature of Secondness, "the cases to which it applies" (*CP*:1.342), Thirdness embodies continuity, the rule of feeling and action by general principles. Since these principles provide logical explanations, all intellectual activity is a Third. Logical thought, Thirdness, creates orderliness, law, and regularity as opposed to, and out of, chaos, randomness, and chance: "The thread of life is a third" (*CP*:1.337). Since it is concerned with continuity, Thirdness is future-oriented and permits us to predict what is to be, and to adapt our attitude accordingly. Peirce argues that

This is the kind of consciousness which cannot be immediate, because it covers a time, and that not merely because it continues through every instant of that time, but because it cannot be contracted into an instant. It differs from immediate consciousness, as a melody does from one prolonged note. Neither can the consciousness of the two sides of an instant, of a sudden occurrence, in its individual reality, possibly embrace the consciousness of a process. This is the consciousness that binds our life together. It is the consciousness of synthesis. (*CP*:1.381)

All "finer" feelings and "deeper" emotions such as love, hope, compassion, and religious fervor, which because of the sophistication are popularly considered to be peculiar of the human species, are Thirds. The same is, *a fortiori*, true of cognition, intelligence, and mental growth. (modified after Gorlée 1987:47)

Peirce taught that, although our cognitive knowledge is not limited to signs, and we have knowledge of objects which are not signified, knowledge is necessarily in signs and we think about signs in signs. "We have no power of thinking without signs", Peirce stated at an early date (*CP*:5.265;*W*2:213,1868); and "life is but a sequence of inferences or a train of thought" (*CP*:7.583;*W*1:494,1868). Thought-signs reflect the different ways in which we make sense of phenomena we observe. In this sense are Peirce's modes of reasoning --"abduction". "induction", "deduction"-- complex, namely threefold, thought-signs; Thirds consisting in turn of signs, and which need to be built upon, and themselves involve, Seconds and Firsts .

Reasoning and logic

Scientific inquiry is always inspired by intellectual curiosity. A phenomenon, event, or fact which is surprising, puzzling to an observer, or which otherwise "strikes him as singular" (*MS*634:5,1909), challenges thereby the inquirer's ingenuity. In order to explain and make sense of the phenomenon, event, or fact, and to make predictions as to its future nature or behavior, it is carefully observed and reflected upon. Seeking to enhance the scientific value of the investigation and its conclusion(s), the investigator adopts a policy which in his or her view minimizes the risk of subjectivity and provides maximum objectivity. To achieve this purpose --objectivity--, the data obtained from sensible and mental perception of the phenomenon --its observation-- are mediated by inferential reasoning, the three-step logical thinking procedure which will yield true conclusions, on Peirce's view, at least eventually.

Customarily, valid reasoning was either deductive or inductive. Peirce revolutionized the traditional dichotomy, which he expanded and re-defined as a trichotomy; this classification is, in Peirce's own words, "the key of logic" (*NEM*4:22,1904). The division which Peirce offered distinguishes between explicatory, or analytic, reasoning and ampliative, or synthetic, reasoning; the latter being in turn of two kinds.

Explicatory, or analytic, reasoning corresponds to what is traditionally called deductive reasoning. It simply substitutes for the facts presented in the premisses, what is implicit in them. As inference from the whole to the parts it does not draw upon the unknown or the partially unknown. This makes deduction the only form of necessary reasoning. On the other hand, ampliative, or synthetic reasoning does not lead to necessary conclusions, but to conclusions which are probable or merely plausible. Ampliative reasoning is further divided by Peirce (in 1866) into two kinds: induction --the traditional probable reasoning-- and abduction --also called by Peirce, its "inventor", hypothesis or retroduction. Since both induction and abduction are forms of inference from the parts to the whole, neither can provide certainty nor lay a justified truth claim. Whereas, in Peirce's words, "Deduction proves that something *must be*" and "Induction shows that something *actually is* operative", "Abduction merely suggests that something *may be*" (*CP*:5.171,1903).

The aforementioned differences aside, all three kinds of logical argument deal, albeit in different ways, with hypotheses. Every inquiry, scientific and practical, uses instinctive reasoning, or abduction; because every inquirer needs to formulate and adopt certain hypotheses on which to further build the argumentation. Using Peirce's famed example of the beanbag, abduction goes as follows:

> *Rule* All the beans from this bag are white.
> *Result* These beans are white.
> ∴ *Case* These beans are from this bag.
> (*CP*:2.623;*W*3:325,1878)

Of the three modes of reasoning, abduction is the only one to "open up new ground" (*NEM*3:206,1911) and to introduce new ideas into intellectual inquiry (*CP*:6.531,1901;*CP*:7.220,1901). Weak as the absolute truth value of abduction may be and in fact is --at least when compared with the probative force of its stronger counterparts, induction and deduction--, it is nevertheless the creative force breathing originality into what would otherwise be a "reasonable" (*CP*:5.174,1903) but utterly rationalistic and, thereby, lifeless procedure.

In his embryonic "Specimen of a dictionary of the terms of logic and allied sciences: A to ABS" (*W*2:108,1867), Peirce coined the technical term "abduction" as a complement and, in a sense, foundation of the traditional pair, deduction and induction. Thereby Peirce re-labeled and christened a mode of thought which, for all its tentativeness, is often more plausible than its previous name, hypothesis, would suggest. For Peirce, abduction is more than gratuitous guesswork, it is responsible for progress in science. Without the ideas generated through abductive inference in a trained mind guided by, Peirce said, "*il lume naturale*, which lit the footsteps of Galileo" (*CP*:1.630,1898), the system of logic would not only be badly lacking in inventiveness and initiative, and therefore be incomplete; more seriously, it would tend to be self-serving, self-actualizing, and, thereby, self-validating; because abductive heuristics is essential to inspired discovery of all kinds.

Abduction corresponds to Peirce's Firstness, the first of his universal categories, which is typically represented by the sign of Firstness, or "icon" --standing for its object in virtue of its similarity or analogy to it[10]. Abduction is iconic argument and the conclusion of an abductive syllogism --the tentative

10 The term "icon" will also be discussed later in this Chapter, in the section on the "Object".

explanation of the puzzling fact observed-- is prefigured iconically in the premisses. The first premiss describes what the beans must be *like* to qualify as beans from this particular bag (*CP*:2.96,1902). The conclusion, or interpretant, of an abduction is an icon. The iconic quality is, in the beanbag example, whiteness.

After abduction, the "sheet anchor of science" as Peirce called it (*MS*691:118,1901), let us next consider briefly the scope of induction, the second type of reasoning:

Case These beans are from this bag.
Result These beans are white.
∴ *Rule* All the beans from this bag are white.
(*CP*:2.623;*W*3:325,1878)

This is an inductive syllogism, by which Peirce meant "a course of experimental investigation" (*CP*:5.168,1903). Induction assumes that "that is true of a whole collection which is true of a number of instances taken from it at random" and therefore "This might be called statistical argument" (*CP*:5.275;*W*2:217,1868). The premiss of the inductive inference constitutes an "index"[11] of the conclusion; the sample points to what all the beans from which the sample is taken will be like. An index is, in Peirce's semiotic conception, a sign of Secondness; a sign which is thought to stand in a physical connection to its object, pointing outside itself to that object. Smoke points in this sense to the maybe hidden but "natural" presence of fire; the latter is the existential component of smoke. Peirce spoke rather graphically of the index as "a fragment torn away from the Object, the two in their Existence being one whole or a part of such a whole" (*CP*:2.230,1910). By this token, induction is indicative argument; for it establishes between premiss and conclusion an evident cause-consequence relation which hardly requires an intelligent interpreter to do so.

There can be no absolute certainty in induction; because the investigator, spurred by intellectual curiosity (*CP*:5.584,1898), is in fact making predictions and judging the unseen by the seen. Reasoning as he or she does from particulars to generals, new knowledge is inferred by extrapolating it from actual, observed fact. By doing this, the inquirer is, or at least should be, aware of the fact that the present factual knowledge as is reflected in the premisses, may be incomplete or even false; but nevertheless "the reasoning proceeds as though all the objects which have certain characters were known" (*CP*:5.272;*W*2:216,1868).

This optimism is a reflection on the so-called "pragmatic maxim" which Peirce formulated in his 1878 paper "How to make our ideas clear" and on which, together with the three universal categories, Peirce's whole semiotic (or logic)

---

11 The term "index" will also be discussed later in this Chapter, in the section on the "Object".

system hinges[12]. In accordance with this principle of pragmatism, Peirce was convinced that "inquiry of every type, fully carried out, has the vital power of self-correction and growth" (*CP*:5.582,1898). Induction will bring the honest and serious inquirer so to speak halfway on the path which, in the Peircean view, must eventually lead him or her from interrogation and doubt to certainty and truth. In this stage, however, "we only know that by accepting inductive conclusions, in the long run our errors balance one another (*CP*:5.350,1868); and thus

> The operation of testing a hypothesis by experiment, which consists in remarking that, if it is true, observations made under certain conditions ought to have certain results, and then causing those conditions to be fulfilled, and noting the results, and, if they are favorable, extending a certain confidence to the hypothesis, I call *induction*. (*CP*:6.526,c.1901)

Induction as defined by Peirce in this crucial period of his thought, yields a "practical truth" (*CP*:6.527,c.1901), one which "shows that something *actually is* operative" (*CP*:5.171,1903) and does no more, and no less, than "affording us a reasonable assurance of an ampliation of our positive knowledge" (*CP*:2.96,1902).

A typical deductive inference goes like this:

Rule	All the beans from this bag are white.
Case	These beans are from this bag.
∴ *Result*	These beans are white. (*CP*:2.623;*W*3:325,1878)

Whereas "Induction is where we generalize from a number of cases of which something is true, and infer that the same thing is true of a whole class" (*CP*:2.624,1878), deduction --which is typified by mathematical reasoning-- is "merely the application of general rules to particular cases" (*CP*:2.620,1878). The inference of a conclusion from the premisses is here a purely methodic operation, which approaches the mechanical (*CP*:5.579,1898). The premiss of a deductive syllogism provides a general rule under which the specific conclusion falls. The premiss is therefore, in respect to the conclusion, a sign of Thirdness. Consequently, deduction is symbolic argument, fundamentally linked to the mode of being of the "symbol"[13] --in the specific meaning Peirce gave to this widely-used term.

In Peirce's conception, a sign is symbolic whenever the relation to its object is abstracted from reality, to the point that it can only signify if it is interpreted according to some agreed-upon, law-like rule or convention. Without

---

12 Peirce's pragmatic maxim will be quoted and discussed in following pages.

13 The term "symbol" will also be discussed later in this Chapter, in the section on the "Object".

such a "common ground", which must be shared by sign-producer and sign-interpreter-- , successful interpretation of the symbol is hardly possible. The fact that, in certain circumstances, a white dove can mean peace (and a flag, one's country, for instance), is "non-natural", culture-bound knowledge which must be acquired at some point by all members of the symbol-using community for it to function in efficient communication. Since symbols are man-made and do not mean naturally but culturally and/or socially, they are signs of belonging (or not belonging) to this community. This means that all linguistic signs, both written and spoken, are, first and foremost, symbolic signs. They can only make sense to an interpreter (reader, listener, etc.) who has effectively mastered the sophisticated set of rules which apply in a particular language, or linguistic sign-system.

Deduction is "the only kind of argument which is compulsive" (*CP*:2.96,1902); as opposed to abduction and induction, it almost "can be worked by a machine" (*CP*:5.579,1898). This would imply that, in Peirce's own words,

> *Theoretically*, . . . , there is no possibility of error in necessary reasoning. . . . In practice, and in fact, mathematics is not exempt from that liability to error that affects everything that man does. Strictly speaking, it is not certain that twice two is four. (*CP*:5.577,1898)

Thus, even deductive inference has no absolute truth value. Given, moreover, that its validity "depends unconditionally upon the relation of the fact inferred to the facts posited in the premisses" (*CP*:5.270;*W*2:215,1868), its truth is wholly a function of this relation, so that "as long as the premisses are true, however, other facts may be, the conclusions will be true" (*CP*:5.271;*W*2:215,1868). For the argument here it is important to underscore that deduction does not question the validity of the hypotheses contained in its own premisses; instead, it is simply taken for granted that they are correct because they "represent our whole knowledge of the matter" (*CP*:5.271;*W*2:216,1868). Since deduction forecloses critical (re)examination and/or (re)evaluation of its premisses, it does not engage in the introduction of new insights, nor in the rejection of hypotheses once they have been adopted. This makes deductive thought strictly explicatory, non-ampliative.

Now the point I wish to make here does not require going into further details concerning Peirce's arguments. The goal of all reasoning is simply and truly "to find out, from the consideration of what we already know, something else we do not know" (*CP*:5.3;*W*3:244,1877). This is the process Peirce typically called the "fixation of belief" (*CP*:5.358-5.387;*W*3:242-257,1877), the process by which he meant a settlement of opinion, from the individual to the collective. This truth-seeking process corresponds to what Ransdell means when he speaks of a "cognitive quest", --to which he also refers, rather felicitously, definitely in Peirce's spirit, and with a somewhat anthropological flavor, as a

> . . . *communal hunt*: "Hey, everybody! I think it went that way! Look; here are the signs. Now I interpret them to mean that...." But it is really no metaphor. Human beings were hunters before they were warriors or growers even, and we will always be on the hunt for something. Objectivity is the form of the communal hunt for the truth, and it seems to me that this is what *scientific* should be construed to mean as well. (Ransdell 1986a:238)

Peirce's mature thought --which can be located from the turn-of-the-century onward-- is likewise focused on the degrees of truth which can be conveyed by the various kinds of argumentation. The idea of truth-providing, that is, necessary reasoning, is abandoned and replaced by shades of "subjective probabilities, or likelihoods" of facts (*CP*:2.777,1901).

Peirce's pragmaticism

Peirce's maxim of pragmatism in its early and best-known 1878 version goes as follows:

> Consider what effects that might conceivably have practical bearings, we conceive the object of our conception to have. Then, our conception of these effects is the whole of our conception of the object. (*CP*:5.402;*W*3:266,1878; cf.later versions: *CP*:5.9,1902;*CP*:5.412,1905;*CP*:5.438,1905;*MS*318:256-257,1907)

Thinking, said Peirce, seeks to establish meaning; a mental action, it removes doubt by establishing a belief which leads to a habit of thought. For Peirce, meaning is an affair of concepts producing logical effects (that is, interpretations) which lead from the first to the second and then to the third and last stage of clearness of thought, the objective truth. In the twenty-five years following the formulation of the pragmatic maxim, Peirce did not work seriously on pragmatism, but was mainly involved in the study of the categories, the classification of the sciences, and the general theory of signs. The insights which he developed in this period are integrated in Peirce's fully developed concept of pragmatism --which he renamed "pragmaticism" to distinguish it from his friend and colleague William James's more general doctrine of "pragmatism". In 1905, Peirce described pragmatism, or pragmaticism, as consisting in "a method for ascertaining the real meaning of any concept, doctrine, proposition, word, or other sign" (*CP*:5.6,1905); and two years later he wrote:

> I understand pragmatism to be a method od ascertaining the meanings, not of all ideas, but only of what I call "*intellectual concepts*", that is to say, of those upon the structure of which arguments concerning objective fact may hinge. (*MS*318:134,1907)

Starting with the series of lectures which Peirce delivered at Harvard University in 1903, he thus associated pragmaticism with Thirdness; it deals with the meaning of the above-mentioned "intellectual concepts" as it is evolved by a mind in an endless series of "interpretants", that is, signs interpretative of previous signs. This "scientific procedure" is no longer guided by personal, practical beliefs as in Peirce's early thought, but by theoretical, scientific beliefs. The latter are experimentally verifiable judgments furnished through controlled abduction, the hypothesis of the man of science. In Peirce's pragmatic doctrine, logically good reasoning is thus controlled sign-action, or in other words "semiosis", the process through which we as thinking persons will come ever closer to the ultimate purpose of rational thought, which Peirce called the *summum bonum*. Thinking is an interpreting, that is a semiosic, activity in that it is deliberate, future-oriented, evolutionary action converging, in the hypothetical long run, toward law-like uniformity, Peirce's thinking-habit, or "fixation of belief"[14].

In 1905, Peirce reworded the pragmatic maxim in semiotic language as follows:

> The entire intellectual purport of any symbol consists in the total of all general modes of rational conduct which, conditionally upon all the possible different circumstances and desires, would ensue upon the acceptance of the symbol. (*CP*:5.438,1905)

In his mature period Peirce has wedded, so to speak, the three categories --and hence his earlier logic in the form of the three modes of reasoning-- with his pragmaticism. In its new formulation, pragmaticism was to play a central role in his semiotics. Beginning with a very "soft" universe consisting of pure irregularity and chance, the pragmaticist embarks upon a process of making such a universe ever "harder". This evolutionary making-process is nothing but experimental science itself; because science, for Peirce, consists in inquiry not in doctrine; and experimentation is a kind of feedback process requiring self-control.

Though Peirce spoke of the pragmaticist's action as of "rational experimental logic" (*CP*:5.430,1905), for him this does not imply that habit-forming, or generality, must rely upon the action of humans. Anthropomorphism is doubtless a plausible conclusion, yet it is possible to analyze other self-controlling mechanisms in nature. For Peirce, the human cognitive process can be "naturalized" and applied to natural phenomena. To show that thinking, or "mind", is not opposed to nature, or "matter", but is in "natural" continuity with it, is the task Peirce, the evolutionary thinker, was engaged in for nearly half a century all in all. On this view, thinking itself is a kind of activity having isomorphic features with all forms of activity in nature, and so if humans interact experimentally with

---

14 For a detailed account of Peirce's pragmatism, see Fitzgerald 1966:91ff. and Kent 1987:192ff.

nature they do not do so exclusively from the standpoint of their subjective self, but place themselves in the "architectonic" processuality of semiosis. As argued above, this starts out as a hypothesis which by being tested is increasingly "clarified", that is, acquires increasing "hardness". This hierarchical procedure has a deductive form, an abductive origin, and an inductive confirmation; it leads ultimately to the *summum bonum* of objective generality, --the truth of reality.

That the three-step processuality is, in Peirce's scheme, universally applicable to all logical (that is, for Peirce, the same as semiotic) processes, may be illustrated below by some examples taken from different domains, or fields of research, in all of which the same triadic scenario --Firstness, Secondness, Thirdness-- may be distinguished:

Logic Hypothesis, Induction, Deduction (*CP*:1.354,1890-1891;*CP*:1.369,c.1885); Names, Propositions, Inferences (*CP*:1.354,1890-1891; *CP*:1.369,c.1885); Sign, Signified, Cognition (*CP*:1.372,c.1885); Terminus, Connection, Branching (*CP*:1.371,c.1885); Icon, Index, Symbol (*CP*:1.369,c.1885); Absolute Term, Relative Term, Conjugative Term (*CP*:1.354,1890-1891).

Metaphysics I, It, Thou (*CP*:1.551,1867); Spirit, Matter, Evolution (*CP*:6.32,1891); Origin, End, Mediation (Betweenness) (*CP*:6.32,1891); Pluralism, Dualism, Monism (*CP*:6.32,1891); Mind, Matter, God (*W*1:83,1861).

Physics Indeterminacy, Haecceity, Process (*CP*:1.405,1890-1891); Chance, Law, Habit (*CP*:1.409,1890-1891;*CP*:6.32,1891); Rest, Velocity, Acceleration (*CP*:1.337,c.1875; *CP*:1.359,1890-1891); Inertia, Force, Causality (*CP*:1.66-1.69,1903).

Biology Sensibility, Motion, Growth (*CP*:1.393,1890-1891; Variation (Arbitrary Sporting), Heredity, Selection (*CP*:1.398,1890-1891;*CP*:6.32,1891); Instinct, Experience, Habit (*CP*:8.374,1908).

Physiology Cell Excitation, Excitation Transfer, Habitual Excitation (*CP*:1.393,1890-1891); Irritation, Reflex, Repetition (*CP*:5.373,1877;*CP*:3.156-3.157,1880).

Psychology Feeling, Willing, Knowing (*CP*:1.375,1890-1891; *CP*:1.382,1890-1891); Feeling, Reaction, General Conception (*CP*:6.32,1891); Feeling, Activity, Learning (*CP*:1.377,1890-1891); Instinct, Desire, Purpose (CP:7.369,1902)[15].

Sign

In order to define and describe Peirce's concept of sign two aspects of the matter need to be touched upon: (1) What kind of "things" can be signs?, (2) What are the characteristics of a sign?

---

15 This section draws heavily upon insights from Esposito 1980:174-175. The triads here (most of which are taken from "A guess at the riddle" or other writings from the same period) are either explicitly mentioned in Peirce; or they are extrapolations from Peirce. Of course, it should be taken into account that Peirce's perspective was time-bound, and occurred before the theory of relativity and quantum theory were to revolutionize the sciences.

Addressing the first question, Peirce explained that he included

> . . . under the term "sign" every picture, diagram, natural cry, pointing finger, wink, knot in one's handkerchief, memory, dream, fancy, concept, indication, token, symptom, letter, numeral, word, sentence, chapter, book, library. (*MS*74:3,n.d.)

And elsewhere Peirce wrote:

> . . . Signs in general [are] a class which includes pictures, symptoms. words, sentences, books, libraries, signals, orders of command, microscopes, legislative representatives, musical concertos, performances of these, . . . (*MS*634:18-19,1909)

Peirce made it abundantly clear that for him anything "Cognizable" (*CP*:8.177,1909) --that is, anything perceptible, knowable, or imaginable-- can be a sign. This includes qualities (signs of Firstness), actually existing or occurring things (signs of Secondness), as well as thoughts, laws, and habits (signs of Thirdness). Yet "a sign is not a kind of thing. The world does not consist of two mutually exclusive kinds of things, signs and non-signs, each with its subdivisions, yet with no subdivision of the one overlapping any subdivision of the other" (Fisch 1986:329-330). There is nothing that may not be a sign; perhaps, in a sufficiently generalized sense, everything is a sign: "all this Universe is perfused with signs, if it is not composed exclusively of signs", Peirce wrote (*CP*:5.448,n.1,1905). All human cognition, including sensory perception, emotive feeling, as well as inferential reasoning, involves signs. But for a sign to *act* as a sign, it must enter into a relation with its "object", be interpreted, and so produce a new sign, its "interpretant". This interpretative process is called sign-action, sign-activity, or, in semiotic parlance, semiosis. The fundamental distinction is therefore not between things that are signs and things that are not (because everything can be a sign, provided it functions as a sign), but between "genuine", triadic sign-relations and what Peirce called "degenerate" sign relations --the dyadic and monadic relations which were for Peirce a sign of immature thinking[16]. This would for Peirce no doubt have included Saussurean, dichotomous thought as practiced in semiology. So the fundamental conception of a Peircean semiotics is not that of the sign but that of sign-action, semiosis.

The second question is in fact the more challenging question of the two: What are the fundamental characteristics of the sign *qua* triadic sign-action? For the sake of brevity let me advance here a short answer: What characterizes it is the

---

16 For a discussion of Peirce's concept of degeneracy, see Gorlée 1990 and the bibliographical references given there.

ability which it possesses to not only represent meaningfully something else, but also to be decoded, understood, and interpreted as such.

Although Peirce redefined his definition of a sign frequently, the following one, from 1897, has become one of his best-known definitions of the sign:

> A sign, or *representamen*, is something which stands for something in some respect or capacity. It addresses somebody, that is, creates in the mind of that person an equivalent sign, or perhaps a more developed sign. The sign which it creates I call the *interpretant* of the first sign. The sign stands for something, its *object*. It stands for that object, not in all respects, but in reference to a sort of idea, which I have sometimes called the *ground* of the representamen. (*CP*:2.228,1897)[17]

At this point Peirce's definition already implies that the ground of a sign is the first element of the sign *qua* relation, and is itself a First; that the object is the second element of the sign relation, and a Second; and that the interpretant is the third element of the sign relation, and a Third. Five years later, Peirce associated explicitly the elements in his definition of the sign, with the three ontological modes of being:

> A *Sign*, or Representamen, is a First which stands in such a genuine triadic relation to a Second, called its *Object*, as to be capable of determining a Third, called its *Interpretant*, to assume the same triadic relation to its Object in which it stands itself to the same Object. (*CP*:2.274,1902)

A sign consists in the meaningful interaction between a First, a Second, and a Third element, in which the Third mediates between the First and the Second. The nature of the sign itself, its own inherent qualities or physical/material makeup, is what is referred to as First; at the same time, however, the triadic sign-relation itself is also called "sign": "A sign is a sort of First [which] brings a Second, its Object, into *cognitive* relation to a Third . . ." (*CP*:8.332,1904). To be sure, this "cognition", or thought is, Peirce said,

> . . . not necessarily connected with a brain. It appears in the work of bees, of crystals, and throughout the purely physical world; and one can no more deny that it is really there, than that the colors, the shapes, etc., of objects are really there. (*CP*:4.551,1906)

The sign-in-itself appears, as has been shown, as the first element in the semiotic triad; yet it may in its turn appear again in three different modalities; it is either a "qualisign", a "sinsign" (also called "token"), or a "legisign" (also called "type"). This is Peirce's first *trichotomy of signs*:

---

17 In Chapter 5 I shall discuss the concept of ground, which Peirce used in his earlier thought.

> . . . in the first place a sign may, in its own firstness, either be a mere idea or quality of feeling [a qualisign], or it may be a "sinsign", that is, an individual existent, or it may (like a word) be a general type ("legisign") to which existents may conform. (*MS*914:3,c.1904)

A qualisign, Savan writes, is

> . . . a sign which signifies through its abstractable quality as such, through the Firstness of quality, apart from any empirical or spatiotemporal relation of the quality of anything else. For example, I use a colour chip to identify the colour of some paint I want to buy. The colour chip is perhaps made of cardboard, rectangular, resting on a wooden table, etc., etc. But it is only the colour of the chip that is essential to it as a sign of the colour of the paint. Or again suppose I am teaching someone to swim and demonstrate a particular arm stroke for my pupil to imitate. Here too there are many aspects of my act that are irrelevant. What is essential to it as a sign is a characteristic sweep of movement. Wherever a quality is a sign that is to be copied, imitated, mimicked, mirrored, it is acting as a qualisign. (Savan 1987-1988:20)[18]

"When we speak of quality" Savan continues, "we think first of the simple sensory qualities of colour, odour, sound, etc." (Savan 1987-1988:29), i.e., of what pertains to the sign, a First, in its Firstness:

> The apprehension of any individual or collection of individuals presents us with some abstractable quality. We can and do speak of complex landscape qualities ("Alpine," "Tropical"), or the qualities of human personalities ("Napoleonic," "Chaplinesque"). (Savan 1987-1988:20)

Next comes the sinsign[19], or "actual existent thing or event which is a sign" (Peirce 1955:101,c.1903). To qualify as a sinsign, which means to embody a First in its Secondness, the "thing or event" must actually owe its signhood to its existence as an individual thing or event. A sinsign must occur in a particular context, thereby eliciting an action:

> The samples of moon rock being analyzed by lunar scientists are sinsigns. Every singularity and peculiarity of the moon rock is recorded, analyzed, and used as a clue of the structure and history of the moon, the earth and the solar system . . . [Another example of a sinsign is] the red traffic signal . . . [which] does not signal stop when it is an

---

18 Note the curious parallelism between Savan's example of the swimming instructor, Wittgenstein's language game of the gymnastics instructor (Wittgenstein *PI*:1:630) and Goodman's example of the gymnastics instructor (Goodman[1968]1985:63), which I discussed in my article "Wittgenstein et Peirce: Le jeu de langage" (Gorlée 1989b).

19 Peirce explained that "the syllable *sin* is taken as meaning 'being only once,' as in *single*, *simple*, Latin *semel*, etc." (Peirce 1955:101,c.1903;cf.*CP*:8.334,1904).

> electrical room decoration, or if it were set up in the middle of a cow pasture, or if observed from his helicopter a few feet overhead by the traffic reporter. (Savan 1987-1988:21-22)

"[T]hirdly, it is of the nature of a general type, when I call it a *legisign*" (*CP*:8.334,1904); its general, regular, law-like character must then be what makes it a sign. All linguistic signs fall first and foremost into the third category, because they typically represent the sign, which is a First, in its Thirdness. In this, Peirce is pretty clearly correct, and it is important to note this feature of linguistic signs[20]. A test for something's being a general is whether it is repeatable as opposed to being a unique individual. It is fairly obvious that words of human language are repeatable, that the very same word, for example, can be spoken or written many times. Peirce called these instantiations "replicas".

Object

After discussing, in the previous section, the sign, let us now turn to its correlate, the "object". The object or "referent" of the sign is represented by and signified by the sign. Any object may be real or ficticious, that is, created in sign-use: "The word Sign will be used to denote an Object perceptible, or only imaginable . . . " (*CP*:2.230,c.1897). The sign exists in the creation of a "standing for" relation, and without representation --that is, the sign-object relation-- we have no sign. Thus, in order to be a sign, a portrait needs to be a representation *of* someone, real or imaginary; the object must be prior to the sign. While a sign presupposes the existence, real or potential, of an object, the reverse is not true. This also implies that the sign must be *other* than the object. In the sign-object relation the sign is influenced by or, as Peirce said: "determined by", the object; the sign is the passive element, the object the active element determining the sign. The object is, however, only knowable through the sign. Peirce wrote that the object of the sign,

> . . . when there are both an utterer and an interpreter, is that which the former has in mind, but which it does not occur to him to express, because he well knows that the interpreter will understand that he refers to that, without his saying so. I am speaking of cases in which the sign stands alone without any context. Thus if the utterer says "Fine day!", he does not dream of any possibility of the interpreter's thinking of any mere *desire* for a fine day that a Finn at the North Cape might have entertained on April 19, 1776. He means, of course, to refer to the actual weather, then and there, where he and the interpreter are alike influenced by the fine weather, and have it near the surface of their common

20 Following Peirce, Pharies states that "All linguistic signs, regardless of their form or meaning, refer to their objects primarily and indispensably by virtue of convention" (1985:44). Despite its broad title, *Charles S. Peirce and the Linguistic Sign*, Pharies limits himself in his book to lexical linguistic signs, or words.

> consciousness. Marine fossils found on a mountain, considered as a sign of the sea-level having been higher than the levels of deposit of these fossils, refer to a distant but indefinite date. Here, there is no utterer; but this is what might have remained unexpressed in the mind of the utterer, though essential to the significance of the sign, if that sign had been devised and constructed to give the human race a first lesson in geology. Where the sign is only a part of another sign, so there is a context, it is in that context that the [object] is likely, in part at least, to be found . . . (*MS*318:69-70,1907)

Each semiosis gives, perhaps, pieces of new information about the object, which thereby gradually discloses itself to the observer/interpreter. But if a sign and its object would be the same, the sign would no longer point toward the object and thus convey no information: "an Object that merely presents itself represents nothing" (*MS*634:21,1909). Self-referentiality between sign and object would mean the inevitable end of the process of semiosis.

Peirce distinguished between two objects in semiosis: on the one hand, the object as it is represented directly in particular sign-use, the "immediate object", and on the other hand the object which is not immediately present, Peirce's "dynamical object" (which he also called the "mediate" or the "real object"). Both objects may be, and often are, quite different from one another.

The immediate object is known by taking the sign at face value; it represents the object, which is a Second, in its Firstness. It can, at least in principle, be a quality, an existent, or a law (*PW*:33,1904). Whereas the immediate object is the object "inside" the sign or "the idea which the sign is built upon" (*MS*318:70,1907), the dynamical object is "that real thing or circumstance upon which that idea is founded, as on bed-rock" (*MS*318:70,1907). The dynamical object is not immediately present: it represents the object, which is a Second, in its Secondness. It is "the Object outside of the Sign" (*MS*318:70,1907), which elicits and informs the sign. Peirce wrote: "The Sign must indicate it [the dynamical object] by a hint; and this hint, or its substance, is the Immediate Object" (*PW*:83,1908). Although the dynamical object is only indirectly expressed by the sign, yet careful examination of the sign in its surrounding context, together with what may be called "experience" and, in Peirce's words, "collateral observation, aided by imagination and thought, will usually result in some idea" (*MS*318:77,1907) of what it is about.

In the final consideration it may be said that the dynamical object, or the object as it is in itself, abstracted from its occurrence and role in a particular sign-use, will correspond to the sum total of the instances of the sign-bound immediate object. And knowledge of the dynamical object, the real meaning of the sign, can only be acquired by "unlimited and final study" (*CP*:8.183,1909) of the immediate object in its spatiotemporal context, and is thus the end result of a semiosic process. This implies that the more one knows, in a general way, about a particular phenomenon, event, or the like, the more the immediate and dynamical object will be the same.

In reference to the dynamical object, a sign can be an "icon", an "index", or a "symbol"[21]. This is Peirce's best-known trichotomy and, of his three trichotomies of signs, it is the one which, as he himself said, "seems beyond criticism" (*MS*339C:499,1905). See the following recapitulation:

> A sign can refer to an Object by virtue of an inherent similarity ("likeness") between them (*icon*), by virtue of an existential contextual connection or spatiotemporal (physical) contiguity between sign and object (*index*), or by virtue of a general law or cultural convention that permits sign and object to be interpreted as connected (*symbol*). (*CP*:2.247-2.249,c.1903)

Here and elsewhere Peirce left no doubt that an icon conveys a First, an index a Second, and a symbol a Third:

> A regular progression of one, two, three may be remarked in the three orders of sign, Icon, Index, Symbol. The Icon has no dynamical connection with the object it represents; it simply happens that its qualities resemble those of that object, and excite analogous sensations in the mind for which it is a likeness. But it really stands unconnected with them. The index is physically connected with its object; they make an organic pair, but the interpreting mind has nothing to do with this connection, except remarking it, after it is established. The symbol is connected with its object by virtue of the idea of the symbol-using mind, without which no such connection would exist. (*CP*:2.299,c.1895)

As I have argued earlier,

> . . . an iconic sign, such as a portrait or a map, represents its object by virtue of its similarity with it. Beyond that --that is, in and of itself-- an Icon, as a First, asserts nothing: "For a pure Icon does not draw any distinction between itself and its object. It represents whatever it may represent, and whatever it is like, it in so far is [sic]" (*CP*:5.74). It is meant to be the picture-image or replica of the object signified. Since, according to Peirce, "The only way of directly communicating an idea is by means of an Icon" (*CP*:2.278), an Icon exhibits meaning and requires no interpretation in order to do so.
>
> While Icons stress likeness, Indices stress difference. Since an Index stands in a causal relationship to the object it signifies, it can only assert something insofar as it points directly to its object; hence its Secondness. The object signified is either materially or virtually present. An example of an Index often used by Peirce is a weathercock, which denotes its object, the direction of the wind. Other Indices are, for example, smoke

---

21 Given the "popularity" of these terms, I give in the following an account which is complementary to the remarks advanced earlier in this Chapter.

> meaning fire and fever meaning illness. An indexical message tends to be a simple one in that its interpretation is straightforward, "natural".
>
> Genuine signs are Symbols. They are the only triadic signs, because in order to function as signs (that is, to stand for something else and be meaningful), they must be interpreted according to some previously agreed general rule. In the absence of the object, Symbols can deceive or lie. The meaning of a Symbol is an "open guess", unless a meaning is agreed upon by consensus. Since the association between the Symbol and its object is arbitrary, the interpretation may be changed at will and overruled by a new agreement. In this way a dove can mean peace, and a piece of cloth attached to a rope can symbolize a country and move us to tears. In this sense, too, language is a system of symbolic signs, because any linguistic sign can in principle be used to represent any object. (Gorlée 1987:48)

It must be added here that these three types of signs are not mutually exclusive, and that the same sign can function, and often will function, at the same time as an icon, an index, and/or a symbol[22]. In Peirce's words, "That footprint that Robinson Crusoe found in the sand, . . . , was an Index to him that some creature was on his island, and at the same time, as a Symbol, called up the idea of a man" (*CP*:4.531,1906); and for the sake of completeness Peirce might have added here that, shapewise, the footprint was first of all an icon of some human foot.

Interpretant

Peirce insisted that "nothing is a sign unless it is interpreted as a sign" (*CP*:2.308,1902). It is not enough, he argued, that the sign "stands for" an object; it must also be interpreted as doing so. Interpretation is therefore as essential a component of the sign relation as representation:

> An inscription that nobody had ever interpreted or ever would interpret would be but a fanciful scrawl, an index that some being had been there, but not at all conveying or apt to convey its meaning. (*NEM*4:256)

Peirce made the "interpretant" a central issue in his semiotic theory. In the sign-interpretant relation, the interpretant -- the sign interpreting a previous sign-- logically follows from --once again, Peirce's "is determined by"-- the sign; the sign acts upon the interpretant, which stands on the receiving end of this transaction. Yet once produced, the interpretant, a Third, becomes again the First element, or sign, in the next triadic sign relation, and so on.

As Peirce wrote to Victoria Lady Welby on October 12, 1904: "A sign mediates between the *interpretant* sign and its object [,the former being]

---

22 This was rightly argued by Greenlee in his *Peirce's Concept of Sign* (1973:86), for which this scholar otherwise has been much criticized, particularly for his assertion that all signs are Thirds.

interpreting thought, itself a sign" (*PW*:31,1904). All interpretants are in principle verifiable, because they ultimately refer back to some feature of reality or culture, on which the series of interpretants forms a running commentary or ongoing interpretation. Peirce wrote:

> It appears to me that the essential function of a sign is to render inefficient relations efficient . . . Knowledge in some way renders them efficient; and a sign is something by knowing which we know something more. (*CP*:8.332,1904)

Each new interpretant provides more complete information on the object in question, so that the infinite chain of interpreting signs will point forward towards eventual truth. In this way the process of semiosis operates both backward towards the object and forward towards the interpretant. As Peirce explained the significance of interpretants:

> The meaning of a [sign] can be nothing but a [sign]. In fact, it is nothing but the [sign] itself conceived as stripped of irrelevant clothing. But this clothing never can be completely stripped off; it is only changed for something more diaphanous. So there is an infinite regression here. Finally, the interpretant is nothing but another [sign] to which the torch of truth is handed along; and as [sign], it has its interpretant again. Lo, another infinite series. (*CP*:1.339,n.d.)

Peirce distinguished between three interpretants in semiosis: To one sign correspond an "immediate", a "dynamical", and a "final" interpretant[23]. The immediate interpretant of a sign is, Peirce wrote,

> . . . a feeling produced by it . . . a feeling which we come to interpret as evidence that we comprehend the proper effect of the sign, although the foundation of truth in this is frequently very slight. (*CP*:5.475,1907)

This first interpretant is thus, to paraphrase Ransdell (1986b:681-682), a mere sign of the interpretability of the sign, i.e., of its identity as capable of being interpreted. It shows the sign's generative power by revealing an as yet rather vague and unanalyzed range of its possible interpretants to be produced under given conditions; it is the interpretant, or Third, as it represents the sign in its Firstness.

---

23 How Peirce's second set of three interpretants --the "emotional", the "energetic", and the "logical" interpretant-- is to be placed in relation to the first one, is at this point still a matter of debate. See, e.g., Eco 1976 and, in recent years, Ransdell 1986b, Short 1986a, Liszka 1990, and Johansen (1993). I shall not attempt here to express an opinion on this issue, and shall use both sets of interpretants, reserving the first trio (immediate, etc.) to refer particularly to the stages in the interpretative process, and the second (emotional, etc.) to indicate them from the perspective of the interpreter (or better, the interpreting mind).

The dynamical interpretant goes beyond possibility and is a really occurring interpretative event involving some direct effort, mental and/or physical (i.e., muscular). As Peirce explained to Lady Welby, the dynamical interpretant consists in the "direct effect actually produced by a Sign upon an Interpreter of it .. that which is experienced in each act of Interpretation and is different in each from that of any other" (*PW*:111,1909).

Whereas the dynamical interpretant may thus be characterized by a diversity of viewpoints and shifting of attention, such versatility is superseded in the case of Peirce's third and final interpretant, the essence of which is rule and habit of interpretation. The teleological, judgmental, and normative nature of interpretation thus points towards "the effect the sign *would* produce upon any mind upon which circumstances should permit it to work out its full effect" (*PW*:110,1909); and this final interpretant is "the one Interpretative result to which every Interpreter is destined to come, if the Sign is sufficiently considered" (*PW*:111,1909). Needless to say that since a sign may be studied over and over again, and from an endless diversity of aspects, producing ever-new interpretations of it, its full meaning will only be known in some hypothetical future.

The meaning of a sign is thus provided, respectively, by the intuition, belief, or habit by which the sign is defined. For example, if someone says he or she regards religion as an affair just for the ignorant[24], the meaning of this proposition or assertion (the sign) is not identical with what it refers to (its dual object, religion and the ignorant) but with the rule or habit (its interpretant) by which one would, under certain conditions, recognize, identify, and manipulate this object. The meaning of a sign is, then, not given by its object(s), but by its (their) interpretation(s). This is also brought home to us by Peirce, who offers the following domestic scene in order to illustrate this crucial piece of his semiotic doctrine in a letter to his friend, William James:

> For instance, suppose I awake in the morning before my wife, and that afterwards she wakes up and inquires, "What sort of a day is it?" *This* is a sign, whose Object, as expressed, is the weather at that time, but whose Dynamical Object is the *impression which I have presumably derived from peeping between the window-curtains*. Whose Interpretant, as expressed, is the quality of the weather, but whose Dynamical Interpretant, is *my answering her question*. But beyond that, there is a third Interpretant. The *Immediate Interpretant* is what the Question expresses, *all* that it immediately expresses, which I have imperfectly restated above. The *Dynamical Interpretant* is the actual effect that it has upon me, its interpreter. But the Significance of it, the *Ultimate*, or *Final*, *Interpretant* is her *purpose* in asking it, what effect its answer will have as to her plans for the ensuing day. I reply, let us suppose: "It is a stormy day." Here is another sign. Its

---

24 I borrow this example from the headline of an advertisement in *The New York Review of Books* of January 31, 1991:5.

> *Immediate Object* is the notion of the present weather so far as this is common to her mind and mine --not the *character* of it, but the *identity* of it. The *Dynamical Object* is the *identity* of the actual or Real meteorological conditions at the moment. The *Immediate Interpretant* is the *schema* in her imagination, i.e. the vague Image or what there is in common to the different Images of a stormy day. The *Dynamical Interpretant* is the disappointment or whatever actual effect it at once has upon her. The *Final Interpretant* is the sum of the *Lessons* of the reply, Moral, Scientific, etc. (*CP*:8.314,1909)

Peirce's third trichotomy, of "rheme", "proposition", and "argument", addresses the relation between the sign and the third or final interpretant. This trichotomy is of particular interest for logicians, for it deals with precisely the sort of signs used for logical reasoning, namely Thirds. A sign may be represented by its interpretant as a sign of possibility (rheme), a sign of fact (proposition), or a sign of reason (argument). A rheme, as a sign which is not true nor false, gives no information about the object; it "leaves its Object, and *a fortiori* its Interpretant, to be what it may" (*CP*:2.95,1902). In reasoning, the rhematic sign, or "qualitative Possibility" (*CP*:2.250,c.1903), is an open suggestion with a very slight truth value. One example of this may be found in the commercial slogan "Coke is It"[25], where the "It" remains unspecified and may therefore be interpreted by anyone as standing for anything whatsoever. In contradistinction to a rheme, which is a Third under its aspect of Firstness, a proposition gives information about the object of the sign; it emphasizes the Secondness of its Thirdness and is, as Peirce wrote, "a sign which separately indicates its object. Thus, a portrait with the name of the original below it is a proposition" (*CP*:5.569,1901). A proposition is "not an assertion, but a sign capable of being asserted" (*CP*:8.337,1904); of course, it may equally be rejected. Peirce added that by uttering a proposition, "One subjects oneself to the penalties visited on a liar if the proposition asserted is not true" (*CP*:8.337,1904). To conclude, an argument is a "sign which distinctly represents the Interpretant" (*CP*:2.95,1902); in other words, "for its interpretant, [it] is a Sign of law" (*CP*:2.252,c.1903). As instrumental in reasoning, an argument is "an argumentation or statement expressly designed to lead to a given belief" (*MS*599:43,c.1902). Peirce wrote that

> . . . upon innumerable questions, we have already reached the final opinion. How do we know that? Do we fancy ourselves infallible? Not at all; but throwing off as probably erroneous a thousandth or even a hundredth of the beliefs established beyond present doubt, there must remain a vast multitude in which the final opinion has been reached. Every directory, guide-book, dictionary, history, and work of science is crammed with such facts. (*MS*1369:24-25,1885)

---

25 I owe this example to my friend and eminent Peirce scholar, Professor Jørgen Dines Johansen of Odense University.

Whereas a proposition is endowed with a better truth value than a rheme, an argument advances a definite conclusion especially intended to give the truth. "[T]he premisses of an argument are a sign of the truth of the conclusion" (*MS*283:107,1905-1906): thus the argument should, of the three, be endowed with the highest coefficient of objective truth, since there is nothing in the system to contradict it, and since it is permitted to unfold all its consequences, on all levels.

In logic, an argument is exemplified by the three modes of reasoning, -- abduction, induction, deduction. As an interpretant may follow from its sign hypothetically (abductively), inductively, or deductively, so inferential conclusions are interpretants which are especially singled out from other possible interpretants. If we erase from an argument its special purpose, it becomes a proposition. A proposition is, in logic, a truncated argument, and a rheme, both a truncated argument and a truncated proposition. In Peirce's words:

> That which remains of a Proposition after removal of its Subject is . . . a rhema called its Predicate. That which remains of an Argument when its Conclusion is removed is a Proposition called its Premiss, or (since it is ordinarily copulative) more usually its Premisses . . . (*CP*:2.95,1902)

Rhemes may be monadic (with one blank space), dyadic (with two blank spaces), or triadic (with three blank spaces): "--- is black" shows only the idea or quality of blackness, "--- is a dog", of "dogness", "--- is either black or white", "--- hits ---", "--- gives --- to ---". In order to create a "sentence" or proposition, the blanks must be filled out with some deictic, that is indexical, entity. This adds a subject[26], and thus a storyline, which is lacking in a rhematic sign. Thus, Peirce said,

> A proposition consists of two parts, the *predicate* which excites something like an image or dream in the mind of its interpreter, and the subject, or subjects, each of which serves to identify something which the predicate represents. (*MS*280:34,c.1905)

Last comes the argument, or perspective under which the utterance is intended to be understood. Since an argument is "a symbol which separately shows by what sign it is led to accept its proposition" (*MS*339b:299,1898), a (linguistic) argument may be a command, question, statement, or other speech act[27]. To venture a terminological suggestion: if a rheme may be called a mere "mood-set", a

---

26 Peirce's subject is a logical concept; it includes the grammatical functions of subject and object. See, e.g., *MS*280:34-35,c.1905, where Peirce also related this to his system of existential graphs.

27 About Peirce's early moves in the direction of what later came to be called speech act theory, see Brock 1981 and Hilpinen 1982, and Ferriani 1987. See also Chapter 10.

proposition is a "fact-set", and an argument a "mind-set".

Semiosis

Semiosis is sign interpretation[28]. As mentioned at several instances of the discussion above, it is a triadic process between sign --"something which stands to somebody for something in some respect of capacity", its ground (*CP*:2.228,1897) --, object --that for which the sign stands--, and interpretant, another sign and caused by the original sign in the mind of some interpreter of it. In semiosis the latter (the interpretant sign) mediates significatively between the two former (the sign and the object). To quote Peirce directly, semiosis is

> . . . an action, or influence, which is, or involves, a coöperation of *three* subjects, such as a sign, its object, and its interpretant, this tri-relative influence not being in any way resolvable into action between pairs. (*CP*:5.484,1907)

Semiosis yields, in the interpretant, again three degrees of "hardness" of beliefs which correspond to Firstness, Secondness, and Thirdness. First comes "maybe" (or "maybe not"); second, "actually is"; and third, "must be".

The third or final interpretant is the rule of action constituting the meaning of a sign as a definitive law or "must be". To transform semiosis into giving final answers is, however, denying its essentially open-ended and infinite nature. And such terminality undercuts unlimited semiosis, because it excludes the possibility that any interpreter at some point will start the interpreting process afresh, that he or she will turn the given interpretant into a new sign and produce a new interpretant, the product of a new semiosis, which, turned again into a sign, may again produce an interpretant, and so on; "There is an endless series of signs, . . . in the same sense in which Achilles runs over an endless series of distances in overtaking the tortoise" (*MS*599:31,c.1902).

Short (1986a:119ff.) speaks therefore of a "non-ultimate" logical interpretant, corresponding to Peirce's "final opinion" but still placed in a living triadic sign relation, and prior to the ultimate logical interpretant, the latter being an essentially hypothetical entity in which sign and object are no longer distinguished and semiosis must come to a standstill. This makes a sign potentially, if not in fact, a member of an infinite sequence of signs, each one interpretive of the one preceding it. In order to give ever-new evidence of the life of the sign, semiosis is and must be an ongoing, goal-directed, but always open-ended processuality.

---

28 Peirce's concept of semiosis will play a central role in my argumentation throughout this book. Therefore, the first presentation here will remain brief.

Peirce did not explicitly include the sign user or interpreter as a fourth component of semiosis, in addition to the interpretant. This is not to say that Peirce did not recognize the existence of an interpreter, because he did in fact refer to a (human) interpreter occasionally. Apparently, what Peirce had in mind here was not one single person nor one specific mind, but in an abstract way an intelligent "quasi-mind" or "quasi-interpreter". The human mind not being, on Peirce's view, a prerequisite for semiosis, the "theaters of the mind" (*MS*318:55,1907) and "footlights of consciousness" (*MS*339C:505,1905) are instrumental in making the sign evolve *itself* as a meaning-generating (that is, object-revealing) entity. Even so, an interpreting agency of some kind has to be somehow implied by Peirce in his triadic (and not tetradic) structure of semiosis; because without the intervention of some interpreting mind --actual or potential, human or non-human--, there can be no interpretation, no action of the sign, and hence no semiosis.

Peirce's trichotomies and the classification of signs

To illustrate the foregoing brief --all too brief-- remarks on Peirce's three trichotomies and sign action, let me quote the following extended passage, from the crucial *MS*318, in which Peirce, the pragmaticist, offered an exemplary inventory of the multifarious dimensions of the semiotic sign:

> Now how would you define a *sign*, Reader? I do not ask how the word is ordinarily used. I want such a definition as a zoologist would give of a fish, or a chemist of a fatty body, or of an aromatic body, --an analysis of the essential nature of a sign, of how the word is to be used as applicable to everything which the most general science of signs must regard as its business to study; be it of the nature of a significant quality, or something that once uttered is gone forever, or an enduring pattern, like our sole definite article; whether it professes to stand for a possibility, for a single thing or event, or for a type of things or of truths; whether it is connected with the thing, be it truth or fiction, that it represents, by imitating it, or by being an effect of its object, or by a convention or habit; whether it appeals merely to feeling, like a tone of voice, or to action, or to thought; whether it makes its appeal by sympathy, by emphasis, or by familiarity; whether it is a single word, or a sentence, or is Gibbon's Decline and Fall; whether it is of the nature of a jest scrawled on an old enveloppe, or is sealed and attested, or relies upon artistic force; and I do not stop here because the varieties of signs are by no means exhausted. Such is the definitum which I seek to fit with a rational, comprehensive, scientific, structural definition, --such as one might give of "loom", "marriage", "musical cadence"; aiming, however, let me repeat, less at what the definitum conventionally does mean, than at what it were best, in reason, that it should mean. (*MS*318:52,1907)

In Peirce's earlier thought (see, for instance, *CP*:2.243,1903), signs were classified according to the three trichotomies, and divided in the ways which were yielded by their triadic relations to (1) themselves, (2) their (dynamical) object, and (3) their final interpretant[29]. This division --corresponding to the monadic sign, the dyadic object, and the triadic interpretant-- provided for the three separate divisions and trichotomies of signs discussed above: qualisign-sinsign-legisign, icon-index-symbol, rheme-proposition-argument.

Peirce's next move was to make the separate divisions interact, and thus form combined sign configurations grounded in different triadic relations. The new sign forms may be relatively genuine, relatively (i.e., singly) degenerate, or genuinely (i.e., doubly) degenerate. These distinctions are fuzzy rather than neat, and should be imagined as located on a continuum --such as a wheel-form (Gorlée 1990)-- meant to highlight the dynamic quality of the ever-shifting interrelations:

> For Peirce, the sign is no fixed entity, but one subject to change, an ongoing process of signs shading into each other. One sub-relation changes --for example, a genuine triad (3) becomes a singly degenerate (2) or doubly degenerate (1) sign relation-- and a new sign-configuration is born. Unless the new threefold *Gestalt* is intrinsically triadic (that is, composed of three sub-relations, all of them Thirds), each sign is an incidental, mercurial phase within a whole kaleidoscopic scenery of signs. (Gorlée 1990:78)

In 1904, Peirce wrote:

> . . . I now recognize ten genera of signs, resulting from three modes of division . . . These do not make 27 kinds, but only 10 because: Every Qualisign is an Icon, / Every Icon is a Rhema, / Every Symbol is a Legisign, / Every Argument is a Symbol. Thus the 10 kinds are:
>
> 1 Arguments
> 2 Dicisignificant Symbols, or Propositions
> 3 Dicisignificant Indexical Legisigns
> 4 Dicisignificant Sinsigns
> 5 Rhematic Symbols
> 6 Rhematic Indexical Legisigns
> 7 Rhematic Indexical Sinsigns
> 8 Iconic Legisigns
> 9 Iconic Sinsigns
> 10 Qualisigns[30]

---

29 For a comprehensive account of Peirce's classifications of signs, see Weiss and Burks 1945; and a more recent study is Sanders 1970.

30 Peirce's letter to Christine Ladd-Franklin of July 27, 1904. I owe this reference to Professor Max H. Fisch. In a postscript to his letter to Victoria Lady Welby of October 12, 1904, Peirce reversed the order:

> 1. Qualisigns
> 2. Iconic sinsigns
> 3. Iconic legisigns

Peirce immediately adds here that "Of course, there are very important subdivisions", and he proceeded to develop them by integrating into his classification those degenerate sign elements --the (degenerate) immediate object, the (doubly degenerate) immediate interpretant, the (singly degenerate) dynamical interpretant-- which he at first seemed to have disregarded.

With the recognition that a sign has two objects and three interpretants, the anatomy of Peirce's sign became ever more complex, abstract, and opaque. Additional trichotomous divisions were required to accomodate all of them, and the result became eventually somewhat as follows:

Divisions according to the nature of

1	*Sign in itself*:		
	Qualisign (Tone, Potisign, Mark)	Sinsign (Token, Replica, Actisign)	Legisign (Type, Famisign)
2.1	*Immediate (degenerate) object*:		
	Descriptive (Indefinite)	Designative (Denominative)	General (Copulative)
2.2.1	*Dynamic object in itself*:		
	Abstractive	Concretive	(Collective (Complexive)

---

4. *Vestiges*, or Rhematic Indexical Sinsigns
5. *Proper names*, or Rhematic Indexical Legisigns
6. Rhematic Symbols
7. Dicent Sinsigns (as a portrait with a legend)
8. Dicent Indexical Legisigns
9. *Propositions*, or Dicent symbols
10. Arguments. (*PW*:35-36,1904)

This enumeration is represented diagrammatically in *CP*:2.264,c.1903, where the following labels are used: 1. Rhematic Iconic *Qualisign*, 2. Rhematic *Iconic Sinsign*, 3. *Rhematical Indexical Sinsign*, 4. *Dicent* Indexical *Sinsign*, 5. Rhematic *Iconic Legisign*, 6. *Rhematic Indexical Legisign*, 7. *Dicent Indexical Legisign*, 8. *Rhematic Symbol* Legisign, 9. *Dicent Symbol* Legisign, 10. *Argument* Symbolic Legisign. In the account of Peirce's division of signs which Lieb appended to his early edition of Peirce's letters to Lady Welby, he gave the following examples: 1. A feeling of "redness", 2. An individual diagram, 3. A spontaneous cry, 4. A weathervane, 5. A diagram abstracting its individuality, 6. A demonstrative pronoun, 7. A street cry, 8. A common noun, 9. A proposition, 10. A syllogism (Peirce 1953:51;also quoted in *PW*:161).

2.2.2	*Dynamic object in its relation to the sign*:		
	Icon (Likeness)	Index	Symbol (General Sign)
3.1	*Immediate (doubly degenerate) interpretant in itself*:		
	Hypothetical	Categorical	Relative
3.2.1	*Dynamic (singly degenerate) interpretant in itself*:		
	Sympathetic (Congruentive)	Shocking (Percussive)	Usual
3.2.2	*Dynamic (singly degenerate) interpretant in its relation to the sign* (manner of appeal):		
	Suggestive (Ejaculatory)	Imperative (Interrogative)	Indicative (Cognificative)
3.3.1	*Final interpretant in itself*:		
	Gratific	Practical (Actuous)	Pragmatistic (Temperative, Moral)
3.3.2	*Final interpretant in its relation to the sign* (intended influence):		
	Rheme (Seme, Term, Sumisign)	Proposition (Dicent, Dicisign, Pheme)	Argument (Suadisign, Delome)
3.3.3	*Triadic relation between sign, object, and final interpretant* (assurance given by):		
	Abducent (Instinct)	Inducent (Experience)	Deducent (Form, Habit)

(cf.*MS*339D:543,1906;*MS*795:2,1906;Weiss and Burks 1945:388)

When Peirce wrote to Lady Welby that he found 28 classes of signs yielded by six trichotomies, he was referring to the first six trichotomies mentioned above. He argued this as follows:

> . . . it follows from the Definition of a Sign that since the Dynamoid Object determines the Immediate Object, / Which determines the Sign itself, / which determines the Destinate [Immediate] Interpretant / which determines the Effective [Dynamical] Interpretant / which determines the Explicit [Final] Interpretant the six trichotomies, instead of determining 729 classes of signs, as they would if they were independent, only yield 28 classes. (*PW*:84,1908)

Indeed, Peirce's architectonic doctrine of signs stipulates that whatever is a First determines only a First; whatever is a Second determines a Second or (degenerately) a First; whatever is a Third determines a Third, or (degenerately) a Second or a First (cf.*CP*:2.235f.,c.1903). This principle led Peirce to include the other four trichotomies and thereby greatly expand the number of possible signs.

By 1906 (see, e.g., *CP*:4.531,1906;1.290f.,c.1908), Peirce had discovered that there are ten trichotomies and, derived from them, sixty-six classes of signs: in addition to one kind of qualisign, there are ten classes of sinsigns and 55 classes (10 + 9 + . . . + 1) of legisigns (Weiss and Burks 1945:387-388). Yet Peirce continued fine-tuning his classifications of signs:

> . . . there are *ten* different respects in which signs may essentially vary as far as my researches have already gone. But I already meet with unmistakable indications that there are more than ten modes . . . If these ten respects were independent of one another that would make 3^{10} or 59,049 kinds of signs. But they are so far from being independent that I think the total number is about 100, I think it an even chance that it lies between 66 and 150. (*MS*499s:8-10,1906?)

Peirce was, however, never able to complete the description and analysis of additional divisions to his own entire satisfaction. One typical example of this is his following remark:

> My classification of signs is not yet fully matured. I have been at work upon it, or at least have had it in mind since 1867, but still confidently expect important improvements in it. If I live to complete it, it will be the contribution to exact logic that has cost me the most labor, and it will be recognized by exact logicians as a very positive and indisputable contribution to exact logic even if I should leave it in its present imperfect state. There remain many hundreds of difficult questions yet to be considered though the majority of them have received an examination which cannot justly be called careless or summary. (*MS*499:39-40,1906)

If Peirce in this statement was still sanguine that he would be granted time and energy to rethink and rewrite this crucial issue --the classification of signs in the framework of semiosis-- , and to bring his argument to a conclusion, in his late years he became less optimistic, and even half-apologetic. To conclude, let me therefore quote Charles Sanders Peirce, the patriarch of modern sign theory, as he confessed unreservedly that

> . . . I am, as far as I know, a pioneer, or rather a backwoodsman, in the work of clearing up what I call *semeiotic*, that is, the doctrine of the essential nature and fundamental varieties of possible semiosis; and I find the field too vast, the labor too great, for a first-comer. I am, accordingly, obliged to confine myself to the most important questions. The questions of the same particular type as the one I answer on the basis of an impression, which are of about the same importance, exceed four hundred in number; and they are all delicate and difficult, each requiring much research and much caution . . . There is my apology, such as it may be deemed. (*CP*:5.488,1907)

04. TRANSLATION AND THE SEMIOTICS OF GAMES AND DECISIONS

"A puzzle is an exercise in hypothetic inference"
(*MS*831:17,1900)
"Adhere to the one ordinance of Play, the law of liberty"
(*CP*:6.460,1908)

Introductory remarks

In translation theory, "translation" is used to refer to both the act of translating and to the translated text which is a result of this operation or, indeed, this sequence of operations. Translating has been considered traditionally as a practical, goal-oriented activity aiming at producing a concrete result, the translation. At the same time has there been a growing awareness that translation is not merely reducible to its end product, but that it is also, and indeed, first and foremost, search, attempt to find solutions for problems. Thanks to the progress made in the study of the heuristic element in translation, the process-oriented activity, aimed at problem-solving, has come to complement the product-oriented approach to translation.

Translation as sign interpretation

In the following I will first propose that translation involves a dual incidence of semiosis. Hermeneutics, almost in the traditional sense, forms the first interpretative instance and precedes heuristic interpretation in translation proper. Following the intuition, based upon empirical evidence, that translating implies a semiotic process of decision-making, I will posit that translation theory and the formal theory of games can and may be considered to be basically the same in kind; i.e., translating is in some way similar to playing a "game with complete information", such as a jigsaw puzzle or chess. Support for this working hypothesis is the practical applicability of the conceptual tools used in game theory to the translation situation. I will not propose a formalized model for translation based on the theory of games. Instead I shall venture a tentative exploration of what may be called the game of translation.

My first proposition is thus that in translation one can distinguish a double incidence of interpretation. The first is of a hermeneutic nature. In order to acquire a full understanding of both surface and in-depth meaning (or meanings) of the text, it involves a penetrating *explication de texte*, including its extralinguistic references. Such a close reading of the text in the light of the sociohistorical and cultural context surrounding and conditioning its production makes cognition of its referential meaning or meanings possible. As the translation theoretician, George Steiner, argues in *After Babel*, "comprehensive reading [is] in the heart of the interpretative process" and is in itself a "manifold act of interpretation" (Steiner 1975:5,17).

This first interpretative step made by the translator, the gaining of insight into the text's "inner world", is followed by, and alternative to, a second interpretative move which is outwardly focused. This creative, or reproductive, interpretation constitutes translation proper and consists of the actual transfer of the text from source language into target language. Steiner reaches the same conclusion when he states that the view of translation as interpretation

> ... will allow us to overcome the sterile triadic model which has dominated the history and theory of the subject. The perennial distinction between literalism, paraphrase and free imitation, turns out to be wholly contingent. It has no precision or philosophical basis. (Steiner 1975:303)

Seen from this perspective, interpretation is inherent in any mode of translation, be it intralingual, interlingual, or intersemiotic translation, i.e., Jakobson's three "ways of interpreting a verbal sign" (1959:233).

The dual occurrence of interpretation, with its inward and outward orientations, is reminiscent of Saussure's signifier and signified. But Saussurean semiology excludes extralinguistic referentiality and restricts interpretation to paradigms of signs. Signifier (that is, sign-vehicle or sound-image) and signified (that is, mental image or concept of meaning) merge into a twofold relation based upon mutual "solidarity", or complementarity. Here, the meaning of a sign is strictly bound by convention. The meaning of a sign, however, is actually twice removed: once by conventional and once by individual, "arbitrary" interpretation. The static quality of Saussure's dyadic signification concentrates on the former and does no justice to the creative potential of interpretation which happens to be the core of the argument here.

If, on the other hand, we follow Jakobson and adopt Peirce's theory of signs and their manifold meanings, we may expand the twosided paradigmatic structure and expediently (re-)introduce the dynamic element which is crucial in interpretation, and hence in the concept of translation put forward here. This dynamic element is embodied in the Peircean concept of interpretant, which is the third dimension in the triadic relation, sign-object-interpretant. In Peirce's much-quoted definition,

> A sign, or *representamen*, is something which stands to somebody for something in some respect or capacity. It addresses somebody, that is, creates in the mind of that person an equivalent sign, or perhaps a more developed sign. The sign which it creates I call the *interpretant* of the first sign. (*CP*:2.228,c.1897)

The interpretant as a sign interpretative of another sign implies that interpretation is a generative process of signification. The idea that the meaning of a sign is always another sign generates an endless series of interpretative signs. This unlimited process of making sense heuristically is called, in semiotic parlance, semiosis; and translation (that is, any translational process in the semiotic sense) is semiosis because it produces interpretant signs that, according to Eco (1979:71), "beyond rules provided by codes, explain, develop, interpret a given sign".

Returning to the definition of sign quoted above, we may now supplement it as follows: "The sign stands for something, its *object*. It stands for that object, not in all respects, but in reference of a sort of idea, which I have sometimes called the *ground* of the representamen" (*CP*:2.228,c.1897). Once we define the object in this way as that which is signified and the interpretant as that in which it is interpreted, the multiplicity of different possible interpretant-signs or translations for each sign is in turn determined by the relation the "first" sign has to its object. The multiplex modes of signifying are counterbalanced by the different modes of representational abstraction. In order to function as a sign, a sign needs to lead to interpretation. And in order to be meaningful, a sign must invariably be embedded in some code or system, which Peirce called "ground". Signs signify because the previous acquaintance their interpreter has with the rules that underlie their particular mode of being encoded, enables him or her in turn to produce interpretant-signs.

Without sign representation there is no possibility of sign interpretation. Interpretation, translation, or any other type of semiosis, means, in effect, tracing out the ground as it is operative in actual sign use. Meaning arises from exploratory interpretation of signs in their natural habitat: the world of context in which humans use verbal (and nonverbal) signs in order to meaningfully (for themselves) organize the reality surrounding them, thereby mastering it. This implies a partly experiential and partly cognitive frame of reference which is Peirce's ground.

Semiosis and game theory

In what follows I intend to show how the language game of translation fits into the framework of a non-formalized "translation" of game theory into semiotic terms[1]. This demonstration hinges upon a view of semiosis as a game with and beyond rules. Semiosis of whatsoever sort requires selection of a specific ground, that is, a point of view in terms of which the object is relevant to the significance of the sign in terms of its practical usefulness, in the same way as playing a language game involves choosing one particular tool or set of tools from the tool-box of language. These tools represent the codes providing the rules which in their turn generate signs. This would lead us back into the rigidity of Saussure's rule-governed signs, were it not that Peirce's concept of rule and habit in semiosis turns out to be quite unconventional and, indeed, almost paradoxical, since it is divorced from blind obedience to a repertoire of fixed rules, and must be interpreted to include even original *ad hoc* behavior. In reference to this, Greenlee writes that "the plausibility of the role Peirce gives to habit . . . is likely to be veiled by the fact that the conventions governing signs are often easily changed by mere fiat and appear to lack the ingrained character of true habits" (Greenlee 1973:91).

Game, play is both fiction and reality. It represents what Benveniste (1947) called "form" or "structure", meaning by this that it must have its own reality and its own logic. Hjelmslev, in his originally 1943 *Prolegomena* (discussing Saussure) and especially Greimas (1980:32), go one step further as they hold that play, like language and other semiotic systems, is a form of communication. Play, like semiotics, relies upon a contract[2] in order to relay meaning. In fact, its essence is arbitrariness. Like the sign, play and all game-like activities act as if meaning is being actually suspended, though in fact they carry meaning only relative to context, --thus, relative to other signs (Houle 1987:372). This Saussurean-structuralist concept of play is differently realized and, indeed, dramatized in a Peircean semiotic paradigm. The latter has none of the fixity or immobilizing traits which characterize the former, and offers a thinking method protagonized by dynamic processuality, --namely semiosis[3].

---

1 A formalization of the idea of language game in a mathematical theory of semantics has been developed by Jaakko Hintikka and his associates. See Hintikka 1973 as well as, for instance, Carlson 1983 and Saarinen 1979. On the application of game-theoretical semantics to translation, see Artosi 1981.

2 See further Chapter 10.

3 That Peirce was an enthusiastic gamesman may be particularly clear from his (so far unpublished) *MSS* 1521-1539 containing undated fragments on chess, tick-tack-toe, whist, backgammon, card tricks and other amusements, which testify to Peirce's recreational approach to mathematics. See, for a more detailed discussion of this aspect of Peirce's thought, Gardner (1978), who also seems to include among Peirce's more ludic pursuits his "two major obsessions"

The notion of strategy based on past experience is what binds together ground in semiosis, the heuristics of interpretation, and rules of play in games of skill, as opposed to games of chance, such as lottery and roulette. Whereas the latter do not require any activity from the player, strategic decisions are crucial elements in games of skill (also called parlor games or games of strategy). These games involve a set of fixed rules; the rules, however, do not dictate the actual behavior of player in a game situation. In fact, they permit, and indeed encourage, creativity and individual skill. Uncertainty as to the outcome (winning or losing) is another element these games have in common: if the end result were known in advance there would be none of the tension generated in games of strategy. This tension is a by-product of both the competition and the decision-making elements, and forms the usual motivation for playing strategic games in the first place. The actual outcome of a game is always the result of a strategy embodied in a series of moves made by supposedly rational players. And according to Rapoport this

---

(Gardner 1978:19), namely firstly, his system of existential graphs, a diagrammatical or pictorial, that is iconic, notation of thought, which Peirce invented in 1896 and developed into a complete treatment of logic of propositions and logic of quantifiers; and secondly, what Peirce himself, tongue-in-cheek, called his own "triadomany": "the anticipated suspicion that he [Peirce] attaches a superstition or fanciful importance to the number three, and forces divisions to a Procrustean bed of trichotomy" (heading of *CP*:1.568,1910). In addition, Peirce's concept of "Musement", a mental state of free speculation or reverie, when the mind indulges in "Pure Play" (*CP*:6.458,1908) and is thus able to generate, through abduction, remarkable flashes of insight, may also rightly be considered as a game of sorts.

To these cursory --all too cursory-- remarks on Peirce's keen interest in games the following addition is in order. The (unpublished) *MS* 1135:99ff.,(1895)1896 contains various drafts of what Peirce composed as alternative versions to *Roget's Thesaurus*, each item carrying elaborate (though, in different versions, differing) number combinations in accordance with Peirce's own triadic categorial scheme. In his classifications Peirce here made, under the general head of "*Amusement*, or occupation having excitement as its object and the impulse to be awake & active as motive" (*MS* 1135:99,(1895)1896) the following varying and not always neatly delimited subdivisions: (1) "*Lusory Contests*, to which emulation is the stimulus and success unimportant"(*MS* 1135:99,(1895)1896), also called by Peirce "Games, or Regular Contests, in which the interest is mainly in the course of the contest not in the stake"(*MS* 1135:108,(1895)1896), (2) "*Amusements not essentially social*", to which the stimulus is the desire to accomplish something for the ultimate sake of amusement. Some of these amusements use other people, but merely as playthings" (*MS* 1135:103,(1895)1896), (3)"*Irregular Contests*", with no definite rules, *Sport* proper", (4) "*Solitary Games*", and (5) "*Public Amusements*, including small gatherings" (*MS* 1135:106, (1895)1896). Peirce's further subdivisions run the whole gamut from chess, bird-keeping, swimming, flirting, and mind-reading to patience, property collecting, pantomime, and religious ceremonies. Quite amazingly, among the long list of multifarious games Peirce mentioned in a section of games "springing from primitive impulses", a curious game (or better "game") called "Keeping women", sandwiched between "Amateur Cookery" and "Killing" (*MS* 1135:119,(1895)1896).

refers to a player who, faced with a certain number of choices that represent alternative courses of action, makes tactical calculations of this sort: "If I do this, that will happen . . ., if I do that, this will happen . . . Since I prefer this to that, I will do this" (Rapoport 1961:130); and the same author defines a rational player as someone who

> . . . takes into account the possible consequences of each of the courses of action open to him [and] is aware of a certain preference order among the consequences and accordingly chooses the course of action which, in his estimation, is likely to lead to the most preferred consequence. (Rapoport 1961:107-108)

This implies that many activities humans engage in, if not the whole of life, may be considered a "game" of sorts, in which strategy appears in the struggle for success. And this also explains the wide acceptance and the numerous fields of application for the mathematical models provided by the theory of games, following its introduction by von Neumann and Morgenstern in their (1944) *Theory of Games and Economic Behavior*. Game theory has become a more or less general problem-solving technique which offers a formal approach to any conflict situation among individuals holding opposing interests. It deals with the choices they make or, better, should make in the course of the "game" in order to reach the most preferred outcome, which is called, in game-theoretical terms, utility.

Decision-making in games of strategy involves making one choice from a well-defined domain of possible choices or alternatives. It depends on the stronger or weaker gamble element in any particular game whether the subsequent choices or moves are made under certainty, risk, uncertainty (or a mixture of risk and uncertainty); this means, with or without knowledge as to the choices made by the other player(s). In order to optimize choice performance and hence personal utility, players adopt decision criteria. The decision maker attempts thus to maximize minimum payoff, which amounts to the same as to minimize maximum loss. To achieve this desired result he or she may employ, and often employs, the so-called minimax principle as a strategic tool. This is a normative choice procedure that stands for prudent game behavior in games where a player has one or more malevolent opponents anxious to ruin him or her. The opponent(s) may be (a) human individual(s) or an impersonal opponent called Nature, "Mr. Nature", or even "a diabolical Miss Nature" (Luce and Raiffa 1967:279). However, the selection by a player of a strategy for which the maximum loss for him or her is as small as possible, concentrates exclusively on the worst possible consequences for this particular player, of each of the possible moves, and thus allows no room for free intuition. It is for this reason that it produces essentially pessimistic and conservative game performances.

Game theory creates a dichotomy between, on the one hand, "games with incomplete information" (such as dominoes, poker, and card games), games, that is, in which chance makes a fair deal of the decisions, and, on the other hand, "games with complete information", that is, "games in which each player at each move is always informed about the entire previous history of the play, so that what is preliminary to his choice is also anterior to it" (Morgenstern 1968:64). This is the case of, for instance, chess and jigsaw puzzles.

Due to the normative character of decision theory as derived from games of strategy and due to the mental tool it uses --mathematics-- , game-theoretical analyses of human behavior have been rather unsatisfactory. Notwithstanding this unfruitfulness in, especially, psychological research, the concepts of game theory yield tools and heuristic hypotheses that may help analyze different games of strategy as well as otherwise game-like situations in which the player is in more or less complete control of the game with his or her decisions. The fact that the moves are non-random, since the decisions are derived in a systematic way, does, however, not exclude the possibility that they are inspired by subjective preferences. There is therefore always an element of risk-taking or betting by the player. This idea is wholly semiotic, because the understanding and use of signs is never a matter of recognition of a stable equivalence, but always a matter of guessing, or creative inferring.

Chess and the jigsaw puzzle

I shall limit myself here to applying some game-theoretical concepts to some games and game-like situations "with complete information". Both chess and the jigsaw puzzle are games requiring skill and reasoning, patience and sustained attention, discipline and perseverance. Both games involve decision-making on the basis of calculation and combination. Chess is a combat-like board game, whereas in jigsaw puzzles, the skill of the player is not related to any explicit competitive drive, and the struggle is rather with the obstacle. However, the element of competition is only apparently absent from solitary games of skill, because, as Caillois affirms,

> As individualized as one imagines the operation of the contraption to be --whether kite, top, yo-yo, diabolo, cup-and-ball, or hoop-- it would quickly lose its capacity to amuse if there were no competitors or spectators, at least potentially. There is an element of rivalry in these varied activities, and everyone tries to vanquish his rivals, perhaps invisible or absent, by accomplishing unpublicized feats, triumphing over obstacles, establishing precarious records for endurance, speed, precision, and altitude --in a word, even though alone, reaping glory from a performance difficult to equal. (Caillois 1961:37)

The role played by rules is different in chess and in jigsaw puzzles. While the latter is essentially a free game with a minimum of fixed rules, chess is characterized by a whole systematic complex of rules, its "grammar", beyond which there is nothing, no connection to any other aspect of life. The choice-of-movement problem in chess is solved by a rule-governed analytical thinking process. Because of its relative fixity, the system of chess has often been compared with the system of language. As a matter of fact, this supposed kinship is a well-nigh classical topic in philosophy of language, and has been referred to by Saussure, Hjelmslev, and Wittgenstein, among others[4]. The inadequacy of the analogy becomes, however, clear if one realizes that the rules for chess are given in advance as a non-negotiable whole; whereas linguistic rules need to be functional in ongoing social interaction and transaction, and are *per se* subject to continuous change by their users. Hence Derrida's semiosis-like metaphor of a "bottomless chessboard" (1973:154) which replaces Saussure's two-dimensional chessboard analogy with its successive linear moves (1966:88ff.)

As opposed to the rule-governed nature of chess, rule-determinacy is less pronounced in the jigsaw puzzle: the player is simply supposed to fit together a disarray of pieces of irregular shape so as to form one pre-defined picture, often some figurative design. Though this game usually does not pretend to be creative or even inventive, it may not be denied certain artistic overtones, an aesthetic quality which seems less evident in chess (de Groot 1965:341). In game-theoretical terminology, a jigsaw puzzle is a one-person-decision-game with a finite set of decision-alternatives (the separate pieces) and with some chance element in the focusing and finding process. The player is expected to make the decisions on his or her own, and tries to maximize his or her profit (utility) as he or she uses some strategy by which to enhance the quality of the game performance. So, for example, the player may choose to start joining together those pieces that form the edges, and fill in the empty space afterwards; or he or

---

4 See also Jakobson's views as formulated by Holenstein: "The rules of chess can be said to correspond to the syntactic rules of language. A chess move either complies with the rules (it is right) or infringes upon them (it is useless). But beyond that it can, like performative speech utterances, only be judged felicitous or infelicitous (as regards the goal of the action), but not true or false, as in the case of declarative sentences. Chess not only lacks a superstructure which allows the question of truth, but also --as Jakobson has emphasized repeatedly-- a substructure corresponding to phonology" (Holenstein 1976:168-169). This means that for Jakobson, "The traditional comparison of languages with chess must not be overrated. By mutual agreement chess players may substitute any object whatever for a mislaid chessman, whereas no constituents of a linguistic system can be arbitrarily replaced, and the choice of a substitute is far from being substantially indifferent. Not only the rules of the game, but also the rules of substitution govern the structure of language, since its constituents are bound by inalterable laws of implication and incompatibility" (Jakobson [1958]1971a:531 quoted in Holenstein 1976:169). For a discussion of the functionalistic interpretation of chess and the analogy with language, see, e.g., Carroll 1980, Eco 1976:89-90, Greenberg 1971, Güttgemans 1980, and Verburg 1961.

she may first sort out the amorphous mass of pieces according to their color, shape, or pictorial pattern. Whichever strategy is followed, its rational methodicalness should never spoil the simple fun of playing. The sheer amusement provided by the game itself accounts in fact for much, if not most, of the player's payoff, aside from the aesthetic gratification resulting from the creation of the mosaic-like arrangement.

Problem-solving and decision-making in the jigsaw game are directed at gathering together piece-by-piece, that is move-by-move, what is scattered and multifarious. The game creates order out of chaos. Before each move the player may have to engage in considerable trial and error before focusing on a piece which fits harmoniously into the total anticipated image. Since in the course of the game the "imagical" quality of the field is subject to continuous restructuring, the eye has to "see the problem" (Taylor 1968:506) at each move in order to perceive the new configuration, or *Gestalt.* To gain structural insight into the nature of each problematic situation, the player needs to "read" the problem in visual, spatiotemporal terms as he or she lets his or her eyes wander over the semiotic landscape formed by the two-dimensional playground, prior to making sense of it, --that is, constructing the information gathered into a three-dimensional, or better a poly-dimensional, picture.

The point of view in the "reading" phase is dual: it is atomistic in that the player examines some concrete detail problem; and at the same time it withdraws from the specific immediate puzzle to an overall vision of the entire game field. Shifting from the miscroscopic to the macroscopic perspective and vice versa enables the decision maker to "look around" with bifocals in the game situation, and subsequently to deal optimally with both factical and strategic choices. This game requires thus an ability to organize and memorize visual and spatiotemporal data, as well as to translate binary choices (yes/no) into moves. Being a binary system (such as that of other "games", the computer and the *I Ching*), the jigsaw game does not involve further alternatives.

Arranging the jigsaw puzzle is mainly a reproductive, mimetic activity, because the player recreates a replica in a rather mechanical way. The "substitute" produced is an iconic sign which, according to one of Peirce's definitions, "may represent its object mainly by its similarity with it" (*CP*:2.276,c.1902). Indeed, in its finished state the picture exhibits a close likeness to its model, at least according to the parameters color and shape. Beyond imitative iconicity, however, this game might also be considered as a more sophisticated, "intelligent" activity. It would then become an inventive process which uses disconnected units as building blocks for the construction of a meaningful structure. The jigsaw pieces are then used as Wittgensteinian tools: though, like the cubes of a mosaic, they possess scant meaning in themselves, they are chosen because of their combinational value. According to the rules of the game, the choice of the right tool at the right place will produce the desired result. And chanciness aside, it would then depend on the player's inventive workmanship how effectively he or she makes the right combinations, that is generates the significant image-sign[5].

Translation, a game[6]

This second characterization, mentioned above, of a simple jigsaw puzzle as a heuristic game, may with good reason seem fanciful at first. It is, however, worth pursuing this view here, because it points towards a more complex game, the language game of translation. My proposition is here that translation may be

---

5 Mention of Lévi-Strauss's jigsaw analogy is in order here. On his view, the kind of structuralist approach to anthropological phenomena which requires "the structure to lie at the level of empirical reality, and to be a part of it" (Lévi-Strauss 1960:52) is a misconception. Social structure, Lévi-Strauss adds, cannot be considered as "a kind of jig-saw puzzle [where] everything is achieved when one has discovered how the pieces fit together. . . [I]f the pieces have been arbitrarily cut, there is no structure at all. On the other hand, if, as is sometimes done, the pieces were automatically cut in different shapes by a mechanical saw, the movements of which are regularly modified by a cam-shaft, the structure of the puzzle exists, not at the empirical level (since there are many ways of recognizing the pieces which fit together): its key lies in the mathematical formula expressing the shape of the cams and their speed of rotation; something very remote from the puzzle as it appears to the player, although it 'explains' the puzzle in the one and only intelligible way" (Lévi-Strauss 1960:52). That such a jigsaw puzzle would only permit one "interpretation" is, of course, due to the structural (that is, iconic) likeness of its parts to the shape of the cams, by which it is, at the same time, indexically determined.

6 It is important to underscore that this comparison is not determined by any "objective" necessity, or by any eternal truth about translation or about games. As Toury reminds us: "Every comparison is by nature both partial and indirect: it is carried out regarding certain aspects only common to the objects compared, aspects constituting but a part of their total properties, and it is done with the aid of some 'intermediary concept' related to these aspects and serving as a fixed, invariant basis for the comparison. This invariant, and with it the comparison as a whole, are theory-dependent" (Toury 1978:93). It should be clear that the common theoretical perspective chosen here is semiotic, sign-philosophical. The analogy between the game concept and translation should, therefore, not be pressed as far as to slide from one to the other, thereby ignoring the characters that distinguish both entities. It would be an error of reasoning to claim, without further warrant, that if they share some characters (such as choice, rules, strategy, and decision-making) they must also share others; they don't. In addition to realizing their common characters in different ways, it is also obvious that they differ in general-theoretical scope as well as practical usage and functionality. Accordingly, the tendency here to assimilate translation (here used in the narrow sense) to the (broader) game concept and to refer to mutual "intermediary concepts" comes only from the strategy to provide a source of creative insight, a strategy geared towards the goal of encouraging to make some connections one might otherwise not conceive of making. See also the relevant epistemological issues raised in Jackson 1992, in which an analogy is drawn between the concepts of game and law.

considered as a game, comparable to the jigsaw puzzle as characterized above[7]. In the "game" of translation, however, the main element is Thirdness, not Firstness. Not only is translation governed by strict rules, but at the same time it challenges ingenuity while also involving logical processes. The game of translation is, it would seem, a more intellectual version of the jigsaw puzzle and represents a superior form of mental gymnastics. The translation problem is further presented in a less tangible and portable form than the jigsaw puzzle, and so represents a higher level of abstraction as it is found in the Peircean symbol, or sign of Thirdness.

All verbal language is mainly symbolic in the sense of Peirce's doctrine of signs. "A symbol" wrote Peirce "is a sign which refers to the object that it denotes by virtue of a law, usually an association of general ideas" (*CP*:2.249,1903). Whereas the icon, or sign of Firstness, bears a physical and static resemblance to the object it evokes, the association between a symbol and its object rests upon an agreement, a consensus. There exists thus an increased, dynamic distance between the symbolic sign and its object. Accordingly, the symbol only becomes meaningful in a practical way because the sign user (or better, the community of sign users) makes logical decisions about its scope and usage.

Iconic and symbolic signs both exclude any chance similarity between the sign-vehicle and the object of reference, and rely on some general, conventionally established connection, which consists in their ground. But symbols differ from icons insofar as the ground of the former stresses differences while that of the latter stresses similarities. What icons and symbols have in common is the idea of replica. This idea is salient to both the jigsaw puzzle and translation: in order to become meaningfully recognized, the symbolic, as the leading element in language-based translation, must even imply the iconic, the idea of replica. This replica need not be conventional, just as convention need not be standard but may, in a Peircean spirit, be or, at least, originate from an individual choice. So, while the referentiality of the jigsaw puzzle limits itself to the singleness of replication, language games, based as they are on linguistic signs, are primarily symbolic activities in the original meaning of the word symbol: "Etymologically", wrote Peirce, "it should mean a thing thrown together. . . But the Greeks used 'throw together' (*symballein*) very frequently to signify the making of a contract or convention" (*CP*:2.297,c.1895)[8].

Whereas the jigsaw puzzle exhibits, so to speak, its meaning, language

7 The cautionary remarks and reservations made in note 6 apply, *a fortiori*, to the analogy between one particular game, the jigsaw puzzle, and the "game" of translation (which is, as pointed out in note 6, discussed as a game for the sake of the argument here).

8 More on contract in Chapter 10.

games are not univocal in the same sense, they do not say what they mean, but possess an inherent polysemy which needs to be deciphered and interpreted. The basic symbolicity of language grants the signs used in language a great mobility. This dynamic quality is what distinguishes the game of translation from the jigsaw game. To be sure, the pictorial text conveying all purported information immediately and simultaneously, appears transformed into a textual "image" consisting of sequentially-ordered linguistic signs which the player is required to translate into a different linguistic mode or code, without violating the rules of the game.

In its pure and traditional form the game of translation is a one-person decision game based on rule-regulated, reasonable choices between alternative solutions. There is commonly one solitary player, the translator, who is engaged in this struggle against Nature, his or her impersonal opponent facing him or her in the text to be translated, embodied in its complex of puzzles. The player knows that each action invariably leads to a specific outcome, while the order and nature of the series of actions build and depend on the previous choices the player him- or herself has made. The game is productive of an intricate interrelational pattern, the generation of which can be symbolized by the game tree proposed by Luce and Raiffa in their (1967) *Games and Decisions: Introduction and Critical Survey* and applied to the translation situation by Levy.[9]

My argument here corresponds essentially to the theoretical perspective in Levy's (1967) article, "Translation as a decision process", in that translation is considered from the viewpoint of both game theory and semiotics. In his article, however, Levy concentrates on the problems found in the translation of literary texts; and within translation as a total semiotic process, he focuses on the pragmatic dimension (following Morris's division of the field of semiotics into syntactics, semantics, and pragmatics) as he pays particular attention to assessment by readers, that is interpreters "in the second degree" (as Peirce might have been tempted to call them). In the framework of translation as a decision process, Levy uses graphs called "decision trees". Levy's trees show how an omniscient translator has to deal with decisions, nodes, and branches that typically arise in the course of the translation process. The method of choice is to select that branch leading to the most desired result. Once one branch is chosen from a set of variants, all other branches are thereby eliminated and other solutions blocked for the rest of the game. Thus when a game situation, such as translating, is entered at one end of the decision tree, current values of variants determine a path to an appropriate action. This would mean that translating is not unlike "finding a way

9 See also Levy 1970. The state-of-the-art of translation as problem-solving and decision-making is discussed in Wilss 1988 (see especially Chapters 4 and 5).

through a maze . . . the first time --not, as in studies of animal learning, to learn to run the maze without error" (Taylor 1968:509).

In contradistinction to the jigsaw puzzle, which aims at finding the one pre-specified solution, the game of translation is a game of seeking and finding "a" solution that is as relevant as possible to the purpose of the game: maximizing the player's expected payoff. In translation, this aim can hardly be specified in terms of straightforward gain or loss, because in this solitary game there are no real points to score. Instead comes the gratification provided by the game itself and by its concrete result, measured in terms of success vs. failure. The translator gains the desired (by him or her) outcome if by his or her choices he or she produces an equivalent[10], well-formed translation; and in order to reach this goal he or she tends to avoid time- and energy-consuming trial and error behavior, and to adopt an implicit or explicit strategy that will help him or her to sort out the consecutive problems. As this rational strategy is, more often than not, the minimax principle discussed above, translators, according to Levy,

> . . . are content to find for their sentence a form which, more or less, expresses all the necessary meanings and stylistic values, though it is probable that, after hours of experimenting and rewriting, a better solution might be found. . . . Translators, as a rule, adopt a pessimistic strategy, they are anxious to accept those solutions only whose "value" --even in case of the most unfavourable reactions of their readers-- does not fall under a certain minimum limit admissible by their linguistic or aesthetic standards. (Levy 1967:1180)

Surely the translator often has no other choice than to be satisfied with his or her own minimax performance (for instance, because exhaustive analysis of the alternatives is impossible, or because he or she has to adapt, as economically as possible, his or her own standards to the constraints of the particular game). But such a policy reduces the translator's choices to his or her own strategic options which, at best, are lucky guesses about his or her own capacities.

Systematization of translational performance as rule-bound step-by-step behavior is, however, only a one-sided view of the language game of translation, one which is based on a view of the linguistic code as a collective entity dealing with combinational rules. In reality, however, this code goes far beyond such categories as "grammar" and other rule-bound linguistic features, however comprehensive they may be. In the game of translation, solutions for problems must often be other than grammar-generated and may be the result of non-systematic search in a certain direction. Rule-consistency in decision-making needs to coexist with free discovery if the game of translation is to yield optimal

---

10 For a discussion of equivalence in translation, see Chapters 7 and 9.

results. Goal-directed heuristics is essential in translation because only this thinking method may produce chance discoveries and intuitive inspirations beyond the constraints of grammatical rules. In a heuristic program --based upon Peirce's abduction[11]-- humans obtain plausible if not perfect solutions without examining all of a (possibly enormous) mass of relevant information. In this way a problem, translational or otherwise, may be solved not by conducting an exhaustive search for a solution but by making use of certain rules of thumb and the various approximations and shortcuts that characterize human judgments. It is precisely this aspect of translation which is largely ignored in the game-theoretical consideration of translation, with its emphasis on rational decision-making[12].

Language is a ludic, open-systemic activity and, consequently, language games are forms of play. This may explain why translation is teachable only insofar as its rule-following aspect is concerned, whereas its creative side must remain resistant to systematization beyond the anecdotal, and cannot therefore be formally taught. Game theory explains translation, yet flattens it: its rational reductionism emphasizes unduly the Saussurean abstraction of *langue*, the socially shared system of rules, the linguistic code or stereotyped "grammar". In doing so it fails to deal fairly with its actualization, *parole*, the concrete speech-act or individual linguistic performance characterized by its openness. *Langue* is static, a fixity; *parole* is event, movement, life. In other words: *langue* means non-semiosis, *parole* means semiosis *par excellence*.

Langue and *parole* have in common a certain structure which in the former is a rigid repertoire based on binary choice, and in the latter takes the form of rule-changing, rule-building, rule-creating. "When a culture shapes itself into an all too rational game", as Aguirre's cautionary remark goes, "freedom *to* chose is a refined form of bondage, and only freedom *from* choice is authentic: the one really

---

11 For a discusion of Peirce's abduction, see Chapter 3, particularly the section on "Reasoning and logic".

12 This is a point which is stressed by Aguirre in an essay on the play element in language and culture, where he argues: "From a formal point of view, it is very tempting to say that, for a description of the game, no other factors need to be considered than its set of unalterable rules, which stipulate everything relevant, from the numbers of players, initial assumptions, conditions or truth-axioms, to the elements to be handled, their values and possible moves, and an end-state. This rule-governed activity would, so defined, constitute what I have called a mechanical equilibrium system . . . Unfortunately, this formal characterization of games will not do . . . Even if chess or some other practically closed game is taken to be paradigmatic, it is by no means exhausted by the formal characterization given. Any description in terms of 'rules' must leave out an essential aspect of the nature of games, namely, the element of 'fun', which Huizinga sees as central to an understanding of play, and without which the game makes very little sense. Every purely formal characterization of games is just a shade too serious, and falsifies the nature of the game by making it too earnest" (Aguirre 1981:193-194).

free choice is 'opting out'" (Aguirre 1981:204); and this analogy, transferred to the game of translating, would mean that anyone playing this language game tries to work out for him- or herself a determinate rule for solving a particular mental problem. In doing so, he or she makes a provisional contract[13] with him- or herself, and decides to act *pro tempore* upon the individually chosen, partly instinctive and partly rational, rule of conduct. Producing such a private operational rule, and working with it, is semiosic behavior involving both habit-taking and habit-breaking, alternatively. Such a process needs to be both irreversible and spontaneous. It requires an open and self-organizing system continuously taking in energy (that is, information) and maintaining a continuous expulsion of entropy as redundant material --that is, the habit become useless or superfluous. In this fashion the system is able to control and maintain its informational equilibrium, while at the same time continuously renewing itself by rejecting old habits, and developing and adopting new habits[14].

Decision-tree vs. associative network

In a Peircean semiotics, a bi-dimensional decision-tree is therefore not a graph able to represent the problem-solving and decision-making process in its full strategic complexity. Following Findler (1978:115-116) it can be more efficiently represented by an associative network: a model which is not arranged in hierarchical levels, where any two nodes can be connected, and any number of connecting lines (corresponding to the tree's branches) can emanate simultaneously from a node. Such a poly-dimensional network has none of the structural "flatness" of the decision-tree. Its nodes and branches may be located on different planes, if the information they contain is classified according to two or more criteria at the same time. Each node corresponds to some element of the game, and each connecting line bears a label characterizing the particular relation between the two nodes it connects. A game situation is entered at a special entry node, which may be imagined at the center of the network, and makes its way through it until a node corresponding to some specific action is reached. The labels act as guides to help the player traverse the network, that is, they help in choosing the line connected to the currently active node, that strategically best applies to the game situation under consideration.

This model recalls several other models representing the universal interconnectedness of things and events. Not only is there Derrida's bottomless

13 More on contract in Chapter 10.

14 More on this in Merrell's recent, thoughtprovoking *Signs Becoming Signs: Our Perfusive, Pervasive Universe* (Merrell 1991:120 & *passim*).

chessboard, mentioned above; we also have what Eco calls his "model Q", a n-dimensional global network which is

> . . . equipped with topological properties, in which the distances covered are abbreviated or elongated and each term acquires proximity with others by means of short-cuts and immediate contacts, meanwhile remaining linked with all the others, according to continually changing relationships. (Eco 1976:124)

One further analogy would be with the picture of universal interconnectedness which emerges as a pattern of probabilities from modern atomic physics. In reference to this "cosmic web philosophy" Capra writes in *The Tao of Physics*:

> Quantum theory forces us to see the universe not as a collection of physical objects, but rather as a complicated web of relations between the various parts of a unified whole. This, however, is the way in which Eastern mystics have experienced the world, and some of them have expressed their experience in words which are almost identical with those used by atomic physicists. (Capra 1976:142)

Strictly speaking, games as referred to in this essay, lack the mystical dimension emphasized by Capra. Yet his dynamic universe, which "moves, grows and changes continually" (Capra 1976:202) is curiously and meaningfully reminiscent of the kind of activity and interactivity a player engages in during his or her mental search, in which connections of many different kinds alternate, overlap, and/or combine, thereby creating a multi-dimensional network capable of generating an unlimited number of perspectives. By the same token, the player, translator, reader, or any other sign user must mentally play back and forth, crisscrossing the structure before eventually reaching a desired solution to his or her problem. Given its complexity, a graphic representation of the whole model is rather beyond the imagination --the human imagination, that is, because a computer simulation can probably be deviced.

The term "sign user", in its varieties, points away from a "pure" game situation towards the broader scenery, that of signs and their meanings, in which it is embedded, at least as reflected in the argument here:

> As can be seen, this model anticipates the definition of every sign, thanks to the interconnection with the universe of all other signs that function as interpretants, each of these ready become the sign interpreted by all the others; the model, in all its complexity, is based on a process of *unlimited semiosis*. From a sign, which is taken as a type, it is possible to penetrate, from the center to the farthest periphery, the whole universe of cultural units, each of which can in turn become the center and create infinite peripheries. (Eco 1976:122)

Such a network of interpretants, in which "all is fluid and every point directly partakes the being of every other" (*CP*:5.402,n.2,1893) represents the essence of Peirce's idea of unlimited semiosis. Its structure is both reparative, generative and regulative. In contradistinction to a bi-dimensional model, it is open and open-ended: it "supposes that the system can be nourished by fresh information and that further data can be inferred from incomplete data" (Eco 1976:124)[15].

After stating "The model Q is a model of linguistic creativity" (Eco 1976:124), Eco subsequently concludes thus:

> When Wittgenstein (1953,I,67) mentioned the existence of "family resemblances" he gave /game/ as an example. The idea of game refers to a family of extremely disparate activities, stretching from chess to ball --games which can have components in common (chess and a ball game between two people have in common the idea of winning and losing), and can be separated by radical dissimilarities (a game of chess and the solitary game of a child throwing the ball against a wall, or a game of chess and ring around the roses). Wittgenstein concludes that "something runs through the whole thread --namely the continuous overlapping of those fibres". This image of a continuous super-imposing of correlations recalls that of model Q. (Eco 1976:124-125)

Though Wittgenstein used the term "game" in the expression "language game" "as routinely as anyone else would use any other philosophical term of art", yet he also made a philosophical point here, bringing home that "we play games with words" (Hunter 1980:293). That language-based activities can be game-like is more than an interesting analogy. As discussed by Hunter (1980), the common features seem to lie less in the obvious characteristics of many games, --that they are played for fun, involve winning or losing, and have definite rules; possible resemblances should perhaps be sought in the presence in the players/speakers of beliefs and doubts, the possibility to freely adopt certain agreed rules, the role of common sense, the responsibility of players/speakers for their own moves/assertions, among others. All these game-and-language-related features are relevant to semiosis as meant by Peirce: that is, constituted by and constitutive of webs of relatively regnant and generative signs of habit, spun in the communicative act and forming an intricate web of significance.

As one example of how Peirce understood semiosic human behavior to

15 In his seminal *Semiotics and the Philosophy of Language* Eco (1984a:46-86;cf.1986b:201-206) elaborates his earlier ideas by pitting a non-semiosic, dictionary-like representation against a semiosic, encyclopedia-like representation. Eco's book contains a discussion of the types of labyrinth which may exemplify each of these categories. According to Eco, semiosis would be represented by the meander, a net-like labyrinth; or, more accurately, by a rhizomatic structure. The vegetable nature of the latter metaphor brings to the fore that it refers not so much to an --always temporally/spatially determined-- object as it is an ever-changing, never-ending, multi-dimensional process of growth.

proceed strategically and rationally (that is, as a language-game), a brief discussion of his essay "Ideals of Conduct" (*CP*:1.591-1.615,1903) is in order. Here, semiosis is discussed as a learning process during which one deliberately subjects one's own action to reasonable rules and habits without, however, thereby losing one's creative freedom. Action as meant here by Peirce (including thought) is regulated by preconceived norms, but it is less controlled by these norms (that is, regulated from the outside) as it is self-controlled (that is, reasoned upon and subsequently either accepted as true and valid, or rejected as unsatisfactory).

Point of departure of this goal-directed action procedure is that "Every man has certain ideas of the general description of conduct that befits a rational animal in his particular station in life, what most accords with his total nature and relations" (*CP*:1.591,1903); they "have in the main been imbibed in childhood" (*CP*:1.592,1903). Man[16] then "formulates, however vaguely, certain *rules of conduct* [which] . . . serve to minimize the effects of future inadvertence" (*CP*:1.592,1903); and whenever some action is required, a plan is made, "or, as one might almost say, a *diagram*. . . a mental formula always more or less general" (*CP*:1.592,1903). This pictorial stage, in which iconic signs take center stage, precedes an experimental stage with strong indexical overtones, --that is involving action and conduct in the narrow sense of these terms. After the image-ideas have thus been tried out in reality by a thinking person, he or she may evaluate and criticize his or her own performance according to the pre-established moral principles he or she has previously acquired. Depending on how the quality of the performance is judged, this will either strengthen the rule, or it may be decided that it be changed or even rejected. Semiosis is rule-governed, symbolic, rational action; yet it builds upon and evolves from iconic and indexical activity; in short, the spark of chance-spontaneity without which rule-building would be wholly acritical, mechanical, and perfectly lifeless.

The rule adopted is what Peirce called a logical interpretant, and it offers solutions which are, in Peirce's terminology, "pragmatic ways of interpreting intellectual concepts" (*CP*:5.467,1907). Insofar as language games try to define a successful rule of procedure, they deal semiotically with such "intellectual concepts". The rule is, for Peirce, a habit of interpretation which is based on a conscious resolution made by the interpreter to act in a certain way. The conjectural foundation of the rule-creating decision appears from Peirce's definition of the resulting growing habit as a "readiness to act in a certain way under given circumstances and when animated by a given motive"

16 Though I follow Peirce in his use of the term "man", I must underscore that I use this term in a gender-neutral sense including womanhood.

(*CP*:5.480,1907). The habit is tried out by experiment but without being earmarked to possess any absolute value; because at each new decision,

> We imagine ourselves in various situations and animated by various motives; and we proceed to trace out the alternative lines of conduct which the conjectures would leave open to us. We are, moreover, led by the same inward activity, to remark different ways in which our conjectures could be slightly modified. (*CP*:5.481,1907)

This makes translational semiosis into a dynamic, purposive, but nonconventional process in which there is no ultimate or "final" interpretant such that with it the signifying process would definitively come to an end. Each move may create a new rule (or modify the primary rule) which, in its turn, may be overruled by any following decision.

Concluding remarks

Translation has here been understood as a heuristic one-person trial-and-error language-game dealing with the generation of moves based on tentative decisions about detail problems, global problems, and the interplay of both. No new moves are discovered, because there is a finite set of linguistic units, --the building blocks that may be used as tools. Instead, meaningful interrelations are created, and creative choices are made from an infinite set of combinations. The semiotic pattern thus created is both rule-governed, rule-changing, and rule-creating. The interpreter is free to shape and change it at will. This makes translating into a kaleidoscopic, never-ending game of creative mental skill.

To conclude, it has not been my prime intention here to demonstrate a fundamental kinship between the jigsaw puzzle and translation, nor to fully elaborate such an analogy along the lines of game theory. I have explored the possibility of considering translation as a game-like activity, and of fitting it into the framework of a general theory of signs. This is exciting because it liberates translation from its exclusively abstract, verbal nature, as it adds to it a visual, aesthetic dimension. At the same time, translation as semiosis unleashes reason and allows the translator's creative potential free play. This perspective enables us, in short, to recapture the play element in translation that has been lost in the labyrinths of rationality.

05. WITTGENSTEIN, TRANSLATION, AND SEMIOTICS

"You need not fear to compromise your darling theory by looking out at its windows"
(*CP*:5.459,1905)

Introductory remarks

Forty years ago[1], the Austrian-born philosopher, Ludwig Wittgenstein (1889-1951) died in Cambridge, England, where he spent most of his working life, -- apart from the years he spent in Skjolden, at the bottom of the spectacular Sognefjord, one of the remotest, wildest, and most inaccessible spots in the mountains of Western Norway. There he worked on his only published work (in 1922), *Tractatus Logico-Philosophicus* before the First World War, and on his posthumously published *Philosophische Untersuchungen* (*Philosophical Investigations*) in the late 1930s.

To conmemorate the event I will, in this essay, look at Wittgenstein's remarks on translation. Wittgenstein's remarks on this phenomenon, though numerically rather modest, are, as I intend to argue, significant in that they reflect the various stages of his thought. Wittgenstein used them to illustrate and clarify key notions in his language-philosophical thought, such as "rule", "use", and "language-game". The language-game issue will be the *pièce de résistance* of this discussion. Subsequently, I will venture a "translation" of Wittgenstein's concepts into the framework of a Peircean semiotics. While there is little likelihood that Wittgenstein and Peirce knew each other's publications[2], their works reveal

---

1 The first version of this Chapter was written in 1988 and published in 1989.

2 As Hardwick points out: "There is a strong pragmatic strain in Wittgenstein's later work. It is a strain that is more than merely pragmatic --it is Peircian in nature. The question is how Wittgenstein came to his pragmatic views. Whether it was the result of a natural evolution, or a

remarkably similar views of language. This conceptual connection will add a new dimension to the study of translation as it is traditionally focused on. At the same time, it will, it is hoped, broaden and enhance both the Wittgensteinian and the semiotic perspectives.

Wittgenstein spent a lifetime philosophizing about language and the function and meaning of its structures. It is, therefore, hardly surprising to find throughout his writings references to intralingual, interlingual, and intersemiotic translation[3]. Nevertheless, many of these references are not meant to discuss translation for its own sake, as the actual linguistic activity in its own right, but rather as a heuristic device aimed at clarifying by analogy some of the fundamental philosophical topics discussed by Wittgenstein throughout his intellectual career. The analogies propounded by him are particularly between different nonverbal (acoustic, visual, kinesic, etc.) sign systems and language.

Picture theory and translation

In his oracle-like *Tractatus Logico-Philosophicus*, belonging to his early period, Wittgenstein addressed the way words are linked to things in reality. He proposed a two-place pictorial relation, or *abbildende Beziehung*, his "picture theory"[4]. In Wittgenstein's picture theory every object has a name attached to it and language simply mirrors the world. Invariant "rules of logical syntax", which differ from one sign-system, or symbolism [*Zeichensprache*] to the next, rule the name-object correlations and form the "logical scaffolding" (*TLP*:4.023) of propositions. The proposition (or meaningful sentence) is a combination of names, or "simple signs" (*TLP*:3.202): "One name stands for one thing, and another for another thing, and they are connected together. And so the whole, like a living picture [*Bild*], presents the atomic fact [*Sachverhalt*]" (*TLP*:4.0311). According to Wittgenstein in his earlier period, the proposition, or word picture, is thus an articulate "picture of reality" (*TLP*:4.01). The logical form of language mirrors the logical form of

---

result of the influence of F. P. Ramsey, or some other close associate, or perhaps through reading Peirce, is still a matter of speculation" (Hardwick 1977:25). One thing is clear, namely that "there is no mention of Peirce by Wittgenstein" (Hardwick in *PW*:xxxi). More recently, Deledalle (1988:14) has claimed Wittgenstein must have known, through Ramsey, at least some of Peirce's work.

3 These are the well-known terms coined by Jakobson (1959:233;1971b:261). For a more detailed discussion of Jakobson's three kinds of translation, see Chapter 8.

4 I shall not discuss in this essay the intricacies involved in the translation of Wittgenstein's works themselves from (Austrian) German into (British) English. Whenever my references are to bilingual editions, I have also consulted the German texts and will, for the sake of the clarity of the argument, make occasional comments upon them. For a more detailed account of Wittgenstein's picture theory see, e.g., Fogelin 1976:16-23.

reality in the same way as the musical score represents the musical piece (*TLP*:4.011):

> The gramophone record, the musical thought, the score, the waves of sound, all stand to one another in that pictorial internal relation, which holds between language and the world. To all of them the logical structure is common . . . In the fact that there is a general rule by which the musician is able to read the symphony out of the score, and that there is a rule by which one could reconstruct the symphony from the line on a gramophone record and from this again --by means of the first rule-- construct the score, herein lies the internal similarity between these things which at first sight seem to be entirely different. And the rule is the law of projection which projects the symphony into the language of the musical score. It is the rule of translation of this language into the language of the gramophone record. (*TLP*:4.014,4.0141)

The musical analogy confirms Wittgenstein's thesis that if the right rules are applied, "Every correct symbolism must be translatable into every other according to such rules" (*TLP*:3.343). For Wittgenstein, the same rules apply to intersemiotic translation as to interlingual translation; in the latter the necessary rules are given in the bilingual dictionary. The strict application of dictionary definitions guarantees a seamless one-to-one correspondence between the words, but not between the sentences; and, as Wittgenstein claimed in the *Tractatus*, this is exactly what translation ought to do:

> The translation of one language into another is not a process of translating each proposition of the one into a proposition of the other, but only the constituent parts of propositions are translated. (And the dictionary does not only translate substantives but also adverbs and conjunctions, etc., and it treats them all alike.) (*TLP*:4.025)

The parenthetical addendum is especially noteworthy because it may be seen as a first sign of Wittgenstein's growing doubts about the legitimacy of his own pictorial view on translating, and indeed of his picture theory *tout court*. Objects may be physically labeled as long as they are present; *in absentia*, however, ostension is not possible and things have to be named by verbal definition. This is more often than not the case, because not all substantives refer to material objects[5]. The problems involved in labeling or naming abstract nouns and other "simple signs" such as pronouns, adjectives, adverbs, and conjunctions, have at this point been rather oversimplified by Wittgenstein. The various word categories

---

5 Eco (1984:50) distinguishes in this connection tentatively between "object words", the meaning of which is given by ostension of the state of the world, and "dictionary words", which, paradoxically, need to be defined in terms of other dictionary words. For the distinction between "objects" and "things" in Wittgenstein's *Tractatus*, see Finch 1971:21-48.

reflect different *Sachverhalte* which, consequently, can hardly be filtered through the same pictorial semantic grid.

In addition to the word problem there is the sentence problem; it is virtually impossible to label or give ostensive definitions to sentences[6]. Wittgenstein, however, appears in his *Tractatus* to elude the sentence question on the (implicit) grounds that language is, like music, a serial, combinatorial sign-system: "The proposition is not a mixture of words (just as the musical theme is not a mixture of tones)" (*TLP*:3.141). Once again the analogy with music purports to support Wittgenstein's picture theory. Yet Wittgenstein's view that the word and not the sentence is the unit of translation, remains ambiguous and will be questioned by Wittgenstein himself. Wittgenstein came to acknowledge unreservedly that "there is no ostensive definition [*Erklärung*] for sentences" (quoted in Hintikka and Hintikka 1986:228). Challenging in so many words his own theory, Wittgenstein was, it seems, preparing the ground for a new conceptual framework to accomodate his rethought ideas on language. This move may be illustrated by the following remark, from 1931:

> The limit of language is shown by its being impossible to describe the fact which corresponds to (is the translation of) a sentence, without simply repeating the sentence. (This has to do with the Kantian solution of the problem of philosophy.) (Wittgenstein 1980c:10e)

In the following I intend to show how Wittgenstein's exact rule of projection was eventually to be superseded by his later thought.

From icon to semiosis

Scattered throughout the pages and in a notoriously laconic style, the *Tractatus*, and Wittgenstein's subsequent works, treat semiotic questions[7]. In the *Tractatus*, which is curiously reminiscent but independent of the work of his contemporary, Saussure[8], Wittgenstein put forward a series of pronouncements on signs and their

---

6 On Wittgenstein's view of ostensive definitions, see Hintikka and Hintikka 1985:*passim*. I am much indebted to this monograph for its clear and thoughtprovoking analyses of Wittgenstein's thought.

7 In addition to the works touched upon in this essay, Wittgenstein's *Über Gewissheit* (*On Certainty*) is, for Hardwick, "a work particularly loaded with Peircian themes" (*PW*:xxxiv). On Wittgenstein as a semiotic language-philosopher, see Chatterjee 1986 (with bibliography).

8 Not only are the *Tractatus* and the *Cours de linguistique générale* thematically related; they even possess a certain formal likeness. The *Cours* is basically a collection of notes and drafts of the outlines Saussure used for his lectures at the University of Geneva, which were posthumously edited into the text as we know it. The *Tractatus* is, in its items presented seriatim, equally unusual. In both works the scope of the discussion seems to be inversely proportionate to its size; in its 75

meaning. I shall have to refrain from dealing any more than in passing with the *Tractatus*'s Saussurean overtones. It is tempting to view the picture theory and the pictorial coupling of words and reality in the light of what Peirce called iconicity --which is one instance of his Firstness. Like the Wittgensteinian *Bild*, the iconic sign, such as a map or a portrait, represents its object by virtue of its similarity with it. Like Wittgenstein's picture, the icon is meant to be the picture-image or model of the thing signified. Further, both *Bild* and icon are meant to directly exhibit meaning without requiring any genuine (that is, genuinely triadic) and intelligent interpretation.

However, a pictorial view on the connection between the word (or sign) and the world (or object) partakes of indexicality (or Secondness), in addition to iconicity. If the word is supposed to refer immediately outside itself to its *alter ego*, the object signified, this pointing function renders the representation clearly indexical. This is also implied in Wittgenstein's "ostensive definition" (e.g., *PI*:1:38). One example of the mixed nature of pictorial signs is provided by photographs. Wittgenstein remarked, "we *regard* the photograph . . . as the object itself (the man, landscape, and so on) depicted there" (*PI*:2:205), but he went no further; whereas for Peirce, photographs are indices as well as icons: because "they are in certain respects exactly like the objects they represent", while at the same time "their resemblance is due to the photographs having been produced under such circumstances that they were physically forced to correspond point by point to nature" (*CP*:2.281,c.1895). Indeed, Peirce taught that every index "necessarily has some Quality in common with the Object" and "does, therefore, involve a sort of Icon" (*CP*:2.248,1903).

In his *Semiotics and the Philosophy of Language*, Eco (1984a:46) reminds us of the basic but often expediently forgotten fact that a sign is not only something which stands for something else (the scholastic dictum, *aliquid stat pro aliquo*), but that in order for it to be a sign it must also function as a sign, i.e., be interpreted, at least potentially. Eco's book contains a semiotic discussion of the scope and structure of the dictionary vs. the encyclopedia (1984a:46-86). This distinction is, as shall be shown, pertinent to mark the transition from a dual sign-relation (sign-object) to a triadic one (sign-object-interpretant): only the latter qualifies as semiosis.

Eco points out that in a sign-theoretical context,

---

pages, the *Tractatus* even exceeds the *Cours* in brevity. It is perhaps interesting to note here that Peirce's *Collected Papers*, despite their voluminosity, resemble the *Cours* in being a product of heavy posthumous editing of mainly unpublished material, which, in Peirce's case has taken a particularly fragmentary and collage-like form. See also note 38.

> . . . *dictionary* and *encyclopedia* are theoretical models accounting for a possible interpretation of the semantic component of a grammar or for a given mental or cultural competence. As such, they do not correspond to the "flesh-and-blood" dictionaries and encyclopedias as practical repertories sold under the form of one or more books, even though, also in this case, a dictionary is supposed to provide mere "linguistic" information while an encyclopedia provides pieces of world knowledge. (Eco 1986b:201)

Eco argues that dictionary(-like) definitions establish bidimensional semantic relations, whereas the encyclopedic universe possesses a labyrinthine quality creating multi-dimensional pragmatic relations which stimulate choice and interpretation, i.e., semiosic competence. I would even broaden Eco's dictionary definition to include Saussure's binary concept of the sign and Wittgenstein's pictorial word-world relation as described above. This labels *signifiant/signifié*, *Bild* relations, and other twofold equivalences which are based upon fixed designation, as nonsemiosic, static, and trivial[9].

These ideas crystallize in the concluding chapter of Eco's book, called "Mirrors" (1984a:202-226), in which the discussion, *sub specie speculorum*, seems to broaden and pertain to the whole of sign theory. According to Eco, the mirror image is an absolute double, an exact replica of the object: "If the mirror 'names'", he remarks in a Wittgensteinian manner of speaking, "it only names a concrete object standing in front of it" (1984a:211). By the same token, the "catoptric experience" mirrors (!) Wittgenstein's twoplace picture model of language and translation; a concept of translation, however, which is its own negation because, in Eco's words, "A mirror does not 'translate'; it records what struck it just as it is struck . . . Our brain interprets retinal data; a mirror does not interpret an object" (Eco 1984a:207-208). The mirror image seems to be more than an icon, an "absolute icon" of the object it represents. "Absolute iconicity" as well as the *Tractatus*'s word-world links and its word-to-word idea of translation, are, however, at best pseudosemiotic concepts:

> We therefore come to discover that the semantics of rigid designation is in the end a (pseudo-)semantics of the mirror image and that no linguistic term can be a rigid designator (just as there is no absolute icon). If it cannot be absolute, any rigid designator other than a mirror image, any rigid designator whose rigidity may be undermined in different ways under different conditions, becomes a *soft or slack designator*. (Eco 1984a:213)

An instructive parallel to the above view of the mirror image, which is indicative of Wittgenstein's early view of language, is encountered in Peirce's remarks on the semiotic implications of "a man looking at himself in a looking-

---

9 See also Chapter 4, n.15.

glass" (*MS*909:41,1890-1891[10];cf.*MS*904:6,1909). Interestingly, Peirce did not regard the mirror image here as typifying the iconic relation (as he did in *MS*599:41,c.1902), but instead construed it as an instance of a kind of upgraded dual relation, -- still degenerate[11], but on the way, as it were, of becoming a triadic, genuinely semiosic relation:

> Here, if we regard the light as a third object besides the man and the mirror, no doubt there is genuine thirdness. But leaving that out of account, the only fact is that the man and the glass are in a somewhat complicated dual relation to one another. Namely the glass imparts to the man the temporary power of self-vision. We may call this a case of a reflective third. Any dual relation may be so regarded as involving a third. (*MS*909:41,1890-1891)[12]

This means that for Peirce a mirror image is not a sign of the person standing in front of it, unless it is interpreted as such by an interpreting mind --for instance, by the person mirrored.

In the final analysis, the isomorphism inherent in Wittgenstein's picture view of language is more rigid than Peirce's iconic relation applied to language. Hintikka states that

> . . . Peirce makes it clear that the resemblance in question need not consist in an unanalyzed qualitative similarity but rather consists normally in a structural similarity. According to him, many icons "resemble their objects not at all in looks; it is only in respect to the relation of their parts that their likeness consists" (2.282). In comparison, in the *Tractatus* the picture view is rather static. (Hintikka 1969:218-219)

---

10 *MS*909 contains the complete text of Peirce's famous essay "A guess at the riddle", only parts of which were published in *CP*:1.354-1.416,1890-1891. The quotations here are taken from an as yet unpublished part of the *MS*.

11 I have addressed Peirce's concept of degeneracy in Chapter 3 ("Peirce's trichotomies and the classification of signs") and elsewhere (Gorlée 1987, 1989b, and, particularly, 1990).

12 That Thirds involve Seconds and Firsts and that Seconds involve Firsts, is repeatedly stressed by the later Peirce: ". . . a symbol, if sufficiently complete always involves an index, just as an index sufficiently complete involves an icon" (*NEM*4:256,c.1904; cp. *CP*:2.293,c.1902;*CP*:2.248,1903). The reverse --namely, that Seconds may involve Thirds, as seems to be suggested here by Peirce-- is to my knowledge a novel and unexplored proposition, which is worth pursuing. The key to this problem may be found by starting from the following, earlier quotation, where it appears to be affirmed nor denied: "The category of first can be prescinded from second and third, and second can be prescinded from third. But second cannot be prescinded from first, nor third from second" (*CP*:1.353,c.1880;cf.*MS*478:37-38,1903, where Peirce posited: "Everything must have some non-relative element; and this is its Firstness. So likewise it is possible to prescind Secondness from Thirdness. But Thirdness without Secondness would be absurd"). See also n. 27.

For Peirce, however, genuine sign-action is threefold and must involve an interpretant, in addition to a sign and its object. The sign only deploys its meaning (that is, becomes meaningful) in the interpretative act or acts. At the same time, however, this triadic action includes and is again built up out of monadic (iconic) and dyadic (indexical) relations. While Seconds involve Firsts, and Thirds involve Seconds and Firsts, the reverse is not true.

Peirce thus allowed signs to give a more dynamic picture of reality than the young Wittgenstein. Interestingly, Wittgenstein's thought in the decade following the publication of the *Tractatus*, would become more and more phenomenologically oriented, thereby becoming, coincidentally or not, close to Peirce's pragmatism, (or, as Peirce called his version of it, pragmaticism)[13].

As Wittgenstein, in a pragmatic spirit, replaced formal-logical determination by a descriptive procedure, learning names is replaced by learning to use language. The sign no longer has a mirroring relationship to its object, the fact signified; it has become one element in a triad which includes, and indeed emphasizes, a user (a human being or any other thinking mind) as one necessary element. This is a user, or interpreter, whose performance may be, for the moment, rather poor, or who might even distort, wilfully or not, the meaning of the message, but one who, as a Peircean pragmaticism teaches, is with varying success involved in a learning process, and who, given time, is bound to reach the reality of truth.

Wittgenstein eventually realized that his bidimensional idea of projection from things into words, and translation from one language into another, was a calculus. That is to say it was a reductionism emphasizing a strict rule. He realized that in doing so he failed to deal fairly with the speech act (in the literal sense of linguistic performance) characterized by its semiosic openness. In this development, the year 1931 seems to be a turning-point where Wittgenstein explicitly and rhetorically started to question his own idea, thus: "Should I say: I am only interested in language insofar as it is a calculus" (Wittgenstein 1931:112; my trans.), by pitting it against his new insights in the relation between the (linguistic) sign and the reality it is intended to reflect. This may be illustrated by the following: "Here we have *this* haunting problem: how it is possible even to think of the existence of things, when we only see images --their projections. . . . (*never the things themselves*)" (Wittgenstein 1931:108-109; my trans.). Subsequently, in the *Blue Book*, which he dictated to his students in Cambridge during the 1933-1934 session, Wittgenstein pointed to "*certain definite* mental processes through which alone language can function" and without which "the

---

13 For a comparative study of Wittgenstein's and Peirce's pragmatism, see Rorty 1961 and Ransdell 1976.

signs of our language seem dead" (*BBB*:3). He then argued that "a thought (which is such a mental process) can agree or disagree with reality" (*BBB*:3-4) and concluded that "if we had to name anything which is the life of the sign, we should have to say it was its *use*" (*BBB*:4).

Indeed, in the beginning of his *Philosophical Investigations*, the text of which was completed by 1945, Wittgenstein advanced his famous analogy of language with tools:

> Think of the tools in a tool-box: there is a hammer, pliers, a saw, a screw-driver, a rule, a glue-pot, glue, nails and screws. --The function of words are as diverse as the functions of these objects. (*PI*:1:11)

Just as things signify according to their uses, "the meaning of a word is its use in language" (*PI*:1:43). Though the use of language is the key to its meaning, yet the workmanlike analogy with carpenter's tools clearly suggests that meaning is not reduced to (linguistic) rules-of-usage as given in "grammar", and that the meaning or use of words has a nonverbal component in addition to its linguistic character[14].

This entails a new perspective on translation. From his middle period, Wittgenstein mentioned translation as the application of a partly linguistic and partly nonlinguistic, psychological rule. In the *Blue Book* he spoke of "two sentences of different languages" sharing "the same sense"; and "therefore the sense is not the same as the sentence", but one interpretation among others, "a shadowy being" (*BBB*:32) capable of lying. Indeed, "it is essential that the sign should be capable of representing things as in fact they are not", Wittgenstein argued (*BBB*:32), thereby explicitly opening the door to semiosis in Peirce's definition. Indeed, in Peirce's elegant definition facts are signified as "fluid extracts of events carrying away so much of them as a proposition will hold" (*MS*478:155,1903).

Meaning had, for Wittgenstein, lost its straightforward referentiality and had become a complex, elusive, semiosic entity. This is once more, and in different instances, exemplified by analogy with paraphonetic, kinesic, and musical translations of verbal signs, functioning as simultaneous interpretations.

---

14 In this connection, Hintikka and Hintikka rightly point out that in the well-known equation of meaning and use in *PI*:1:43, Wittgenstein used the German word *Gebrauch*, which not only means "use" in the sense of "habit", "custom", but "can also signal that something is being *utilized* or *put to use*" (Hintikka and Hintikka 1986:217-218). Indeed, in the tool analogy Wittgenstein used the related term *Verwendung* meaning "application". *Anwendung* is equally used by Wittgenstein in the sense of "utilization", both verbal and nonverbal. On this point, see also Finch 1977:27ff.

While in 1931, Wittgenstein, the language philosopher, had asked himself the following question:

> Why do I say: the feelings, emotions, etc. accompanying a sentence, do not interest me? Because what interests me is only the symbolic structure. Are they [the feelings, emotions, etc.] of a vague nature, because they don't belong to the symbol, because they may be like they are as well as different, even when the symbol is the same? (Wittgenstein 1931:113; my trans.)

Subsequently, Wittgenstein came to rephrase this problem as follows:

> A process accompanying our words which one might call the "process of meaning them" is the modulation of the voice in which we speak the words; or one of the processes similar to this, like the play of facial expression. These accompany the spoken words not in the way a German sentence might accompany an English sentence, or writing a sentence accompany speaking a sentence; but in the same sense in which the tune of a song accompanies its words. This tune corresponds to the feeling with which we say the sentence. (*BBB*:35)[15]

Emotions and thought (that is, mental images) are more or less translatable into spoken words, and these may be translated again into (nonverbal) outward signs. These and other forms of intersemiotic translation in Wittgenstein's thought suggest a new, assymetrical view on translatability or, in general, describability. The contrast between isomorphism and semiosis (and the possibility of the transition from the former to the latter) is apparent from the use of the dictionary as a concrete tool and a thought-sign, respectively:

> Let us imagine a table (something like a dictionary) that exists only in our imagination. A dictionary can be used to justify the translation of a word X by a word Y. But are we also to call it a justification if such a table is to be looked up only in the imagination? -- "Well yes; then it is a subjective justification." -- But justification consists in appealing to something independent. -- "But surely I can appeal from one memory to another. For example, I don't know if I remembered the time of departure of a train right and to check it I call to mind how a page of the time-table looked. Isn't it the same here?" -- No; for this process has got to produce a memory which is actually *correct*. If the mental image of the time-table could not itself be *tested* for correctness, how could it confirm the correctness of the first memory? (*PI*:1:265)[16]

---

15 Similar ideas are expressed in the *Brown Book* in one of Wittgenstein's picturesque tribal language paradigms (*BBB*:102-104).

16 In his critique of Bunn's (1981) *The Dimensionality of Signs, Tools, and Models*, Pazukhin distinguishes likewise between conventions such as "time-tables and schedules used in communications, production, and everyday events . . . called upon to coordinate dispersed magnitudes, duties, and actions" and, on the other side, "agreements that enable some things to

It could not. Semiosis may, of course, produce truthful ("correct") interpretant-signs, but it is *per se* unconcerned with producing signs with this quality.

From his middle period onwards, Wittgenstein argued that the rule of projection adopted in translation refers to its object "in some queer way" (*BBB*:37). Henceforward, he would be engaged in the pursuit of investigating as he put it in the *Brown Book* (dictated in 1934-1935), the nature of this "mysterious relation" (*BBB*:183). Subsequently, in his principal work, the *Philosophical Investigations*, the Austrian philosopher would put forward a full-fledged exposition of how signs signify through their being used in manifold human activities. Wittgenstein coined the term "language-games" for these activities[17].

Language-games

Toward the beginning of his *Philosophical Investigations*, Wittgenstein listed a number of language-games:

> Giving orders, and obeying them --
> Describing the appearance of an object, or giving its measurements --
> Constructing an object from a description (a drawing) --
> Reporting an event --
> Speculating about an event --
> Forming and testing a hypothesis --
> Presenting the results of an experiment in tables and diagrams --
> Making up a story; and reading it --
> Play-acting --
> Singing catches --
> Guessing riddles --
> Making a joke; telling it --
> Solving a problem in practical arithmetic --
> Translating from one language into another --
> Asking, thanking, cursing, greeting, praying. (*PI*:1:23)

The penultimate language-game on this list is, significantly, "Translating from one language into another", Jakobson's interlingual translation. It is necessary to

---

represent other things, ideas, actions, and/or properties in social intercourse . . . Owing to such agreements, traffic signs can inform us about certain traffic conventions while specific graphic images and symbols are used to denote phases of planned activities, functions, ranks, appointments, roles, prices, nominal values, etc. It is only the latter kind of agreements that may be studied with the help of *semiotic analysis*, whereas the agreements of the former type are plainly unaccessible to such investigations. Surely, a semiotician is in a position to understand and describe the principles of the employment of traffic signs, but he is unable to give any professional account of road and street circulation problems and their eventual solutions" (Pazukhin 1985:271).

17 See also Gorlée 1989b.

understand Wittgenstein's concept of language-game before it can be applied to translation theory.

What the above-mentioned language-games have in common, their "family resemblances" (*PI*:1:67;cf.*BBB*:17) lies perhaps first and foremost in their rule-governed nature, in the culturally established social situations in which they appear, and in the language(-like) symbols which are used in them[18]. All of these language-games are accompanied and supported by appropriate systematic (that is, rule-governed) nonlinguistic action or actions. In the framework of one language-game the speech signs and the behavioral, kinetic signs are mutually translatable: usually, they convey the same message and produce one meaning in an intersemiotic textual totality[19].

Language-games (such as asking a question, making a confession, apologizing, or, for that matter, writing this essay) are different ways of dealing semiotically with language and reality, and with the interplay between the two. Language-games organize both language and reality. In order to make sense of reality humans play such "games", "countless different kinds of use [*Verwendung*] of what we call 'symbols', 'words', 'sentences'" (*PI*:1:23). The latter constitute the tools with which language-games are played. That these tools possess *per se* a purely utilitarian value is true; but when instrumentalized in linguistic activities they are enhanced and, thanks to their mediating role, elevated to a semiotic status[20].

According to the later Wittgenstein, the basic semantic links between language and reality are thus established through the practice of a myriad of such human activities involving language. They are forms of purposeful, meaningful rule-following action; for obeying a rule by chance or unwittingly does not qualify as a language-game. Indeed, Hintikka and Hintikka (1986:187ff) strongly emphasize the primacy of playing language-games over the rules which govern them, but which may at any point be changed or disobeyed. A language-game is prior to "any experience, feeling or imagined reality" (Finch 1977:74), a "proto-phenomenon" (*PI*:1:654): "Look on the language-game as the *primary* thing", Wittgenstein taught, "[a]nd look on the feelings, etc., as you look on a way of regarding the language-game, as interpretation" (*PI*:1:656).

Not surprisingly, the rule-governed behavior displayed in language-games involves the spontaneous use of language. At the same time, however, Wittgenstein recognized the existence of an extralinguistic component in the

---

18 The word "symbol" is used here in the broad Wittgensteinian sense (corresponding to Peirce's concept of sign) and includes words, drawings, thoughts, and even music.

19 The semantic relation between the verbal signs and their nonverbal "illustrators" may be one of emphasis, repetition, substitution, complementation, or contradiction (Nöth 1990:397).

20 See note 16.

language-games: "I shall also call the whole, consisting of language and the actions into which it is woven, the 'language-game'" (*PI*:1:7). Indeed, Wittgenstein underlined that "the term language-*game* is meant to bring into prominence the fact that the *speaking* of language is part of an activity" (*PI*:1:23). The key term here is perhaps the word "part", often unduly overlooked. Wittgenstein's formulation seems to imply that language-games are acts of language, speech-acts in the literal sense of this compound noun; instances of "operating with words", with a built-in nonverbal component which makes them forms of play-acts, programmed to suit human needs. As opposed to animal behavior, this combination comes naturally to human beings: "Commanding, questioning, recounting, chatting, are as much part of our natural history as walking, eating, drinking, playing" (*PI*:1:25). All these are social activities, games entered with the (explicit or implicit) intention to provide new ways of interpreting (that is, looking at and commenting upon) the world.

Culture

The above interpretation of Wittgenstein's language-game is confirmed by the crucial passage in which the concept of language-game is explained by Wittgenstein: "Here the term language-game is meant to bring into prominence the fact that the *speaking* of language is part of an activity, or a form of life" (*PI*:1:23). The last part of this explanatory clause is decisive because it places the games in the wider context of human culture as a whole. Though primarily language-based, language-games do not function in a social vacuum, but are inscribed in so-called "forms of life". A form of life is, according to Finch's definition, "a pattern of meaningful behavior in so far as this is constituted by a group"; this definition is to distinguish it,

> . . . on the one hand, from behavior which does not have such meaning as, for example, physical or biological happenings, and, on the other hand, from totally individual behavior which, while it may be "meaningful" in some sense, is not an *established group meaning*. Shopping, for example, is something which people do in some societies and which is shared by them as a meaningful activity. (Finch 1977:91)

Shopping behavior involves various language-games. So do teaching behavior, courting behavior, and (Wittgenstein's example) hoping behavior: "That is to say, the phenomena of hope are modes of this complicated form of life" (*PI*:2:176). Forms of life are thus culturally determined behavioral *Gebräuche* or *Gepflogenheiten*, that is, uses in the sense of "customs". As such they counterbalance "use" in the sense of "application" or "utilization" as embodied in the language-game[21].

Each form of life represents a cultural unit in Eco's sense (1979:66ff). In his semiotic parlance, cultural units are "the meaning to which the code makes the system of sign-vehicles correspond" (Eco 1979:67). In an encyclopedic semantics, Eco identifies the cultural system as a whole with the dynamic process of semiosis, and therefore, cultural units with Peircean interpretants. In the indivisible Peircean triad sign-object-interpretant, the interpretant is a sign interpretative of another sign. Here the formulation of one of Peirce's better-known definition of the sign as a semiosic agent is in order, namely ". . . anything which determines something else (its *interpretant*) to refer to an object to which itself refers (its *object*) in the same way, the interpretant becoming in turn a sign, and so on *ad infinitum*" (*CP*:2.303,1901). The idea that the meaning of the sign is always another sign generates an endless series of interpretative signs. This unlimited process of signification upon which culture hinges is called semiosis; and interpretants are cultural units, the verbal and nonverbal signs which together pattern our ever-changing sociocultural life:

> . . . [C]ulture continuously translates signs into signs, and definitions into definitions, words into icons, icons into ostensive signs, ostensive signs into new definitions, new definitions into propositional functions, propositional functions into exemplifying sentences, and so on; in this way it proposes to its members an uninterrupted chain of cultural units composing other cultural units, and thus translating and explaining them. (Eco 1979:71)

Eco's semiosic conception of culture as an ongoing process generating ever-new interpretants by a society of interpreters, accords with Wittgenstein's later view on words and the world. Indeed, forms of life are for Wittgenstein the basic condition, "what has to be accepted, what is given" (*RPP*:2:687); otherwise said, the set of rules, or codes. And cultural codes form the common ground upon which humans may (and do) play their language-games.

Signs signify because the interpreter of them has previous acquaintance with the rules or forms of life that underlie the way the signs are encoded. This enables the interpreter to produce interpretant signs. If, in the final consideration, forms of life enable interpreters to generate meanings, this signification is also made possible because of the representative nature of all signs. Indeed, representation is as much a condition for interpretation as the opposite.

---

21 See note 14.

Ground

Representation means that a sign is related to an object in such a way that the sign, in Peirce's words, "stands for the object not in all respects, but in reference to a sort of idea, which I have sometimes called the *ground* of the representamen" (*CP*:2.228,c.1897)[22]. This ground is an abstract but knowable idea serving as justification for the mode of being manifested by the sign: "there must exist, either in thought or in expression, some explanation or argument or other context, showing how (that is, upon which system or for what reason) the Sign represents the Object or set of Objects that it does" (*CP*:2.230,1910).

Peirce's ground is a selective abstraction (Greenlee 1973:64ff), while in Wittgenstein's language-games language is used like one uses a tool-kit. Just as tools can be used for multiple purposes (that is, to do many different jobs), so language may serve as a working and workmanlike instrument to play different "games". Ground and language-game are semiosic agencies conveying a standpoint which determines one or more modes of being --that is, the possible assertions implied in particular instances of sign-use. Ground and language-game are concerned with acts of encoding, decoding, and interpreting signs, that is, with the signifying process as grounded in communication. Grounding and playing language-games are (non)verbal practices bound by the social context but not confined by it. The social context is, however, the consensual framework in which these activities must ultimately function and "work".

For Sheriff, Peirce's ground and Wittgenstein's language-games "are similar if not exactly the same" (1981:70;1989:95). But if I have understood Sheriff's argument correctly, he regards both notions as being, in fact, identical. However, I would instead suggest that they can only be the same if "ground" means ground-in-use, or operational ground. Not only can a human activity hardly be the same as the idea underlying its production, use, and/or modification; more importantly, meaning cannot, on Wittgenstein's operationalist view, be realistically considered apart from the use of sign structures in context.

Ground corresponds perhaps better to Wittgenstein's "intention" to play a language-game, a "kind of super-strong connexion [which] exists between the act of intending and the thing intended" (*PI*:1:197); and ground would then refer not to the language-game itself, but to this "causal connexion" (*PI*:1:198), the inner motivation to play it, and to play it in accordance with the rules accepted, adopted, or adapted. Intention is, Kevelson writes, "idealized by the act of entering into the

---

22 This is, exceptionally, a late reference to ground; the last, isolated offering being *MS*7:15,1904. In Peirce's published work one finds only sporadic references to the concept of ground. Despite this, ground seems to have been a fundamental concept in Peirce's earlier thought. Peirce abandoned the concept of ground in his later years.

game [, at which point] [a]n objective is projected as realizable by means of the game" (Kevelson 1977:41). The language-game is, for Wittgenstein, a resemblance which mediates as a sign between existing reality and possible reality; and "[a]n intention is embedded in its situation, in human customs and institutions" (*PI*:2:335). This idea would also open the possibility for individuals to initiate the practice of new language-games by creating new rules determining the game process[23]. In other words, it would make possible the kind of nonmechanical sign-use or sign-action referred to by Peirce as semiosis[24].

The Peircean concept of ground is the point of view which renders the representation meaningful; therefore, Short describes significance as "grounded significance" (1986b:105). If the grounding of the sign-object relationship is monadic and is based upon similarity, the sign is an icon, or sign of Firstness. If the sign and its object have a dyadic relationship, which is dynamically and/or causally grounded, the sign is an index, or sign of Secondness. And if the relationship is triadic and grounded in virtue of an agreement and/or habit, the sign is a symbol, or sign of Thirdness. The triadic sign is the only genuine sign. All words and, more generally, all linguistic signs, are first and foremost symbols, so in their analysis there are no pure icons or indices. An icon is doubly degenerate --twice removed from the written or spoken word; an index is singly degenerate -- once removed from it.

Firsts, Seconds, Thirds

Scattered through Wittgenstein's works there are references to what Peirce would call Firsts; for example, his remarks on "the sensation of red" being a pure "private experience" (*PI*:1:272ff) and the impossibility to describe the aroma of coffee (*PI*:1:610)[25]. Wittgenstein also discussed Seconds, as he spoke of indices such as the sign-post which "leave[s] no room for doubt" (*PI*:1:85) and the arrow which points in a definite direction without any "hocus-pocus" (*PI*:1:454). However, genuine semiosis only emerges where the preconceived rule breaks down and the possibility of ambiguity begins, that is in Thirdness. Peirce's three modes of being yield many interplaying tripartite divisions, among which sign, object, interpretant; icon, index, symbol; instinct, experience, form (*CP*:8.374,1908). To this last trichotomy Wittgenstein offered an instructive parallel: "Instinct comes first,

23 On the language-game of reciting poetry, Jakobson stated that "A Serbian peasant reciter of epic poetry memorizes, performs, and, to a high extent, improvises thousands, sometimes tens of thousands of lines, and their meter is alive in his mind. Unable to abstract its rules, he nonetheless notices and repudiates even the slightests infringements of these rules" (Jakobson 1960:364).

24 Not surprisingly, therefore, Kevelson (1977:42) draws a close parallelism between the Peircean interpretant and Wittgenstein's intentionality in language-games.

25 See the discussion of solipsism in Finch 1977:105ff.

reasoning second. Not until there is a language-game are there reasons" (*RPP*:2:687). At this point Wittgenstein's concept of language-game and Peirce's "regular progression of one, two,three" (*CP*:2.299,c.1895) overlap[26]; because when Peirce declared Firstness and Secondness to be irrational, he in effect identified rationality with Thirdness (*CP*:1.354f,1903;*CP*:1.405f,1890-1891).

Language-games involve language and hence ontological Thirdness; but since they tend to include more "motivated" nonverbal signs (exclamations, bodily movements, and/or facial expressions), they also partake of Firstness and Secondness. Moreover, one and the same sign can function at once as an icon (First) and an index (Second) as well as a symbol (Third). In fact Peirce held (in his essay on "Consequences of four capacities") that we can get to know the latter, (thought-)signs, and their meanings by studying how they translate themselves, as it were, into sensations, feelings, and actions: "There is some reason to think that, corresponding to every feeling within us, some motion takes place in our bodies" (*CP*:5.293;*W*:2:230,1868). In Peirce's sweeping theory of mental activity , the reverse may also be true: namely that emotional and bodily emotions can be developed and converted into thought-signs. By this translational operation, "animal motions" such as "blushing, blenching, staring, smiling, scowling, pouting, laughing, weeping, sobbing, wriggling, flinching, trembling, being petrified, sighing, sniffing, shrugging, groaning, heartsinking, trepidation, swelling of the heart, etc." precede and determine not only action (Secondness) but also thought (Thirdness); this would presuppose, however, the presence of a "real effective force behind consciousness" (*CP*:5.289;*W*:2:227,1868), a force which must be a "physiological force" (*CP*:5.289,n.2; *W*:2:226,n.3,1868)[27].

This may be illustrated by the language-game of saying goodbye, in which the verbal, symbolic farewell signs may be accompanied, at least in face-to-face encounters, by such iconic-indexical actions as are embracing, hugging, kissing, waving (hand/arm/handkerchief), and weeping. And Wittgenstein himself referred to the language-game of evoking a past emotion, of remembering how

> At that moment I hated him . . . And if I were to rehearse that moment to myself I should assume a particular expression, think of certain happenings, breathe in a particular way, arouse certain feelings in myself. I might think up a conversation, a whole scene in which that hatred flared up. And I might play this scene through with feelings approximating to those of a real occasion. (*PI*:1:642)

---

26 For a more detailed discussion of Wittgenstein's language-game from the perspective of a (Peircean) semiotics, see (besides Kevelson 1977, see n.24 above), Ransdell 1976 and Gorlée 1989b.

27 See also note 12 and Callaghan 1986:134-135.

Such a remembered event consists again in mutually translatable (or, at least, mutually complementary) "thoughts, feelings, and actions" (*PI*:1:642) --i.e., in a combination of Peirce's three modes of being.

The fundamentally symbolic nature of language-games appears further from the openness of language-games, their susceptibility to change. Language-games are "not something fixed, given once for all: but new types of language, new language-games, as we say, come into existence, and others become obsolete and get forgotten" (*PI*:1:23). Likewise, Peirce argued that

> Symbols grow. They come into being by development out of other signs, particularly from icons, or from mixed signs partaking of the nature of icons and symbols. We think only in signs . . . If a man makes a new symbol, it is by thoughts involving concepts. So it is only out of symbols that a new symbol can grow. *Omne symbolum de symbolo*. A symbol, once in being, spreads among the peoples. In use and in experience, its meaning grows. Such words as *force*, *law*, *wealth*, *marriage*, bear for us very different meanings from those they bore to our barbarous ancestors. (*CP*:2.302,c.1895)[28]

These remarks on the symbol-making process place the language-game in the framework of Peirce's symbolicity and seem to be especially well-chosen to characterize one Wittgensteinian language-game, the game of translation, as a perhaps paradoxical instrument of both convention, methodicalness, responsive interaction on the one hand, and change, innovation, invention on the other.

Language-game of translation

At this point a distinction has to be made between language-games involving translation and the language-game of translation. The former have been discussed above; it has been shown that intersemiotic translation, or transcoding from a verbal into a nonverbal code and vice versa, is a phenomenon which is shared, at least potentially, by all full-fledged language-games. The language-game of interlingual translation, or translation proper, will be the next, and last, issue taken up in this essay. Following Wittgenstein (*PI*:1:23), translation is here regarded as

28 By the same token, Huizinga's remark that the function of play "can largely be derived from the two basic aspects under which we meet it: as a contest *for* something or a representation *of* something" (Huizinga 1964:13) is interpreted by Kevelson as applying to the sign-nature of language-games, thus: "Representation is allied with the idea of display and not repreduction; it is primarily an activity or dramatization of ideas, imaginatively, in opposition. In the language-game, as in Play in general, perception is heightened, and all moves are charged with a significance similar acts lack in ordinary activity. The instrumental purpose of the language-game us to create something of novel value that can carry over into everyday life" (Kevelson 1977:34).

a language-game[29], and will be viewed in the semiotic framework sketched above.

The language-game of translation is meaningful rule-governed behavior aimed at producing a concrete result, the translation. Like all language-games, translation is basically something we do, a praxis. We can play this game because we have mastered a technique, not because we have learned a set of rules. Therefore, it is wholly possible to practice translation without consciousness of the rules, which are implied in the game itself. The language-game of translating is embedded in rules, customs, codes, and grammar, but not reducible to them.

According to Wittgenstein, "Following a rule is analogous to obeying an order. We are trained [*abgerichtet*] to do so; we react to an order in a particular way" (*PI*:1:206). However, translating is more than just obeying rules in the same way as animals are taught to perform certain tricks, or humans are trained to enact certain rituals such as the robot-like recitation of prayers and the use of certain verbal clichés in specific social settings. Such human behavior corresponds to Wittgenstein's "[a]sking, thanking, cursing, greeting, praying" (*PI*:1:23): language-games, that is, which are based on ceremonial use of words and trivialized action. Ritual activity is, "in a certain sense, *pure action --ungrounded action--* because it has no purpose beyond itself and no further basis or explanation" (Finch 1977:211). Such groundless (in Finch's, not Peirce's, sense) action is primarily rooted in instinct, familiarity, and repetition; that is to say, in Firstness. Language is nothing but a vacuous component part of ritual "games". Its Thirdness has become interchangeable with feeling (Firstness) and action (Secondness); its rational-informational purport has weakened, thereby becoming (in Peirce's terminology) degenerate. At the same time, however, these ritual "games" are socially meaningful forms of life, which serve to weld people together and enhance their group spirit.

Translation is a form of cross-cultural human communication. As the so-called Sapir-Whorf hypothesis argues, different linguistic communities have different ways of experiencing, segmenting, and structuring reality. On the basis of these diverse patterns different word-world connections are established which translation aims to bridge for the sake of communication. The game of translating

---

29 See also Chapter 4 and, particularly, notes 6 and 7 there, which are equally timely here. If I propose now to assimilate translation to Wittgenstein's concept of language-game, this is not done because I wish to refer to the one in place of the other, nor to treat the characters of the one as definitive of the other. Wittgenstein used language-games as, in his own words, "*objects of comparison* which are meant to throw light on the facts of our language by way not only of similarities, but also of dissimilarities" (*PI*:1:130). Following Wittgenstein, my argument is to show that translation is one example of language-game, one that exemplifies its semiosic nature. With this proviso it is hoped that no unwarranted moves will be made.

consists in the transformation of an uneconomical source-code into a more economical target version. Finch stresses the systematizing, ordering aspect (Thirdness) of the exercise when he explains translation as "the language-game which includes many kinds of definitions, projections, correlations, transcriptions, decipherings, etc. And it is obviously related to such activities as indexing, cataloguing, briefing, reviewing" (Finch 1977:86). But Finch then adds that "[w]e cannot translate from one *language-game* into another, because language-games are independent of each other, but we can translate from one language into another in the many different ways in which we do" (Finch 1977:86).

These remarks would imply that translating is at the same time rule-following, rule-changing, rule-building, and rule-creating[30]. The coexistence of systematic (rule-generated) and creative (rule-generating) behavior is called, in semiotic terms, semiosis.

Translation as semiosis

Translating is semiosis[31]. It takes as its point of departure the (simple or complex) verbal sign (such as a word, sentence, or text) as referring to its object (or set of objects). Tracing back the particular way in which a sign is encoded (its ground) is followed by the creation, in the mind, of an interpretant, the meaning of which is equivalent to, or a more developed version of, the meaning of the first sign. This interpretant also becomes a sign, which is the starting point of a second triadic relation. In cooperation with the (immediate) object (or better, its second version), a second interpretant-sign is produced which refers, albeit mediately, to the same (dynamical) object as the primary sign. In this fashion, the second interpretant-sign is produced with codes and language-games which are transformations of the original sign. Semiosis in the language-game of translation means that the interpreter/translator interprets and translates in fact his or her own interpretants.

The translator embodies the sign user or interpreter which Peirce did not include as an explicit fourth component of semiosis, in addition to the interpretant. This is not to say that Peirce did not recognize the existence of the interpreter, because he did in fact refer to an interpreter occasionally. Apparently, Peirce did not have in mind one single person or one specific mind, but in an abstract way an intelligent "quasi-mind". As Peirce wrote, semiosis "not only happens in the cortex of the human brain, but must plainly happen in every Quasi-mind in which Signs of all kinds have a vitality of their own" (*NEM*4:318,c.1906). A "quasi-

---

30 For a discussion of (language-)games as open-systemic activities, as forms of play, see Aguirre 1981 and Chapter 4 here (particularly n.12).

31 For a general account of Peirce's concept, see Chapter 3 under "Semiosis".

interpreter" is such a "quasi-mind" (*CP*:4.551,1906). However, in the language-game of translating there is commonly some individual interpreter at work; accordingly, reference to the interpreter is in this connection a practical necessity. This interpreter is either a human being or a computer --the latter a nonhuman artifact, but nevertheless an extension of the human being. Machine translation is carried out by an electronic device programmed to obey orders blindly --as Wittgenstein might have put it. The human translator, however, plays a genuine language-game, semiosis, the result of which is an interpretant sign, the translation, which can itself be interpreted by an interpreting mind "and so on *ad infinitum*" (*CP*:2.303,1901).

Wittgenstein pointed to what Peirce called unlimited semiosis as follows: "When I interpret, I step from one level of thought to another" (*Z*:234). Translation produces what Peirce called logical interpretants because it deals with Thirdness, the "pragmatic" process of making sense of intellectual concepts. Parallelling Wittgenstein's idea of rule, the essence of Peirce's logical interpretants is the habit of interpretation. Just as in language-games rules are not fixed entities, in the process of semiosis habits are developed, adopted, and changed at will. The solution of intellectual problems occurs, in Peirce's paradigm, in three stages showing different degrees of "hardness" (cf.*CP*:5.467,1907): first, second, and third (or final) interpretants. As a mental problem-solving process the language-game of translation follows the same, perhaps partly overlapping, stages.

In the first instance there is Peirce's first logical interpretant. It arises in puzzling situations of an intellectual nature as a more or less fleeting belief suggesting, and suggested by, a potential habit:

> [Readiness] to act in a certain way under given circumstances and when actuated by a given motive is a habit; and a deliberate, or self-controlled, habit is precisely a belief. (*CP*:5.480,1907)

Peirce referred to the author of such speculative ideas, or "airy nothings", as the "muser" (*CP*:6.455,1908). In doing so he drew a parallel between the first, heuristic stage of scientific inquiry and the "Pure Play of Musement" (*CP*:6.452ff,1908)[32]. Indeed, the muser's playful attitude, characterized by

32 The sphere of musement has been explored by Sebeok in his *The Play of Musement* (1981). In cooperation with Eco, Sebeok also published *The Sign of Three* (1983), in which thoughtprovoking parallels are drawn between musement, conjectural thinking in Peirce's abduction, and the methods used in criminal detection, especially by Sherlock Holmes.

Peirce as intellectual reverie (*CP*:6.458,1908)[33], is equally relevant to who plays the game of translation and first lets his or her thoughts flow, ostensibly without serious purpose. In this fashion creative ideas generated by a conscious being are given free play. In the translation situation the first logical interpretant corresponds to the impromptu translation generated almost intuitively by the trained translator's mind.

Next the mind is struck by second thought which disturb the dreamy "meditation". And second logical interpretants are prompted by the first more or less lucky guesses. Peirce wrote that

> . . . those first logical interpretants stimulate us to various voluntary performances in the inner world. We imagine ourselves in various situations and animated by various motives; and we proceed to trace out the alternative lines of conduct which the conjectures would leave open to us. We are, moreover, led, by the same inward activity, to remark different ways in which our conjectures could be slightly modified. (*CP*:5.481,1907)

In this second phase, the working hypotheses are put to the test and verified by solid judgment. In the translation situation this step corresponds to what Peirce, albeit only in passing, referred to as "transsociations", or "alterations of associations" (*CP*:5.476,1907). What arose in the interpreting mind in the form of a spontaneous but provisional translation, is now put on the dissecting table and analyzed with a clear head. The result is "a" translation, which proposes "a" solution to the problem. It may certainly offer a successful solution which "works" in the intended communicational situation and makes sense in the target culture. Yet it cannot pretend to give the absolute, unique solution, because it does not establish an ultimate rule of procedure.

The perfect solution would be the third or final logical interpretant, the single unfailing habit with which (though itself embodied in a sign relation and therefore susceptible to further interpretation[34]) semiosis would in principle come to an end:

---

33 To refer to the idea of musement, Peirce also used, in the same passage, the term "vacancy", curiously reminiscent, etymologically, conceptually, and otherwise, of Wittgenstein's statement that "philosophical problems arise when language *goes on holiday* [and] the philosopher tries to bring out *the* relation between name and thing by staring at an object in front of him and repeating a name or even the word 'this' innumerable times" (*PI*:1:38). Recitation of a mantric formula is, of course, one well-known technique to empty the mind.

34 The seemingly paradoxical nature of the concept of "final interpretant" has been addressed in Greenlee 1973:122ff and later in, for instance, Short 1986. The finality of unlimited semiosis is equally questioned by Wittgenstein in the following passage: "And what about the last definition in this chain? (Do not say: 'There isn't a 'last' definition': That is just as if you chose to say: 'There isn't a last house in this road; one can always build another one'.)" (*PI*:1:29).

> . . . the conclusion (if it comes to a definite conclusion) is that under given conditions, the interpreter will have formed the habit of acting in a given way whenever he may desire a given kind of result. The real and living logical conclusion *is* that habit; the verbal formulation merely expresses it . . . The deliberately formed, self-analyzing habit --self-analyzing because formed by the aid of the exercises that nourished it-- is the living definition, the veritable and final logical interpretant. (*CP*:5.491,1907)

While these "habits in themselves are entirely unconscious" (*CP*:5.492,1907), the language-exercises (that is the language-games) embody, describe, and convey them. In the exercise of translation, the final logical interpretant stands for "the" perfect translation. This is a utopic project, because absolute normativeness in translation can only be of interest ideally. Translators actually prefer the "normal" to the "normative", and thus, on personal, cultural, and other grounds, they "settle for" a "softer" level of professional performance. Though semiosically more tentative, the game will still be played, according to Wittgenstein,

> . . . to give the final interpretation; which is not a further sign or picture, but something else --the thing that cannot be further interpreted. But what we have reached is a psychological, not a logical terminus. . . [where] we shall . . . be inclined to think that there is no further possibility of interpretation. (Z:231)
> What happens is not that this symbol cannot be further interpreted, but: I do no interpreting. I do not interpret, because I feel at home in the present picture. (Z:234)

At this point, the interpretant-sign has arrived at "a stopping place that is natural to me, and its further interpretability does not occupy (or trouble) me" (*Z*:235).

Here it is crucial to remember that the translator in fact interprets verbally his or her own nonverbal interpretants: thus producing interpretant-signs which are twice, thrice, etc. removed from the primary sign. The fact that the interpreter produces meaningful Thirds, logical interpretants, does not necessarily mean that these must possess a high truth value. Although they are the product of reasoning, their truth value may actually be slight. In Peirce's semiotic jargon (*CP*:2.250ff,c.1903), a particular translation, taken as a whole and as a single sign, may be realistically experienced as a "dicent indexical sinsign"[35] (or, according to the qualification rule, dicent sinsign), a highly informative sign of actual existence, or Secondness, capable of being asserted. As such it will embody a "rhematic icon", which is neither true nor false but serves to make recognizable the likeness between the sign itself and what it "is about"[36]. But a translation may

---

35 See the section on "Peirce's trichotomies and the classification of signs" in Chapter 3.

36 See also the discussion on equivalence in Chapter 9. In addition to its basic symbolicity, a translation (that is, the actual translated text) displays a strongly indexical and iconic character. The information provided by the individual translation as well as the text itself refer directly back to the

also be transformed into an "argumentative symbolic legisign" (or argument, for short), an elaborate thought-sign accepted as law and regarded as authority[37]. The translated text will then have acquired a new and sophisticated status, that of genuine final Thirdness. To transform the language-game of translation into giving final answers is, however, denying that the translator is essentially a craftsman, and translation is essentially dynamic. Such totalization undercuts unlimited semiosis because it excludes the possibility that any interpreter, now or in the future, will start the interpreting process afresh; that he will turn the given interpretant into a new sign and produce again "an" interpretant, a new head-made and hand-made translation.

Translation: Wittgenstein and Peirce

That Peirce's manner of philosophical writing, interlaced as it is with technical terms, would not have been congenial to Wittgenstein, is hardly doubtful. However, the latter's laconic and simple style and manner of writing do not make his thought any more readily accessible. The point is to show that, contrasting language usage aside, the ideas of both philosophers are basically consistent with each other. I hazard the suggestion that by being coupled, both insights gain both in methodological scope and in clarity of argumentation. This may be illustrated in the concluding part of this chapter from the passage in which Wittgenstein pronounced himself most elaborately on (interlingual) translation:

> Translating from one language into another is a mathematical task, and the translation of a lyrical poem, for example, into a foreign language is quite analogous to a mathematical *problem*. For one may well frame the problem "How is this joke (e.g.) to be translated (i.e. replaced) by a joke in the other language?" and this problem can be solved; but there was no systematic method of solving it. (Z:698)[38]

---

object, so that the translation is in that sense complementary to the original. At the same time, a translation is based on equivalence and likeness, both of information and of actual physical shape. The iconic aspect adds an esthetic --that is, sensuous-- dimension to translation, which deserves particularly to be studied more fully in its visual, auditory, and even tactile manifestations.

37 This is especially problematic in translation of the Bible, the Hebrew Torah and Talmud, and other texts of a religious (or, more generally, a sacred) nature. See the classic on this issue, Nida 1964.

38 This text also appears in *RPP*:1:778, albeit in a slightly variant translation (but, curiously, delivered by the same translator, G. E. M. Anscombe). The original German text is, apart from one question mark and one case of italicization, identical in both editions. Both *Z* and *RPP* contain fragments of manuscripts dictated by Wittgenstein in the later 1940s and left by him as a collection of mere slips of paper. This material has subsequently been assembled, organized, and partly reconstructed by the editors. Semiotically, their job was to create some sequential order, or Secondness, out of a multifarious welter of Firsts, to make possible the construction of a meaningful Third. Indeed, a painstaking intellectual *bricolage*. See also note 8.

The language-game of translation is, for Wittgenstein, analogous to the language-game of "Solving a problem in practical arithmatic" (*PI*:1:23) in that both are meaningful rule-governed praxes aimed at problem-solving and producing a concrete solution. As such both language-games are again related to the language-game of "Guessing riddles" (*PI*:1:23)[39]. This illustrates how different language-games cluster in groups. If we include "Making a joke: telling it" (*PI*:1:23), the passage quoted above connects four consecutive games on Wittgenstein's list of examples in *PI*:1:23. The two analogies put forward in *Z*:698 to clarify translation, hinge on mathematics and jokes.

As argued by Schwayder,

> Wittgenstein held that mathematics is derivative from the use of language . . . that it is this civil application which gives mathematics its meaning . . . [and] that mathematics at its most characteristic is the conceptual investigation of (other) language-games. (Schwayder 1969:69)

This would explain why Wittgenstein advanced the analogy with interlingual translation. Indeed, what is really done in the most concrete parts of mathematics is actual calculation and, Schwayder specifies,

> Wittgenstein not surprisingly lays stress on calculation and on . . . "Intuitive Mathematics", on that kinds of non-systematic thinking well illustrated by classical thought-experiments typically conducted outside of mathematical theory by methods which are indeed methods of *demonstration* and not of logical derivation. (Schwayder 1969:68)[40]

Indeed, for Wittgenstein "A mathematical question is a challenge. And we might say: it makes sense if it spurs us on to some mathematical activity" (Z:697); and "We might then also say that a question in mathematics makes sense if it stimulates the mathematical imagination" (Z:697). This means that the rules and routines of mathematical thinking have to be complemented by original insights (Firstness) in order to make a genuine semiosic language-game possible. This is in full accordance with Peirce's abductive guess as a plausible problem-solving device, within mathematics and elsewhere. While Peirce held that the one universally valid logical method is that of mathematical demonstration, and

39 Note the interesting parallel with Peirce's "A guess at the riddle".

40 Peirce's wish to acquire a "demonstrative knowledge of the solution of a certain problem of reasoning" (*CP*:5.490,1907; also quoted in Eisele 1979:220), which explains his tendency to use examples like the Achilles-and-the-tortoise in his mathematical theory (*CP*:4.202,1897, for instance), points in a similar direction.

mathematicians typically are deductive reasoners, all their hypotheses are, he argued, abductively created[41].

Wittgenstein also stated that "the translation of a lyrical poem . . . is quite analogous to a mathematical *problem*" (*Z*:698). This analogy serves to highlight the formal, prosodic, and acoustic restraints imposed upon the poetic translator, and which cause this specialized language-game to be commonly regarded as practically unworkable[42]. But if the problems involved do not stifle the translator and instead prompt his or her creativity, poetry can be translated: like in Wittgenstein's version of mathematics, here too a solution can be found[43].

Wittgenstein's second analogy is with translating a joke. This equally specialized language-game is really a combination of "Making a joke: telling it" and "Translating from one language into another" (*PI*:1:23)[44]. Verbal jokes are often strongly bound to one language and one culture. They are normally linked to specific social habits, or Wittgensteinian forms of life. In this connection jokes tend to question and even break a presupposed rule (Eco 1984b). When different frames of reference are thus juxtaposed, one feels, Kevelson writes,

> . . . surprise --a comic reaction-- and begins to doubt what was formerly believed to be true. Peirce says that it is not the perception of disorder that provokes surprise, but the discovery of an unsuspected order which jars belief, and which leads to further questions. (Kevelson 1985:204)

All this makes jokes hard to translate without making the implicit explicit, thereby spoiling the joke. The translator's job is to decide to follow a certain procedure, a pragmatic combination of generally accepted and self-made *ad hoc* habits; and if the translated joke "works" in the new frame of reference, the new linguistic

---

41 About Peirce's triadic logic of reasoning, see Chapter 3 (particularly "Reasoning and logic"). For Peirce as a mathematician, see the four volumes of *NEM* and Eisele 1979.

42 Wittgenstein stated that "in the sense in which it [the sentence] can be replaced by another which says the same", in poetry it "cannot be replaced by any other" (*PI*:1:531). This does not mean that lyrical texts are not actually translated. Theoretically, the problem has been addressed, from various methodological angles, in Levy 1969, Day-Lewis 1970, Lefevere 1975, de Beaugrande 1978, and Raffel 1988, among others.

43 See also Steiner 1975:275. This monograph is to my knowledge the only major study in the field of translation theory, which treats Wittgenstein any more than cursorily. According to Steiner (1975:295,n.1), Wittggenstein pronounced himself on translation in *PI*:1:23, 206, 243, and 528; however, in *PI*:1:206 and 243 no mention is made of the subject.

44 By the same token one can easily imagine many other combinations between language-games; e.g., opera is a mixture of "play-acting" and "singing catches"; one may "lie" while "describing the appearance of an object"; "telling a dream" may include "reporting", and vice versa.

(and hence, cultural) community --that is, if it has the desired comic effect--, it has fulfilled its purpose. The game has then achieved its "point"[45].

The analogy with the translation of jokes is cleverly chosen, because it combines the playful (Peirce's Firstness) with the methodical (Peirce's Thirdness); indeed, as Wittgenstein concluded, "this problem can be solved; but there was no systematic method of solving it" (Z:698). Translating provides no rule beyond the anecdotal evidence given in the actual translation. Neither the one ever-successful rule of projection, nor the one faultless translational habit can be created.

Peirce himself stressed the open-ended nature of any intellectual exercise in his own analogy, the saga of the "imaginary inventor" (*CP*:5.490,1907), whom he also called an "investigator" and "interpreter"; a man already skillful in handling a given sign (that has a logical interpretant) and who wishes to "acquire a demonstrative knowledge of the solution of a certain problem of reasoning" (*CP*:5.490,1907). In Peirce's tale this scholar sets out to find the mathematical solution to the so-called map-coloring problem[46]; and

> Under the high stimulus of his interest in this problem, and with that practical knack that we have supposed him to possess in coloring maps without too frequently being obliged to go back and alter the colors he assigned to given regions, we need not doubt that our inquirer will be thrown into a state of high activity in the world of fancies, in experimenting upon coloring maps, while trying to make out what subconscious rule guides him, and renders him as successful as he usually is; and in trying, too, to discover what rule he had violated in each case where his first coloration has to be changed. This activity is, logically, an energetic interpretant of the interrogatory he puts to himself. Should he in this way succeed in working out a determinate rule for coloring every map . . . , there will be good hope that a demonstration may tread upon the heels of that rule, in which case, the problem will be solved in the most convenient form. (*CP*:5.490,1907)

"But", Peirce hastened to add, "while he may be very likely to manage to formulate his own usually successful way of coloring regions, it is very unlikely that he will obtain an unfailing rule for doing so"; so that, as Peirce concluded his argument, "We may assume with confidence, then, that our imaginary interpreter will, at length, come to despair of solving the problem in that way" (*CP*:5.490,1907).

Peirce was an investigator of logical methodology; this explains his extensive work in the heuretic branch of mathematics and topology, among others. Considering his lifelong search for a universal method applicable to all sciences

---

45 Wittgenstein's *Witz* is because of its dual meaning in German, co(n)textually translated in *PI* as either "joke" or "point".

46 This mathematical problem was in fact only solved in 1976, more than one hundred years after it was raised.

alike, it is, however, quite possible to substitute Peirce's above-quoted[47] remarks on the map-coloring problem for any other intellectual problem, such as the one we confront in translation. In this sense translation demonstrates the ongoing and open-ended process of continuity, or semiosis, the habitual and sustained effort which may (or may not) in the end result in the problem's final resolution. The absence of a final logical interpretant is thereby not a weakness in semiosis, but a living and constant appeal to the interpreter's (that is, in this case, the translator's) creative resources; for the latter enable and invite man to engage himself in the never-ending pursuit of generating what is an infinite series of energetic, nonfinal interpretants. In this sense the language-game of translating proposes workable solutions and is to be regarded more definitely as a process-oriented than as a result-oriented activity. This is, in closing, a view Wittgenstein would probably have shared with Peirce, and such an approach brings both philosophers and their ideas on translation to a potential meeting ground from which, it is hoped, translation theoreticians, semioticians, and language philosophers may benefit alike.

47 For other references, see Eisele's paper on "The four-color problem" (Eisele 1979:216-222).

06. PEIRCE AND THE PROBLEM OF TRANSLATION : SOUL AND BODY[1]

"When you speak . . . of Man as *translating* vegetal and Brute strength into intellectual and spiritual vigor, that word *translating* seems to me to contain profound truth wrapped up in it." (Peirce to Lady Welby in letter of March 14, 1904) (*PW*:111)

Introductory remarks

References to translation may be found throughout Charles Sanders Peirce's writings, published as well as unpublished. However, many of these references were not meant by him to discuss translation for its own sake, and even less to limit translation to a linguistic activity. Rather, Peirce used translation as a heuristic device aimed at clarifying some of the fundamental sign-theoretical issues he raised throughout his intellectual career. To show this will be the core of my argument in this chapter.

Peirce as translator

Peirce, the polymath, was also a practising translator. The first two pages of his *Illustrations of the Logic of Science*, "The fixation of belief" (*W*3:242-257,1877) and "How to make our ideas clear" (*W*3:257-276,1878), were after their composition translated by Peirce himself and appeared subsequently in French in *Revue philosophique* as "Comment se fixe la croyance" (*W*3:338-355,1878) and "Comment rendre nos idées claires" (*W*3:355-374,1879). Although the French

1 The subtitle of this chapter is taken from "Soul and Body", the title Peirce had given to Volume VI of his *magnum opus*, *The Principles of Philosophy: Or Logic, Physics, and Psychics, Considered as a Unity, in the Light of the Nineteenth Century*. This giant work, which Peirce conceived of by 1893, was to comprise twelve volumes, none of which Peirce was able to finish (see Esposito 1980:158).

varies in quality (see the "Editorial notes" in *W*3:531-535), Peirce was doubtless a man endowed with an unusual gift for, and interest in, languages, alongside his many other interests; and the French language was, for many reasons, professional as well as private, particularly close to his heart.

That Peirce was an insightful polyglot is also, and quite eloquently, shown in other translations which he composed in later years (*MSS*1514-1520;see Robin 1967:160-161) and to which he owed much of his livelihood after he left his longstanding position at the U.S. Coast and Geodetic Survey, on 31 December 1891, and thus missed this source of regular income. Wiener comments that, by the year 1901, "Peirce's lack of a steady position and income left him poverty-stricken and dependent on reviewing and hackwork like translating scientific papers for the Smithsonian Institution" (Wiener in *SW*:275).

To be sure, the translated texts are, from the perspective of translation studies today, often less interesting than the annotations which Peirce had the habit of placing in the margins. These marginal notes include miscellaneous technical comments, emotional exclamations, as well as occasional "sharp criticism of the author [of the original]" (Robin 1967:160), thus providing a wealth of information, musement, and even amusement.

For the sake of brevity, anecdotal evidence of this, in the form of a few more or less random examples, must suffice here. A propos of one passage, from the work of the pioneer of gas illumination, Philippe Le Bon (1767-1804), Peirce offered, in a translator's note, an elaborate counterargument to what he called the French engineer's "enigmatic hypothesis", namely that "at that temperature [500° Celsius], the light is converted into heat as fast as it is absorbed" (*MS*1516:12,n.d.). Apparently overcome by professional frustration, Peirce jotted in the margin: "This sounds like nonsense" (*MS*1516:12,n.d.). In a different *MS* Peirce placed, in the same personal vein, the following critical remark in a frame which he had drawn at the end of a Dilthey quotation: "I can make no sense at all this nonsensical stuff. Germans are so logically inaccurate in writing, that it is sometimes hard to guess what they mean. This is awful and nauseous" (*MS*1517:46,1896). Another commentary by Peirce pertains to professional ethics not allowing this translator to retranslate in good faith a German version of a passage by Tolstoy into English:

> Upon the principle that translations two deep are to be avoided, the translator would prefer to insert a direct translation from Russian if any exists. Otherwise, it would be a small matter to get the requisite translation. The present translator does not read Russian. (*MS*1517:76,1896)

That Peirce was an extremely conscientious translator is also testified to in his correspondence. In a letter dated June 1, 1905, addressed to the then Director of the Smithsonian Institution, Samuel P. Langley --who "took a generous interest in helping to support Peirce" (Wiener in *SW*:275)-- , Peirce wrote:

> By the way I noted one time, . . . , that you *hinted* that some error or errors had been found in some translation of mine. You would oblige me *most particularly*, when such a thing happens, if you would please communicate the whole thing to me; and if you can *without trouble* do so about the former criticism I should be obliged to you. In the first place justice to me requires it. I have always got the best aids possible & that fact would very likely come out in regard to any doubtful case. German writers frequently express themselves so loosely that an accurate translation sometimes reverses their meaning. At least, I took the trouble to ascertain that such was the case on one occasion. However, after having done all the work I have on dictionaries I know very well how absurd it would be to maintain that any translation of mine were impeccable . . . (Peirce's underlining)[2]

Special mention deserves further the text which Peirce translated "from the second German edition" of *Genius and Degeneration*[3], which contains some curious renderings into English of parts of the libretto of Wagner's opera-cycle, *Der Ring des Nibelungen.* Peirce placed the original German texts in footnotes, which for the interested student facilitates a comparison between original and translation. Unsuited to be sung in a real operatic performance (if only because Peirce's versions are often longer (that is, have more syllables) than the original German lyrics), they are also unable to tune into the lyrical mode and are hardly evidence of artistry and poetic sensitivity[4]; rather, they affirm the widely accepted view that artistic texts are in so far basically untranslatable. One typical example of this is the following key-passage from Wagner's *Rheingold*:

> Only who Eros'
> Power denies,
> Only who love's delights
> Chases away,
> Can attain to the magical power
> To bend around the gold to a hoop.
>
> [Nur wer der Minne

---

2 This is a reference from Professor Max H. Fisch's personal file cabinet. I thank Professor Fisch for his kind permission to inspect and quote from the thousands of fiches which he has assembled in a lifetime of devotion to Peircean studies.

3 The German original was W. Hirsch's *Genie und Entartung: eine psychologische Studie* (first edition 1894), now fallen into oblivion.

4 See Apter 1989 for a more detailed discussion of the problems involved in translating opera, --a complex syncretic art form involving the musical, literary, and scenic arts (as noted in Sebeok 1985a:79).

Macht versagt,
Nur wer der Liebe
Lust verjagt
Nur der erzielt sich den Zauber
Zum Reif zu zwingen das Gold.] (*MS*1517:136,1896)

Translatability

In the whole of Peirce's work his own translations were a marginal aspect. It is crucial to emphasize here that Peirce characteristically used "translation" and related terms in a very broad sense, and mostly abstracted from what Jakobson (1959:233) would come to call "interlingual translation, or *translation proper*". Peirce's concept of translation being of a general sign-theoretical nature, it is, however, wholly applicable to this and other types of translation involving language, without however being identical with it.

For Peirce in his earlier period, the meaning of any sign, verbal and nonverbal, lies first and foremost in its translatability, and sign translation is thus sign comprehension:

> Everything may be comprehended or more strictly translated by something: that is has something which is capable of such a determination as to stand for something through this thing; somewhat as the pollen-grain of a flower stands to the ovule which it penetrates for the plant from which it came since it transmits the peculiarities of the latter. In somewhat the same sense, though not to the same degree, everything is a medium between something and something. (*W*1:333,1865)

This means that something carries no meaning, and can therefore not be considered to be a sign, if the "peculiarities" or essential characters which it contains and which would make it a sign, cannot be perceived, captured, and comprehended; accordingly, the "matter's conveying a notion" (*W*1:50,1861) is a defining property of what Peirce used to call a "representation", or sign. Indeed, significance (that is, signhood as Peirce saw it in his earlier years[5]) is made possible because of the standing-for character of all signs: thus "We are capable of understanding representations only by having conceptions or mental representations, which represent the given representation as a representation" (*W*1:323,1865). The sign, in order to be one, must not only have a material form, its "body", and thus be perceptible and cognizable. It must also have a "soul", that is, it must embody a recognizable message, at least potentially; and recognition is

5 For the sake of clarity it must be noted that initially Peirce identified "sign" only with what he called "symbol" --that is, with a general sign, word, or other sign having a relation of Thirdness to its object, and thus requiring thought for its interpretation.

based upon prior experience with, or imagination of, the objectual universe determining a particular sign-use.

Short (1986:105) has described significance as "grounded interpretability", thereby meaning that the Peircean concept of ground must be considered as the point of view which renders the representation variously meaningful --that is, intelligible, decodable, and comprehensible. By retracing a sign's ground, the observer is led to take the sign as embodying its object iconically, indexically, symbolically, or (as commonly is the case) as a mixture of two or all three of these modes. By ground must Peirce thus have meant "the pure form or abstraction which is the original of the thing of which the concrete thing is only the incarnation" (*W*1:474,1866). In other words, and to continue the Peircean imaginery, if the sign has a (concrete) body, its ground indicates the idea of the (abstract) soul which animates it.

This concept of sign seems to imply the Cartesian idea of separating soul and body: that signs make no sense unless they are capable of being translated, on the basis of their ground(s), into other, pre-existing systems of signs, and this would in fact make the notion of translation referred to here, a "respect of likeness" (*W*1:474,1866), that is, a matter of Firstness. That it was ostensibly not Peirce's intention to identify translation of signs wholly with their interpretability or groundedness was, however, shown by Peirce in many other writings, both of the same period referred to here, and of later years. There, Peirce placed sign translation no longer in the domain of Firstness, but of Thirdness, thereby resolving the problem of Cartesian dualism into something with three components, one of which being the mediating force aimed at bridging the separation between the other two. I would venture the suggestion that this is not the bold leap it looks like. What seems like a change of heart --self-contradicting or even paradoxical-- is in fact a natural outgrowth of Peirce's theory of meaning, which is again built upon the doctrine of the three categories as Peirce came to develop it over the years.

Indeed, as argued by Murphey (1961:313ff.), Peirce's earlier theory of meaning, upon which his concept of translation is based, oscillates between two poles, Firstness and Thirdness. Given that, for Peirce, intellectual inquiry and, more generally, thought, aim at the "fixation of belief", they revolve around developing mental habits which render such beliefs increasingly general, solid, "harder". The perfect illustration of how meaning is constructed through a teleological truth-seeking process running from tentatively suggested Firstness, through actually present Secondness, to final Thirdness, may be found in Peirce's own pragmatic maxim: "Consider what effects, which might conceivably have practical bearings, we conceive the object of our conception to have. Then, our conception of these effects is the whole of our conception of the object" (*W*3:266,1878).

One of the implications of Peirce's maxim is that meaning (the process of making sense) needs to start out as a First, a belief, or embryonic habit, in terms of which the sign may be interpreted, or translated, thereby becoming potentially meaningful, but no more. Yet for the sign to deploy its full meaning what is needed is more than such a habit *in statu nascendi*, adopted more or less *ad hoc* for the sake of mere intelligibility. Through an experimental process a rule needs to be worked out: only such a general rule, one which may be applied to an infinite number of sign instances and successfully generate meaning there, will in the final analysis be able (if still hypothetically) to reveal the whole meaning of the sign. Therefore must genuine semiosis, or generative sign-action, be a matter of Thirdness building upon Secondness, which again builds upon Firstness. In Peirce's words,

> . . . the intellectual character of beliefs at least are dependent upon the capability of the endless translation of sign into sign. An inference translates itself directly into a belief. A thought which is not capable of affecting belief in any way, obviously has no signification or intellectual value at all. If it does affect belief it is then translated from one sign to another as the belief itself is interpreted. (*W*3:77,1873)

The use by Peirce of the verb "translate" is in this and similar contexts more than a poetic license or a felicitous metaphor. It can even be carried further: the sign's ground, that is the rule governing its mode of representational being, would then suggest a possible meaning through a process of what may be called "back translation". This is a First. On the other hand, future conduct can only be controlled through "forward translation". It requires the production of a potentially infinite series of ever-stronger habits of interpretation, in reference to which Peirce coined in 1866 the word "interpretant" --though Savan (1987-1988:41), quite interestingly in the context of my argument here, notes that "translatant" would have been an equally adequate term. In Peirce's semiotics, the interpretant, or forward translation, embodies the category of Thirdness, which mediates between Firstness and Secondness. It is both the third element in the semiotic triad sign-object-interpretant, and itself a threefold sign-relation; both the sign's *tertium comparationis* and, in the event of so-called (by Peirce) intellectual signs, or signs of Thirdness, a sign which may again occur as first, second, and third logical interpretant (*MS*318:168ff,1907).

Translation as semiosis

As early as in 1865, Peirce had distinguished, within semiotics, between logic in the narrow sense of representation and what he called "symbolistic":

> I define logic therefore as the science of the conditions which enable symbols in general to refer to objects. At the same time *symbolistic* in general gives a trivium consisting of

> Universal Grammar, Logic, and Universal Rhetoric, using this last term to signify the science of the formal conditions of intelligibility of symbols. (*W*1:175,1865)

By placing what he then called the "force of symbols, or their power of appealing to a mind" (*W*2:57,1867) in the realm of universal rhetoric, Peirce extended his earlier emphasis on representation (the sign-object relation) and highlighted the relation the sign has to "the Consciousness being thinkable, or to any language as being translatable" (*W*1:174,1865). This sign-translational process is obviously a matter of genuine semiosis or Thirdness, the category of the thought-sign which brings sign and object together in a meaningful interpretation:

> Indeed, the process of getting an equivalent for a term, is an identification of two terms previously diverse. It is, in fact, the process of nutrition of terms by which they get all their life and vigor and by which they put forth an energy almost creative --since it has the effect of reducing the chaos of ignorance to the cosmos of science. Each of these equivalents is the explication of what there is wrapt up in the primary --they are the surrogates, the interpreters of the original term. They are new bodies, animated by the same soul. I call them the interpretants of the term. (*W*1:464-465,1866)

Peirce's foregoing 1866 argument on sign translation as a semiosic "process of nutrition" producing interpretant signs, "new bodies animated by the same soul", would not be echoed, continued, and "further developed" by him until no less than 35 years later, when Peirce affirmed in his 1903 essay on "Pragmatism and Pragmaticism" that thought

> . . . is in itself essentially of the nature of a sign. But a sign is not a sign unless it translates itself into another sign in which it is more fully developed. Thought requires achievement for its own development, and without this development it is nothing. Thought must live and grow in incessant new and higher translations, or it proves itself not to be genuine thought. (*CP*:5.594,1903)

In this and subsequent years, Peirce would continue to develop thoughts on translation as a goal-directed, evolutionary process, which define it unreservedly as a Third, the category of the interpretant. In doing so, Peirce did, however, not at all mean to exclude the other, "lower" categories. Indeed, in those same years, which were crucial for his sign-theoretical thought, Peirce argued convincingly that the reverse is true. This will be discussed in some detail in the following pages of this essay, together with Peirce's later remarks on translation which include ideas, both implicit and explicit, on the types of translation characterized later by Jakobson (1959:233) as intralingual, interlingual, and intersemiotic translation. These types of translation involve language, that is Thirdness, in some way or another, but are not reducible to it and must be accommodated in the broad scenery of thought-signs as it was elaborated by Peirce.

By 1902, when Peirce returned to his theory of meaning, he had definitively identified it with interpretive semiosis, or translation implying "two infinite series, the one back toward the object, the other toward the interpretant . . . The type of a sign is memory and delivers a portion of it to future memory" (*MS*599:37,c.1902). This two-way informational process includes both back-translation and forward-translation; but it is in the latter that the sign realizes its meaning-potential. It does so by producing, through an interpreting mind, Peirce's "quasi-mind", a virtually endless sequence of interpretants, or translated signs, each of them adding new pieces of information on the nature of the object. This makes forward-translation the goal toward which the life of all genuine signs must be oriented: "There is no exception, therefore, to the law that every thought-sign is translated or interpreted in a subsequent one, unless it be that all thought comes to an abrupt and final end in death" (*CP*:5.284;*W*2:224,1868).

There is, in a Peircean semiotics, no reason to doubt that semiosis is also what transpires in the different kinds of translation involving linguistic signs. Let us quote, in this connection, a rather extended passage from one of Peirce's unpublished manuscripts, in which is demonstrated that all translational processes are, for Peirce, illustrative of how the "summum bonum" is achieved:

> What does it mean to speak of the "interpretation" of a sign? Interpretation is merely another word for translation; and if we had the necessary machinery to do it, which we perhaps never shall have, but which is quite conceivable, an English book might be translated into French or German without the interposition of a translation into the imaginary signs of human thought. Still, supposing there were a machine or even a growing tree, which, without the interpolation of any imagination, were to go on translating and translating from one possible language to a new one, will it be said that the function of signs would therein be fulfilled?

And Peirce's continued by asking:

> What are signs for anyhow? They are to communicate ideas, are they not? Even the imaginary signs called thought convey ideas from the mind of yesterday to the mind of tomorrow into which yesterday's has grown. Of course, then, these "ideas" are not themselves "thoughts", or imaginary signs. They are some potentiality, some form, which may be embodied in external or in internal signs. But why should this idea-potentiality be so poured from one vessel into another unceasingly? Is it a mere exercize of the World-spirit's *Spiel-Trieb*, --mere amusement? Ideas do, no doubt, grow in this process. It is a part, perhaps we may say the chief part, of the process of the Creation of the World. If it has no ulterior aim at all, it may be likened to the performance of a symphony. The pragmaticist insists that this is not at all [text unreadable] signs which should be merely parts of an endless viaduct for the transmission of idea-potentiality, without any conveyance of it into anything but symbols, namely, into action or habit of action, would not be signs at all, since they would not, little or much, fulfill the function of signs; and further, that without embodiment in something else than symbols, the principles of logic

show there never could be the least growth in idea-potentiality. (*MS*283:97-101,1905-1906)

The above passage seems to sum up Peirce's mature conception of sign translation. It shows that for Peirce signs are evolutionary agents aimed at engendering interpretant signs, which evolve, through time, their informational content, or "idea-potentiality". They would not be able to fulfill this mission if there were no mind available to process and translate the meaning they contain; because then no interpretant could be produced to carry, convey, and transmit further their "ideas". Interpretation is, in Peirce's later thought, as crucial to the life of signs, and hence to survival in general, as is representation.

In this brief exercise in futurology of sorts, Peirce further prefigured the possibility of machine translation (or, more accurately, translation by a "quasi-mind", or thinking organism, non-human but programmed by the human mind), which was to become, for better or worse, such a burning issue for later linguists, scientists, and philosophers[6]. By placing translation systematically in a wider framework than that of linguistics[7], Peirce anticipated the later interdisciplinary approach. Indeed, Peirce, the pragmaticist, had enriched his earlier version of logic focused exclusively on (symbolic) thought-signs, with their iconic and indexical counterparts. In Peirce's later thought, Thirds are no longer exclusive entities; in order to fulfill their role as efficient vehicles of communication, they must involve Seconds and Firsts (in the same way in which Seconds must involve Firsts): ". . . a symbol, if sufficiently complete, always involves an index, just as an index sufficiently complete involves an icon" (*NEM*4:256,c.1904)[8]

6 Peirce's anticipation of translation by computer was preceded by his work on developing a new kind of cable code, to be used in transferring letters to a code. In a fragment of a letter draft to Henry Cabot Lodge, he wrote: "I could make a machine which would write a cipher dispatch, as secure as a combination lock, and as readily as an ordinary typewriter, and a companion machine would translate it as fast as a stock ticker, --every dispatch in a different sipher which the machine itself would discover. This would be valuable to merchants in war times" (*MS*L254:12,1898?).

7 "I do not, for my part, regard the usages of language and forming a satisfactory basis for logical doctrine", Peirce noted in the important *MS*517, and "the appeal to language appears to be no better than an unsatisfactory method of ascertaining psychological facts that are of no relevancy to logic" (*NEM*4:245,c.1904).

8 That the reverse is not necessarily true is shown, in Peirce's text under discussion, in his question whether the communication of ideas is to be considered as "a mere exercize of the World-spirit's *Spiel-Trieb*, --mere amusement" (*MS*283:99,1905-1906), that is, as Firstness. While Firstness --Peirce's "Pure Play of Musement" (*CP*:6.452-6.465,1908)-- doubtless is the source of creativity in the use of signs, yet it lacks *in itself* the dimension of "action or habit of action" (*MS*283:101,1905-1906) represented by signs of Secondness and Thirdness, and without which no genuine semiosis can occur.

The different translational modes proposed by Jakobson partake of the same characteristics of signhood described above. His intralingual, interlingual, and intersemiotic translation are three types of interpretive sign-action, or semiosis)[9]. They hinge on the production of interpretants, in Peirce's sense of the term interpretant, which he defined as "an equivalent sign, or perhaps a more developed sign" (*CP*:2.228,c.1897). "An equivalent of a proposition is the same proposition, differently materialized", Peirce stated a propos of what Jakobson would later call "interlingual translation or *translation proper*"; and he continued, "For the proposition consists in its meaning" (*MS*599:62,c.1902;cf.*CP*:5.138,1903). What happens is that this meaning-content --pure thought, the soul of the message-- receives a different material form --a new body which both incarnates it and is given new life by it.

Peirce referred repeatedly to the three types of translation in his later period. In the following quotation he discussed intralingual and interlingual translation, thus:

> Note that a proposition is nothing existent, but is a general model, type, or law according to which existents are shaped. Here, for instance, are half a dozen existent writings:
>
> Solomon built himself an house.
> Σολομῶν ᾠκοδδόμησυν αὑτῳ όἰκον.
> Solomon built him a house.
> Salomon aedificavit illi domum.
> Solomon built a house for himself.
> Solomon a adeiladodd dy iddo ef.
>
> But they are all existing singular *instances* of one self-same proposition. (*MS*280:29,c.1905)

What is under discussion here is, however, translation as a product, not as a process. Peirce focused here not on semiosis itself, but on the end-product(s) of transcoding interpretation. He found, to use his own parlance, that Seconds (actual sentences) are generated partaking of Thirds (the "grammar" of language) in such a way that these Seconds, though differing in linguistic code, are nonetheless logically equivalent[10].

Jakobson's intersemiotic translation is inter-medium translation moving away from language (Thirdness) into the vast and highly diversified realm of the nonverbal (Secondness and Firstness). Peirce was particularly interested in one

---

9 For a detailed discussion of this, see Chapter 8.

10 The concept of equivalence is discussed from a Peircean perspective in Chapter 9.

mode of intersemiotic translation, namely, the translation of language into what he called the "moving images of Thought" (*MS*298:13,*CP*:4.8,1906):

> [T]hat thought needs language and could not have taken place before men possessed language [is] in so far right that speech is man's instinctive vehicle of thought... But every mathematician and every logician will tell the linguists that they are in possession of quite other systems of signs into which they are accustomed to translate words and forms of words and so to render them more intelligible. One such system, equivalent to a syntax... is called the system of Existential Graphs. (*MS*654:5-6,1910)

This system, which Peirce invented in 1896, made "literally visible before one's eyes the operation of thinking *in actu*" (*CP*:4.6,1906). The pictorial notation has, said Peirce, "none of the ordinary parts of speech; for the indivisible elements are, one and all, complete assertions" (*MS*654:6,1910). As opposed to the fragmented way of verbal signs to reflect thought, existential graphs offer *totum simul*. Its iconic nature gives the system of existential graphs more than one dramatic advantage over language:

> Namely, instead of being merely protracted in time, its expressions are diagrams upon a surface, and indeed must be regarded as only a projection upon that surface of a sign extended in three dimensions. Three dimensions are necessary and sufficient for the expression of all assertions; so that, if man's reason was originally limited to the line of speech, (which I do not affirm) it has now outgrown the limitation. (*MS*654:7,1910)

Signs are translated here from a linear, symbolic code into a nonlinear, iconic code. This diagrammatic mode expands the meaning-content of the originary verbal signs, and this expansion of their "idea-potentiality" enables the observer to see new interrelations and connections, and to reason upon them in a novel way. This form of intersemiotic translation is, it would seem, an excellent illustration of how thoughts may grow through translation.

Metempsychosis

The dynamic-idealistic thoughts on translation, linguistic or otherwise, which Peirce left later in his life, are embedded in his ideas on evolutionary growth through dialogue of ideas, methods of inquiry, and language. They appear to elevate sign-translation to higher spheres and to transmogrify it into a phenomenon with somehow "mystical and mysterious" (*NEM*4:262,c.1904) overtones, --a kind of supersymbol.

Of the "three Universes of Experience" Peirce addressed in this "perfect sign" the third and highest one, corresponding to the category of Thirdness: "The third Universe comprises everything whose being consists in active power to establish connections between different objects, especially between objects in different Universes" (*CP*:6.455,1908). Peirce described this mediating power again in terms of his earlier soul-body metaphor, thus:

> Such is everything which is essentially a Sign --not the mere body of the Sign, which is not essentially such, but, so to speak, the Sign's Soul, which has its Being in its power of serving as intermediary between its Object and a Mind. Such, too, is a living consciousness, and such the life, the power of growth, of a plant. Such is a living constitution --a daily newspaper, a great fortune, a social "movement". (*CP*:6.455,1908)

From such a soul --hidden, perhaps, but always present-- comes the meaning of a genuine sign; and this soul and its commitment to growth, both mental, spiritual, and intellectual, are sure signs of Thirdness, and hence of life.

In order to grow, however, sign and soul need one another; one must serve as interactor to the other, and vice versa. A soul, Peirce noted, "cannot live without a body, though it will preserve its identity through all the metempsychoses and through all the oblivia thereto pertaining" (*MS*298:13,1906)[11]; and Peirce continued thus:

> The soul *without the body* is simply an impossibility and an absurdity. The soul in the body certainly has characters utterly incongruous to those of a body without a soul, however. A *sign* must have an interpretation or signification or, as I call it, an interpretant. This interpretant, this signification is simply a metempsychosis into another body; a translation into another language. This new version of the thought received in turn an interpretation, and *its* interpretant gets itself interpreted, and so on, until an interpretant appears which is no longer of the nature of a sign; . . . (*MS*298:15,24,1906)

---

11 For the sake of clarity it should be noted here that Peirce used metempsychosis here as an object of analogy, and that he was sharply critical of this and similar aspects of the spiritualism of his days. He placed belief in transmigration of the soul among "those superstitions that have inspired or terrified mankind --fountain of perpetual youth, philosophers' stone, fairies, ogres, ghosts, magic, personal devil, jinns sealed up by Solomon, archei, oracles of Apollo, Eleusinian mysteries, metempsychoses, and all other romances about substantial spirits . . . The essence of these rapidly-decadent beliefs is the doctrine that soul . . . is able to feel and act independently of its animal body" (*CP*:6.576-6.577,c.1905). In reference to the relation between soul and body, Peirce began his 1902 essay on "Mind and body" by affirming that "[t]here can be no better touchstone of a psychology" (*CP*:7.368,1902). In the same year, in a letter to Samuel P. Langley, he expressed his criticism of "the different theories now held concerning the connection between soul and body, and the nature of the soul, glancing at unconscious mind", and then added: "I have a new theory of the relation between body and soul which I have not yet published or said anything about. Whether it is correct or not is a question which elaborate researches would be necessary in order to ascertain; but the mere possibility of the thing at once knocks the bottom out of the principal argument for 'psycho-physical parallelism', which is the theory most widely entertained at present" (*SW*:288,1902). For an enlightening discussion of the body-soul connection as Peirce saw it, see Colapietro 1989:58 & *passim*.

The sign perfects itself "pragmatically", by translating itself into subsequent signs: "for intellectual concepts", Peirce wrote, "[this] is a conditional determination of the soul as to how it would conduct itself under conceivable circumstances" (*MS*298:24,1906). To continue in spiritualistic parlance, one might say that the sign's soul, determined by the force of karma, uses semiosis as a way to attain self-perfection. The translational process is therefore more than an ongoing change of clothes, through which the body, with varying success, seeks to renew and embellish its outward appearance[12]. It can be compared to a mystical quest of the sign's immortal inner essence, a cycle of incarnations leading eventually to a final apotheosis, the enlightenment of nirvana[13]

As a variation on the metempsychotic theme, the supreme adventure called semiosis, or sign translation, brings now success now failure, gain and loss, erosion and growth. It comes to an end only when the sign's soul has broken through all its limitations and has reached, through its successive embodiments, its ultimate purpose. This makes the truly final interpretant --the definitive translation of the sign on the threshold of self-fulfillment and release-- "the ripe fruit of thought", as Peirce called it (*MS*298:15,24,1906). Translation in all its guises is aimed at revealing this "ultimate signification of the sign" (*MS*298:15,24,1906); in short, the truth of complete knowledge.

Translation as motion

In his middle period, following the appearance of his pivotal "On a new list of categories" (1867), Peirce appeared to have become less committed to his work on sign-theoretical issues. In fact, the 1870s, 1880s, and part of the 1890s were his most productive years as a professional mathematician and scientist (chemist, astronomer, geodesist, metrologist, *inter alia*). As his work in logic and semiotics was marginal to these multiple pursuits, it is hardly surprising that Peirce did not make spectacular progress in his sign-theoretical thought in the narrow sense.

---

12 In his discussion of translational metaphors, Koller (1972:50-52) also includes "Übersetzung als Kleiderwechsel" and in this connection mentions Pascoli's 1946 metempsychotic metaphor, which Koller traces back to von Wilamowitz-Moellendorf's 1891 article on "Was ist Übersetzen". I might add here that Nabokov refers in his 1941 article on "The art of translation" to the "[t]hree grades of evil [which] can be distinguished in the queer world of *verbal transmigration*" (Nabokov 1941:160,emphasis added).

13 See the interesting parallel (and, seen from Peirce's categorial progression, the interesting contrast) with the following observation put forth by Barthes: "[T]hat fabric of deliberations and decisions that perhaps makes up our lives - resembles the Buddhist karma, the interlocking causes that constantly oblige us to act, to respond. The opposite of karma is nirvana. And so, when one is suffering a great deal from karma, one may postulate or fantasize a kind of nirvana. Idleness then takes on a dimension of annihilation . . . There is a Taoist precept on idleness, I think, on 'doing nothing' in the sense of 'moving nothing', determining nothing" (Barthes 1985:342).

Interestingly, though, Peirce's concern with what may be called translational phenomena remained unchanged in this long middle period, albeit translation was now taken in an entirely different sense, namely in the part of mathematical geometry addressing so-called "rigid bodies". Peirce defined a rigid body in two ways: (1) in terms of its visual (or better, considering the abstract nature of this field of research, its visualizable) properties: "every particle of such a body always occupies a single indivisible place", "every flat film of such a body . . . always continues (there being no stress upon the body) to occupy a plane. It neither breaks nor bends . . . [I]n any straight fibre of such a body . . . the order and continuity of the particles remain always the same" (*CP*:7.307,n.d.); and (2) in terms of the positional properties of its particles when rotated or otherwise moved in relation to one or more chosen axes or dimensions in isotropic space (*CP*:7.308,n.d.)[14]. Peirce showed how the fixation of one particle reduced in several ways the freedom of motion of all other particles of the same body.

A translation is in geometry to be understood as the movement of abstract bodies, which may change of position without being actually moved and without change of physical orientation in space[15]. This "mysterious" movement takes place under the influence of invisible natural forces, such as magnetic, optical, and electrical forces, and gravity, and it occurs mostly as a result of the movement of a second body. What we are most inclined to call motions in practical life are translations and rotations of detached objects, such as Newton's falling apple, the flying arrow, and the launched spacecraft. According to Peirce's non-empirical viewpoint, however, translation is "equivalent to an infinitely small rotation about an infinitely distant axis; so that all particles are moved along rays through equal distances and toward one 'vanishing point' in the firmament" (*NEM*2:441-442,1894)[16], in such a way that "every accessible particle moves along a ray, and in a perspective picture all those rays have one vanishing point" (*NEM*2:443,1894)[17].

As opposed to rest or immobility, translative or rotative motion of bodies,

---

14 Peirce also used "ray" instead of "axis".

15 The "classical" doctrine inherited by Peirce separated mechanical interactions of tangible objects by contact or impact, from those physical phenomena which were less tangible, and affected objects distant from one another.

16 Note also the following, alternative definition: "Translation is an infinitely slow rotation about an axis infinitely distant" (*NEM*2:442,1894). These definitions would imply that for Peirce all translation would be reducible to rotation.

17 The notion of vanishing point comes from artificial, pictorial perspective, the theory of the picture plane; the parallel edges of an object project to straight lines which go into the distance, and out of sight, by minification of the solid angle to a vanishing point at the horizon. Abstract geometry is, of course, concerned with idealized objects moving along and around the three axes of coordinate space.

their relative physical displacement, would seem to be "regulated by the old formula of causation" (*CP*:7.483,c.1898). A patient body (the phenomenon under observation) is acted upon by a force coming from some agent, the result of which is a motion along invisible but straight lines leading directly from the one to the other and converging to the vanishing point. There seems at first blush to be no doubt that translation in this sense is anything but a straightforward event, which in Peirce's categorial scheme should be explained "naturally", in mechanical terms, as a phenomenon governed first and foremost by Secondness, the category of action and reaction, of cause and effect, of *vis viva*, Leibniz's term for active and living force. Force, the moving agent, confronts hereness with thereness, thisness with thatness, and sameness with otherness. Like Secondness, it is about the creation of active but non-creative relations. The change brought about by translative motion is thus, in the classical conception, determined by this "principle of duality" (*NEM*2:435,1894) and adheres strictly to the grammar of deterministic mechanics.

Such a "rude idea of a cause" inherent in the "idea of Force in general" (*W*3:268,1878) is however, as Peirce argued, only the first and mechanical part of the explanation:

> Ancient mechanics recognized forces as causes which produced motions as their immediate effects, looking no further than the essentially dual relation of cause and effect. That was why it could make no progress with dynamics. The work of Galileo and his successors lay in showing that forces are accelerations by which [a] state of velocity is gradually brought about. The words "cause" and "effect" still linger, but the old conceptions have been dropped from mechanical philosophy; for the fact now known is that in certain relative positions bodies undergo certain accelerations. Now an acceleration, instead of being like a velocity a relation between two successive positions, is a relation between three; so that the new doctrine has consisted in the suitable introduction of the conception of threeness. (*CP*:1.359,1890-1891)

Peirce's assertions here seem to be in tune with the turn-of-the-century transformations in theoretical physics from "classical" physics into what may be called, with a key term, "relativity" and "quantum theory". He argued that "all force cannot be positional attractions and repulsions. There is therefore some law additional to the last" (*CP*:1.508,c.1896), an anti-dualistic (that is, anti-Cartesian and anti-Newtonian) argument, which is illustrated by the Peirce-based triad "Rest, Velocity, Acceleration" (Esposito 1980:174)[18]

---

18 A similar argument may be found in the article on "Uniformity" which Peirce composed for *Baldwin's Dictionary* and in which he (in a pioneering spirit, considering the dyadically static mainstream physics of his time) pitted the "usual and in some sense standard opinion" (*CP*:6.101,1902) on uniformity vs. variety, against his own, evolutionary view. See the following,

Space-time laws are the principles of geometry which must be considered as part of physics. Yet, from Peirce's phenomenological point of view, inherent motion, and hence translation in the technical sense, is not simply governed by an unattainable model like a Newtonian universe or the equation for energy: it is more than a causal process, the direct effect of physical force, such as that of gravitational or electrostatic attraction. It must be regulated by a blended scenario of a higher order and greater complexity than a dyadic causal mechanism. Indeed, the mechanistic thinking-model had yielded, in the early 1880s (Rosensohn 1974:68), to a vitalistic one, and Newtonian mechanics "turn[ed] into statistical mechanics with its concern for aggregations and transatomic properties" (Esposito 1980:169).

In the new, evolutionary view, motion had acquired triadic overtones which lifted it, as it were, from mere piece of clockwork to the more sophisticated status of a complex machinery with a great number of moving parts, each of which is one detached object interacting with all the others within the whole. The result is a hierarchical configuration of concurring events, of (in Peirce's terminology) habits requiring purposeful (teleological) rational judgment for its interpretation. This makes motion like a living organism in continuous motion --continuously rearranging its parts and thus continuously reshaping itself. What is followed on this view is rather the Stoic model of seeing natural phenomena as alternate states of a continuous *pneuma* or "breath", and which provide a representation not just of single atoms and their interactions, but too of a whole system of energy. Thirdness, in short; although its built-in component of Secondness prevents it from being any more "genuine" than a "degenerate" version of rationality[19].

---

somewhat extended quotation: "The majority of physicists, at least of the older generation, hold, with regard to the physical universe, that its elements are masses, their positions, and the variations of these positions with time. It is believed that every motion exactly obeys certain laws of attraction and repulsion; and there is no other kind of law, except that each atom or corpuscle is a centre of energy arranged in equipotential surfaces about it, which follow a regular law; and that this is permanency. But the equations of motion are differential equations of the second order, involving, therefore, two arbitrary constants for each moving atom or corpuscle, and there is no uniformity connected with these constants. At least, no such uniformity is, with the least probability, discoverable. . . . The hypothesis suggested by the present writer is that all laws are the results of evolution; that underlying all our laws is the only tendency which can grow by its own virtue, the tendency of all things to take habits. Now since this same tendency is the one sole fundamental law of mind, it follows that the physical evolution works towards ends in the same way that mental action works towards ends, . . ." (*CP*:6.101,1902).

19 If I interpret this rightly, this would be another case of the phenomenon of what could be called "upward mobility" touched upon in n. 7 (see also Chapter 5, n.12). On Peirce's speculative cosmology with reference to his theories of space and time, see Murphey 1961:388ff. I would like to add here that Peirce spoke of "quasi-translation", in addition to "translation": "Like rotation it

Motion as discussed here is a translational process, the only one in which a physical body or material object both changes and stays the same: it changes its position relative to other objects, while at the same time preserving its own identity and the identity of its environment[20]. Identity being substantially a matter of Firstness, and Firstness being a necessary substratum of Secondness and Thirdness, motion thus involves, when construed in Peircean terms, all three sign-configurations: monadic, dyadic, triadic. Depending on the relative weight of each of the three elements, it is in certain cases possible to upgrade motion to genuine semiosis. Provided that the element of purposiveness, or Thirdness, dominates the other two, translational motion may then be considered as a semiosic process of changing position in time. By this process, which runs from the past through the present towards the future, energetic and dynamic habits are being developed which affect the physical body not only in its ever-shifting external *personae* (that is, from the perspective of bodily transfer), but which also, in a deeper and futuristic sense, guide the movements of its "soul", through the mechanism of "rebirth" and in accordance with the norms and ideals of Peirce's evolutionary pragmaticism.

Concluding remarks

In this chapter I have tried to cover, in a tentative way, what I conceive to be the subject of translation, sign-theoretical and otherwise, as it appears in subsequent periods of Peirce's work. In his earlier, semiotic thought, in which representation (the sign-object relation) took center stage, Peirce held that signs are meaningless unless translated (back-translated) into other, already familiar sign-systems. This is a matter of Firstness. In his later years particularly, translation was fully identified by Peirce with interpretation, or Thirdness. In being transmitted from past to future, embodied in an endless sequence of interpretants (forward-translated), signs grow, thereby realizing their meaning-potentiality. Between these two periods, in the 1890s, Peirce, the practising scientist and laboratory man,

---

is either elliptic, hyperbolic, or parabolic" (*NEM*2:435,1894;cf.*CP*:6.582,c.1905). This tripartition is reminiscent of Peirce's concept of degeneracy (and its opposite, generacy); and the analogy -- which fell outside the scope of my own essay on degenerate signs (Gorlée 1990)-- would certainly deserve further study.

20 Interestingly, Nagel (citing Koehler's *Die physische Gestalten*) uses a somewhat similar case to illustrate the argument on summative vs. organic wholes or systems: namely "a group of three stones, one each in Africa, Australia, and the United States. The system is held to be a summative grouping of its parts, because displacement of one stone has no effect on the others or on their mutual relations. However, if current theories of physics are accepted, such a displacement is not without *some* effects on the other stones, even if the effects are so minute that they cannot be detected with present experimental techniques and can therefore be practically ignored" (Nagel 1963:149).

was concerned with translation mainly in a different, mathematical sense, as relevant to geometry. In this framework translation refers to motion of rigid bodies --an affair of degenerate Thirdness or, in other words, Secondness including Firstness and approaching, on Peirce's pioneering view, Thirdness.

Despite appearances to the contrary, there is no break in Peirce's thought. Topically, Peirce's conception of translation moved from Firstness to Thirdness, and subsequently from Secondness to Thirdness. Chronologically, Peirce addressed the phenomenon of translation in three configurations which correspond, coincidentally or perhaps not, to the three universal categories and reflect Peirce's "regular progression of one, two, three" (*CP*:2.299,c.1895), --a sequence, it would seem, which runs from the body to the soul.

07. IDENTITY VS. DIFFERENCE : BENJAMIN AND PEIRCE

"What the world was to Adam on the day he opened his eyes to it, before he had drawn any distinctions, or had become conscious of his own existence . . . "
(*CP*:1.357,1890-1891)

Introductory remarks

Much present-day theoretical speculation on translation is, unfortunately, dreary and rather unproductive stuff. This is at least partly due to the widespread assumption that translation consists in extracting from the words of the original their message or sense which is then rendered by the translator into the target language through a paraphrasing (or interpretive) operation. This common-sense proposition that translation is transfer of meaning, is evidently a reductionism of the real scope of the translation problem. Yet it has resulted into a steady stream of publications in which the equivalence issue has taken center stage --meaning by this the stipulation, recurrent in almost any text in translation theory, that there be between source text and target text, identity across codes.

The resulting perennial discussions regarding the fidelity or infidelity of a translation (as it is often called with a moralizing flavor) have been conducted within a plurality of methodological and conceptual frameworks. This is unsurprising, because translation is an "interdiscipline" (or rather "transdiscipline") combining an approach from (general and applied) linguistics with an approach from (general and comparative) literary studies, in addition to contributions from such disciplines as information theory, logic, and mathematics on the "scientific" side, and social anthropology, sociology, and theology, on the more humanistic side. What is perhaps somewhat surprising is that this language-based transdisciplinarity has not been able to put forth one unified theory, or even to provide consistent answers to the fundamental questions translation-theoretists have time and again asked themselves. In his monumental *After Babel*, George Steiner writes that despite the rich tradition and high caliber of translation critics,

> ... the number of original, significant ideas in the subject remains very meagre. ... Over some two thousand years of argument and precept, the beliefs and disagreements voiced about the nature of translation have been almost the same. Identical theses, familiar moves and refutations in debate recur, nearly without exception, from Cicero and Quintilian to the present day. (Steiner 1975:238-239)

To remedy this rather alarmist situation, I would suggest that what appears to be needed here is a theoretical approach to the phenomenon of translation which concentrates upon something radically other than reproduction of meaning. One such theory has been put forth by the German-Jewish hermeneutic critic of the Frankfurt School, Walter Benjamin (born in 1892 and who killed himself while in flight from the Nazis in 1940). This theory was developed by Benjamin with profound insight and inspired by the Kaballah and Judaic mysticism, particularly in his essay "The task of the translator", which was written in 1923 but first published in 1955.

Benjamin went sharply against common sense as he wrote here in a rhetorical vein:

> For what does a literary work "say"? What does it communicate? It "tells" very little to those who understand it. Its essential quality is not statement or the impairing of information. Yet any translation which intends to perform a transmitting function cannot transmit anything but information --hence, something inessential. (Benjamin 1968:69)
> What can fidelity really do for the rendering of meaning? Fidelity in the translation of individual works can almost never fully reproduce the meaning they have in the original. (Benjamin 1968:78)

From these short quotes it should already be clear that in "The task of the translator" the conception of translation finds a completely novel expression, one which not only, as I intend to argue in this essay, sheds a new light on many taken-for-granted translation-theoretical conceptions. At the same time it displays a striking affinity not only with the later representative in our century of what may be called the Kaballistic/romantic tradition of the theory of literary translation, George Steiner, but also (an even more significative parallelism in the context of my argument in this chapter) with some essential themes of the earlier doctrine of signs of Charles S. Peirce[1], much of which is again an expansion of Kant's position in *The Critique of Pure Reason.*

Benjamin's philosophy of language

Benjamin's work has long been confined to the outer periphery of research in linguistics and, more specifically, translation. It reveals a prophetic, spiritual view of language and translation which, in its literal and allegorical implications, is as far remote from the cold spirit which often permeates language-philosophical modernity, as it approaches the evolutionary vitalism of Peirce's general theory of signs as it is only in recent years beginning to become known among some linguists. This reappraisal of older sources of scholarly inspiration is of course as much a reflection on a general dissatisfaction with the overly dehumanized nature of much modern linguistic thought, as it shows that the philosophically-oriented approach to linguistic problems may have been neglected during the last decades, and dismissed as antiquarianism, but apparently without thereby losing its vigor, suggestiveness, and fruitfulness. Linguistics in the post-Chomskyan era seems to penetrate beneath the study of surface structures as exemplified by transformational grammars, and to develop a renewed interest in more comprehensive thinking-models such as provided by the *Sprachphilosophie* of Walter Benjamin, with its roots in religious-metaphysical thought.

The crux of Benjamin's philosophy of language is the meaning of language. As argued by the Benjaminian critic, Andrew Benjamin (1989), it is aimed at defining and delimiting the communicable, and hence translatable, content in language as seen from a temporal dimension: the concern is with the life and afterlife of literary works, their capacity to live on. "Art is never concerned with response . . . Art is concerned with redemption" (Robinson 1991:242) would synthetize rightly how verbal art-forms survive according to Benjamin's romantic theory. For Benjamin, translation has its starting point in the plurality of languages, but which serves at the same time to exhibit the ultimate affinity among them. This is for Benjamin where its goal and essence lies, and not in the commonsensical transfer of informational content.

Benjamin built his particular view of language and translation upon a Biblical-historical paradigm. As told by Fischer-Lichte (1986) and Menninghaus (1980), Benjamin's creation story goes about like this. Originally, in paradisal language as believed to be the result of Adam's naming, things and the words which referred to them, were at one, unmediated by reason, and conceived to

---

1 The Benjamin-Peirce connection has also been explored --poetically/creatively explored-- in the poetic essay, "Más allá del principio de la nostalgia (Sehnsucht)", by Haroldo de Campos (1987a).

correspond directly. This word was the Word, and according to St. John's gospel, the Word was with God, and the Word was God. This Edenic situation came to an abrupt end with the Babelic confusion of tongues, which created a new phenomenon: the so-called arbitrary (i.e., non-motivated) sign, or sign of rebelliousness, confusion, and exile. Naming needed thereafter to be based upon social agreement, which made language a wholly man-governed affair. Meanwhile, God was hidden, out of sight and speaking only from a burning bush. Since verbal signs no longer prompted meaning, an acute need was created for sign exegesis and sign interpretation, that is for different forms of translation. Since then, attempts are continuously made to bridge the distance between the thing and its name, to restore the primal innocence of language and meaning which existed prior to the Fall, when there was but one truth, and man had not yet been tempted to eat the fruit of the Tree of the Knowledge of Good and Evil, which compelled him to produce forever normative judgments. Seen against this background, Benjamin's language and translation view is a crisis model illustrating man's destiny to retrace his steps until regaining a pre-Babelic paradisal unity, the original identity of thing-meaning and word-meaning[2].

Benjamin's view on translation

In Benjamin's view languages are no fixed repertories; they are in a constant state of mobility and flux, and only become temporarily "solidified" in the form of linguistic units as we know them (be they words, sentences, paragraphs, or texts); entities, that is, with "specific linguistic contextual aspects" (Benjamin 1968:76). The mediating force between them, what must set them into motion, is translation. Translation dramatizes "the idea of life and afterlife" of texts, which means that a text is a living organism which, by being translated, undergoes a "maturing process" (Benjamin 1968:73), the goal of which is "a final, conclusive, decisive stage of all linguistic creations" (Benjamin 1968:75). Through the sequence of translations language eventually achieves total transparency, rest, and fulfillment unburdened with meaning. On Benjamin's view, the primary aim of translation is the annulment of the differences between languages through the harmonious evolvement of its linguistic plurality into one greater, unique, and all-embracing language which Benjamin called "pure language":

---

2 On Benjamin's view, as reformulated by Robinson, "The translator remains a tool . . . of the imagination that the romantics imagine to be messianic behavior, the liberator from internal oppression. This entails a belief in the imaginative power of words not to *record* or *transmit*, but to *create*, specifically to re-create, to demolish the deadening institutional barriers to freedom and restore us to primeval paradise" (Robinson 1991:68). The Babelic origin of translation as interpreted by Benjamin and re-interpreted by Derrida, is addressed in van den Broeck 1987.

> In this pure language --which no longer means or expresses anything but is, as expressionless and creative Word, that which is meant in all languages-- all information, all sense, and all intention finally encounter a stratum in which they are destined to be extinguished . . . It is the task of the translator to release in his own language that pure language which is under the spell of another, to liberate the language imprisoned in a work in his recreation of that work. (Benjamin 1968:80)

In this universal language all individual languages are again reconciled and all the hitherto hidden secrets of meaning revealed; because in it sign-vehicle and meaning are no longer dissociated, but at one and thus self-referring. Translation as processuality is fated to go on until this ideal state-of-affairs will be achieved, because a final and "real translation is transparent; it does not cover the original, does not block its light, but allows the pure language . . . to shine upon the original . . ." (Benjamin 1968:79), at which point the "text is identical with truth or dogma" (Benjamin 1968:82). Needless to say that the univocity of this ideal translation makes issues such as the translatability vs. untranslatability and fidelity vs. infidelity, wholly redundant.

The object: Benjamin and Peirce

The Peircean overtones of Benjamin's equally non-empirical approach to translation should, even from these short remarks, be clear. What Benjamin discussed in his messianic vision of translation may be identified with what Peirce called, long before him, semiosis. For Benjamin, as for Peirce, the translator is the means or agency enabling the text (that is, at least for Benjamin, the literary or sacred text, in which communication of meaning is not the essential) to realize itself rather than to be realized. In Peirce's semiosis, too, the sign is the active element, and the interpreter the passive element[3]. The translator must let his or her mind flow freely. Instead of concentrating on the informational content, the translator must make his or her mind available to capture the intention of the text confronting him or her; it is this, the text's "mode of signification" (Benjamin 1968:78), its "intentio" (Benjamin 1968:79), which needs to be transmitted and expressed. The text translates itself and thereby transforms a certain potential which it carries. Benjamin wrote in reference to this verbal magic that "a specific significance inherent in the original manifests itself in its translatability" (Benjamin 1968:71).

According to Peirce's doctrine of synechism (or continuity), ideas and more generally signs, "once in being, [spread] among the peoples"

---

3 See Chapter 9 for a Peirce-based discussion of the role of the translator in the process of translation.

(*CP*:2.302,c.1895); and in this process, which amounts to a process of translation, they tend to

> . . . spread continuously and to affect certain others which stand to them in a peculiar relation of affectibility. In this spreading they lose intensity, and especially the power of affecting others, but gain generality and become welded with other ideas. (*CP*:6.104, 1892)

This implies that, given time, all ideas and signs are bound to converge. The truth of reality is reached through the successive translational semioses, in the course of which the (interpretant-)sign as a vehicle of meaning becomes more and more transparent. This process of "clarification", semiosis, is, however, a never-ending process. Peirce warned that "If the series is broken off, the Sign, in so far, falls short of the perfect significant character" (*CP*:2.92,1902). The dynamical object, which under "normal" circumstances is only accessible through the sign, through the immediate object, and in the course of the successive semiosic events, will be more and more "stripped of irrelevant clothing" (*NEM*:4:309, 1895) and in the end expose itself wholly unmediated. Just as in Benjamin's achievement of "pure language" identifying sign and meaning, this will, however, only happen ideally and hypothetically; because Peirce made it clear that until the time of what Benjamin called "pure language" will have come, "naked thought itself" must always remain to some degree clothed in a "garment of expression" (*NEM*:3.406,1903)[4].

If we follow Benjamin we may adopt his view that translation is motivated by the multiplicity of languages which need to be redeemed from their differences regarding their mode of intention:

> The words *Brot* and *pain* "intend" the same object, but the modes of this intention are not the same. It is owing to these modes that the word *Brot* means something different to a German than the word *pain* to a Frenchman, that for them these words are not interchangeable, that in the end they strive to exclude each other. (Benjamin 1968:74)

This disjunction between the mode of intention and the intended object, --between the way something is expressed in language as it (pre-)exists, and what it is supposed to mean--, has been shrewdly discussed by Paul de Man by identifying it with the dichotomy between *lexis* and *logos*, between *dire* and *vouloir dire* (de Man 1985:40). In the following paragraphs I will propose that it can be

---

4 See also Chapter 6, the section on "Metempsychosis" and particularly n. 11. For a general discussion of the vestimentary metaphor for translation, see Koller 1972:50-52.

assimilated as well to what Peirce called the two objects (in the technical sense of object as referent of the sign), the immediate object and the dynamical object.

In a general way the object is represented and signified by the sign. In fact, the sign exists in the creation of a "standing for" relation, and without representation we have no sign. Thus a drawing cannot be a diagram unless it is a diagram *of* something. While a sign presupposes the existence, real or potential, of an object, the reverse is not true. This also implies that the sign must be other than, and different from, the object. In the sign-object relation the sign is informed and influenced (Peirce would say, determined) by the object. In this semiotic transaction, the sign is the passive element, the object the active element. The object is, however, only knowable through the sign. Each semiosis gives, perhaps, new information about the object, which thereby gradually discloses itself. But if sign and object would be or become identical, the sign would no longer point toward its object; and "an Object that merely represents itself represents nothing" (*MS* 634:21, 1909). The sign's self-referentiality would mean the inevitable end of the process of semiosis; because it would represent Benjamin's ideal construct, "pure language", which does not stand for something else but is identical to it. The medium will then have become the message, thereby ceasing to be what Peirce called a "medium of communication" (*MS*283:14,1905-1906)[5].

Peirce distinguished, however, between two objects in semiosis: on the one hand, the object as it is represented directly in particular sign-use, the immediate object, and on the other the object which is not immediately present, Peirce's dynamical object. The general remarks advanced above apply in particular to the dynamical object. Both objects may in fact be quite different from one another. Whereas the dynamical object is "an independent agent determining the sign" (*MS*292:16,c.1906), the sign determines its immediate object. The immediate object is the object as the sign itself represents it, and it is known by taking the sign at face value. It represents the object, which is a Second, in its Firstness[6]. This implies that the immediate object is a degenerate Second, unable to fully partake of the law-like, which represents Thirdness, which is again the primary constituent of linguistic signs.

In linguistic signs the immediate object is the direct notion of what is being said or written. Whereas the immediate object is located "inside" the sign, and is determined by it, the dynamical object is "the Object outside of the Sign . . . The

5 Note that Peirce's characterization of the sign as a "medium of communication" was conceived and formulated more than 60 years before McLuhan's aphorism made communication theory "fashionable".

6 Peirce affirmed that it can be a quality, an existent, or a law (*PW*:33,1904). Yet some years later he wrote that although each of the two objects "may be said to be capable of either of the three modalities, . . . in the case of the Immediate Object, this is not quite literally true" (*PW*:83,1908).

Sign must indicate it by a hint; and this hint, or its substance, is the Immediate Object" (*PW*:83, 1908). The dynamical object is thus only indirectly expressed by the sign, though experience and "collateral observation, aided by imagination and thought, will usually result in some idea" of it (*MS*318:77,1907). In linguistic signs the dynamical object is the "real" underlying message which is being put across, independently of whether it is identical to or different from the linguistic fact or facts which the words, sentences, etc. express on the grammatical level.

In the final consideration the dynamical object, or the object as it is in itself, abstracted from its occurrence and role in a particular sign-use, corresponds to the sum total of all instances of the sign-bound immediate object. And knowledge of the former (the dynamical object) can only be acquired by "unlimited and final study" (*CP*:8.183,1909) of the latter (the immediate object) and is thus the end result of a semiosic process, in which the dynamical object is a participant only indirectly. This would explain the distance between the meaning of a statement --Benjamin's *das Gemeinte* or intended object-- and the (linguistic) means by which it is expressed --his *Art des Meinens* or mode of intention. Construed in Peircean terms Benjamin's distinction implies that semiosis, or sign translation, leads the serious inquirer from "the idea which the sign is built upon" to "that real thing or circumstance upon which that idea is founded, as on bed-rock" (*MS*318:70,1907); and sustained consideration of the sign-object relationship is bound to take care of the constraints --both sign-internal (immediate object) and sign-external (dynamical object)-- which make sign-interpretation such a hazardous, fallibilistic (in Peirce's terms) business.

Let us return to language and translation. Each language, or better, each linguistic system, impinges specific structures (such as morphological, lexical, and grammatical structures) upon the semiotic signs in which it needs to express what is a non-linguistic entity, called meaning, content, idea, or otherwise. Herein lie the sign-internal constraints. It is clear that any language-based text possesses such a code-governed material form, which is translatable without recourse to the underlying meaning. What is translated here is the sign in so far as it concerns its immediate object, that is Benjamin's intention, and no more. The translatability of the dynamical object is, it would seem, a more problematic affair. This is due to the fact that its mode of informing the (linguistic) sign is non-linguistic; and the sign-external domain of meaning is untouched by Benjamin's translator, who "gives voice to the intentio of the original not as reproduction but as harmony, as a supplement to the language in which it expresses itself" (Benjamin 1968:79). This translator produces a transliteration of the original, a translation which, on the grounds indicated above, is destined to remain a fragmentary version of the original.

Translation as fragmentation

Jakobson was here, as so often, a true pioneer. He was the only linguist to be acutely aware of this "nearly unexplored" question, namely that every verbal message

> . . . may be and must be dealt with as a temporal interval within a verbalized or nonverbalized, continuous or discontinuous temporal context . . . A contiguous question is the dependence of the message on the simultaneous environmental situation. . . . The spatio-temporal framework of the message becomes one of the crucial problems for any objective approach to language. From a realistic standpoint, language cannot be interpreted as a whole, isolated and hermetically sealed, but it must be simultaneously viewed as a whole and as a part. (Jakobson 1963:159)

If this passage already brings home the fact that a verbal message is something broken out of a partly verbal, partly nonverbal whole, Jakobson's subsequent remark places the problem of the interrelation between message and context wholly in the framework of a semiotic linguistics:

> The comparison of incomplete and explicit messages, the fascinating problem of fragmentary propositions, challengingly outlined in Charles Peirce's perusal of "blanks" and in the semiotic studies of Frege and Husserl, strange as it may seem, have found no response among linguists. The artificial treatment of messages without reference to the superposed context once more exemplifies the illicit conversion of a mere part into a seemingly self-sufficient whole. (Jakobson 1963:159)

Following Jakobson and Peirce there is now a growing awareness among linguists that texts, original and translated, are no self-contained unities but fragments, elliptic entities, which may be described and analyzed as such, as parts of a both intratextual and intertextual whole. The "task of the translator" is to provide the missing link (or links) which would restore the linguistic sign as a whole, which (as argued above) is again a part of the whole meaning of the sign. Derrida points out in his essay on Benjamin's theory of translation:

> The "tower of Babel" does not merely figure the irreducible multiplicity of tongues; it exhibits an incompletion, the impossibility of finishing, of totalizing, of saturating, of completing something on the order of edification, architectural construction, system and architectonics. What the multiplicity of idioms actually limits is not only a "true" translation, a transparent and adequate interexpression, it is also a structural order, a coherence of construct. (Derrida 1985:165-166)

And on behalf of Benjamin this writer cautions both the translator and the translation critic as he writes: "If there be between the translated text and the translating text a relation of 'original' to version, it could not be *representative* or *reproductive*. Translation is neither an image nor a copy" (Derrida 1985:180).

In Peirce's terminology, an arbitrary relation between sign and object which is based upon pure convention, or Thirdness, is symbolic. On the other end, if it stresses similarity (as in the image and copy which Derrida mentions), it is iconic. Halfway, as it were, stands the indexical relation, which builds upon contiguity and expresses the idea of the fragment, which makes full sense as soon as it may be matched with its missing counterpart. In Peirce's doctrine of signs, "a fragment [is] torn away from the Object, the two in their Existence being one whole or a part of such whole" (*CP*:2.230,1910). By the same token, in the Benjaminian paradigm, translation is not based upon resemblance, nor is it the "task of the translator" to produce a copy of the original. The translation repeats, but with a difference. At the same time referring back to its previous form, and pointing forward toward "pure language", the translation has a relation of complementarity to both[7]. In his essay on Benjamin's "The task of the translator", de Man speaks of a double fragmentation:

> . . . any work is totally fragmented in relation to this *reine Sprache* . . . and every translation is totally fragmented in relation to the original. The translation is the fragment of a fragment, is breaking the fragment . . . (de Man 1985:44)

Translation is supposed to show that texts and languages, as material as well as referential entities, are broken and fragmentary, but not mutually exclusive. They rest on interlinear relationships, their "family resemblances", in Wittgenstein's words. Source language and target language are not autonomous entities but must be understood as parts of an interlingual (or translingual) web interweaving all languages together into one symbiotic design; and the same may be said about source text and translated text.

Benjamin saw original and translation as hinging upon each other in several ways which may be construed in Peircean terms. Consider Benjamin's analogy with the broken vase:

> Fragments of a vessel which are to be glued together must match one another in the smallest details, although they need not be like one another. In the same way

7 In reference to the unstable status of the fragment, Quéré speaks of its "double deprivation" creating "states of tension or restlessness, such as suspense, expectation, and a whole strained environment; a pathos which, if oriented towards the 'no more' is called regret or nostalgia, or even becomes tinged with despair; whereas on the axis of the 'not yet' it may be charged with resignation or apprehension, while also containing the hope of a promise fulfilled, thereby prefiguring achievement" (Quéré 1988:49;my trans.). This also approaches the idea underlying contract, which will be discussed in Chapter 10.

> a translation, instead of resembling the meaning of the original, must lovingly and in detail incorporate the original mode of signification, thus making both the original and the translation recognizable as fragments of a greater language, just as fragments of a vessel. (Benjamin 1968:78)

That a text-sign, original as well as translated, must first and foremost be treated as a sign of synthesis, or Third, is implied in the extreme importance of language in literary works --the preeminence of the poetic function over the referential, to use Jakobson's (1960) terminology. At the same time, however, it may be argued that translating --seen as the act of (re)assembling separate meaning-units or, put otherwise, fitting together the pieces of a linguistic jigsaw puzzle[8]-- means that "languages are not strangers to one another" (Benjamin 1968:72), as would have been the case had they been pure, unmotivated Thirds. Their relations must necessarily imply Firsts and Seconds, both in the gluing and in the translating business.

Interrelations between languages

Benjamin argues that "it stands to reason that kinship does not necessarily involve likeness" (Benjamin 1968:74) and "the kinship of languages is brought out by a translation far more profoundly and clearly than in the superficial and indefinable similarity of two works of literature" (Benjamin 1968:72). This implies that some form of iconicity is a necessary component of the mutual relations between different languages, but that their kinship need not consist in a straightforward morphological, lexical, phonological, etc. isomorphism. It may rather lie in the kind of qualitative, relational, or processual similarities which Peirce called "hypoicons", or First, Second, and Third Firstnesses - images, diagrams, and metaphors (*CP*:2.277,c.1902) - , emerging by semiosic referral. On Benjamin's view, all signs somehow fit together; and by semiosic referral any sign or idea can, according to Peirce, be considered to refer to, and thereby to be somehow equivalent to, any other sign or idea[9].

The kind of similarity implied in Benjamin's conception of the interrelations between languages, is thus not synonymous with iconicity. Rather, it is germane to the concept of equivalence as Peirce saw it[10], --an equivalence

8 More on this analogy in Chapter 4 and Gorlée 1986.

9 Like all Peircean signs, the icon is essentially shifting and manifold. Though primarily a sign of Firstness, it occurs in three ranges: "For example, it is obvious that a theoretical model will have more Thirdness about it than a simple drawing or diagram, or that a territorial map will be more assertoric than a hypothetical one, or than an explanatory model will seek to articulate rules of operation. . . . In short, the more the iconic model participates in Thirdness, the more the model will seek to articulate the nature of law - be it natural, logical, or whatever" (Spinks 1991:446).

10 A discussion of Peirce's equivalence may also be found in Chapter 9.

which presupposes Firstness but is a product of semiosis and therefore cannot live by Firstness alone. In Peirce's semiotics, two signs are logically equivalent whenever their dynamical objects are interpreted to be identical, although their immediate objects would be different. Equivalence does not lie in the way a sign represents its object, to wit, its likeness to the object. It obtains whenever a sign is interpreted, and thereby produces an interpretant (or rather a series of interpretants). Two signs which are thus equivalent can be derived logically (that is, for Peirce, semiosically) from one another.

Peirce's concept of equivalence is thus teleological and governed by Thirdness; yet he left no doubt that in his inclusive, semiosis-based view Thirdness involves Secondness and Firstness, while Secondness involves Firstness. Besides Firstness there is therefore also Secondness involved in the relations from one linguistic sign to another, thereby moving linguistic interrelations, and hence translation, away from mimesis amd atemporality toward otherness and a sequential time-order[11]. In a similar spirit, Benjamin remarked that a translation must reproduce in the target language "the echo of the original" (Benjamin 1968:76). Interestingly, for Peirce an echo is a degenerate Second; because, as he wrote, "my own voice coming back to answer itself" (*CP*:1.366,1890-1891) stresses difference in addition to identity. But note the following passage, in which Benjamin refers to the translation in terms of what for Peirce would be a relation of genuine, non-degenerate Secondness[12]:

---

11 This point is also stressed in Andrew Benjamin (1989:90ff.). Since I have chosen here to look at the translation problem from a Peircean viewpoint, I must, however, partly disagree with the conclusions in the following remarks: "It is often thought, and with good reason, that Benjamin is an advocate of mimesis. In his 1933 paper 'On the Mimetic Faculty', he argues that for reasons already advanced within the paper, 'language may be seen as the highest level of mimetic behaviour' (p. 33). For Benjamin mimesis refers to what he calls 'non-sensuous similarity' between language and what is signified. It is not however the case that the relationship posited between language and the signified is the same as the relationship between the translation and the original. The difference between the 'mode of intention' and the 'intended object' can be understood in mimetic terms, the relationship between the translation and the original cannot" (Andrew Benjamin 1989:186,n.15). I hope to have sufficiently argued my proposition that the mode of intention and the intended object may be assimilated to, respectively, the immediate (i.e., sign-internal) and the dynamical (i.e., sign-external) object. More often than not they will be of different nature, which makes any characterization of their relation in mimetic terms a problematic affair. However, to the extent that the relation between translation and original has an implied element of Firstness, besides Secondness and Thirdness, it may insofar be called mimetic.

12 Strictly speaking, of course, the only sign to be "genuine" in all respects is the Third, all of whose three terms are equally Thirds: this means that all Seconds (and, *a fortiori*, all Firsts) are degenerate. On Peirce's concept of degeneracy, see, for instance, text and references of Gorlée 1990 and, in a less theoretical vein, Gorlée 1987.

> We may call this connection a natural one, or, more specifically, a vital connection. . . . A translation issues from the original --not so much from its life as from its afterlife. For a translation comes later than the original. (Benjamin 1968:71)

The translation is here explicitly presented by Benjamin as a direct result of the original: as an index, that is, pointing back in time to its source, thereby safeguarding the survival and enrichment of the latter's spiritual essence.

Concluding remarks

To wrap up my argument, I have tried to show that Benjamin's metaphysical view of "the task of the translator" approaches what Peirce seems to have meant by semiosic engenderment. Semiosis and the three categories in which it is rooted, have opened for several novel ways of dealing with translation, --both translation as an activity and as the resulting text generated by this activity. The three-term interaction of the sign involves the sign in itself, in its relation to the object, and the relation of both to the interpretant. In the same way, a meaningful Third must involve, or be accompanied by, a First and a Second.

One of the extrapolations of this piece of Peirce's doctrine of signs is that it liberates the linguistic sign, both original and translated, from the determination of pure Thirdness, and places it in the Heraclitean stream of semiosis. Linguistic signs are primarily arbitrary; but in order to be meaningful in human communication they must also be contextually connected to one another as well as to the reality they are intended to reflect. The ensuing coexistence, in linguistic signs, of identity, difference, and equivalence makes their power and purpose, as concretized in their interpretative development (their translational growth, for Benjamin as well as for Peirce), the object of such perennial debate and controversy. As a final note I may perhaps venture the suggestion that had Benjamin known Peirce's works, he would probably have welcomed a theory of translation based upon semiosis unlimited.

08. TRANSLATION AFTER JAKOBSON AFTER PEIRCE

"Can we translate messages in Van Gogh's pictures, violin concertos, or Navajo rug designs?"
(Lawendowski 1978:280)

Introductory remarks

Roman Jakobson (1896-1982) was the first among linguists to assimilate Peirce's sign-theoretical thought and to apply some of its now well-known concepts (icon, index, symbol) to linguistics --in the broad sense including poetics in which Jakobson defined this field of study.[1] Since Jakobson's reappraisal of Peirce happened in the early 1950s, at a time when Peirce was still virtually unknown in the field of Jakobsonian "linguistics and poetics", Jakobson's insight dramatically broadened the horizons of the humanities, --even though it must be noted that Jakobson used Peirce's *general* theory of signs in special reference to one subdiscipline of linguistics, namely verbal arts, particularly those of prose and poetry. How momentous Jakobson's insight really was, and still is, is, however, something which will not be appreciated in its full scope until linguistics and poetics have been studied in a thoroughgoing Peircean framework. Despite many valuable attempts to this effect, this ambitious project has as yet not been carried out. Unfortunately, Shapiro's 1980 judgment that "linguistics and poetics have yet to undergo what must eventually become a full-blown Peircean revolution in the humanities and social sciences" (Shapiro 1980:97) is still essentially true.

1 In his famous "Closing statement: Linguistics and poetics" Jakobson stated that "Poetics deals with problems of verbal structure, just as the analysis of painting is concerned with pictorial structure. Since linguistics is the global science of verbal structure, poetics may be regarded as an integral part of linguistics" (1960:350).

The primary aim of this paper is to discuss translation as singled out by Jakobson among Peirce's sign-theoretical concepts, and which Jakobson utilized again in a more restricted sense than originally intended by Peirce. For Jakobson, and in contradistinction to Peirce, translation is a metalinguistic process always involving language. I will propose and argue that the three kinds of translation put forth by Jakobson (1959:233;1971b:261) can be construed and (re)refined in terms of Peirce's three ontological categories, or modes of being. While this aspect of Jakobson's thought will here be traced back to Peirce, it is at the same time wholly an extrapolation from Peirce's thought. I hope to show that instead of forcing Peirce into a structuralist straightjacket (as has been done by Jakobson) it is more fruitful to broaden the structuralist concept of "sense" into what Peirce, the evolutionary pragmaticist, understood by "meaning".

Jakobson and/vs. Peirce

The binary paradigm is the epistemological postulate of semiology (or, as it is more commonly known, structuralism). It was no invention of the so-called Paris School of semiotics; before Greimas (and his colleagues Lévi-Strauss, Kristeva, Todorov, among others) it had been a leading feature of classical European structuralism, building on Saussure, Hjelmslev, Jakobson, and others:

> Saussure's basic definition of differential units as "negative, relative and oppositive" has been seminal. The idea of opposition as the primary logical operation universally arising in humans from the first glimmerings of consciousness in infants and from youngsters' initial steps in the buildup of language was viewed as the natural key to the inquiry in to verbal structure from its highest to its lowest levels. The inalienable property of opposition which separates it from all other, contingent differences is, when we are dealing with one opposite, the obligatory copresence of the other in our minds, or in other words, the impossibility of evoking *long* without a simultaneous, latent idea of *short*, or *expensive* without *cheap*, 'voiced' without 'voiceless', and vice versa. (Jakobson and Waugh 1979:20).

Saussure's binary concepts (signifier/signified, *langue/parole*, paradigm/syntagm, matter/form, sound/meaning, synchrony/diachrony) are echoed in Hjelmslev's dichotomies (expression/content, form,/substance) and in Jakobson's binarism (code/message, selection/combination, metaphor/metonymy, etc.). Traditional structuralism has thus generated "this pervasive habit of the linguist of bifurcating his cosmos [which] continues to permeate semiotic method" (Rauch 1986:917).[2]

---

2 Outside French semiotic theory it is found, for example, in Sebeok's mutually opposite categories (inner/outer, vocal/nonvocal, verbal/nonverbal, witting/unwitting, etc.) and in Lotman's distinction between primary and secondary modeling systems, internal and external communication, closed and open cultures, etc. (see, for example, Sebeok 1985a and Lotman's essays in Lucid

That it was not Jakobson's intention to universalize and perpetuate the Saussurean binary model, is, however, demonstrated in his early interest in the thought of Peirce, the patriarch of American semiotics. As an alternative to Saussurean dichotomies, Peirce's radically triadic thought was "discovered" by Jakobson as a new thinking model to be introduced, he hoped, into all language-oriented fields of research.

Towards the end of his intellectual career, Peirce described himself as "a pioneer, or rather a backwoodsman, in the work of clearing and opening up what I call *semeiotic*, that is, the doctrine of the essential nature and fundamental varieties of possible semiosis" (*CP*:5.488,1907). In Jakobson's view, Peirce is not only a "pathfinder in the science of language"; in addition must he, as Jakobson claimed already in 1952, be regarded as "a genuine and bold forerunner of structural linguistics" (quoted in Jakobson 1977:1027). Jakobson's attempts to transmogrify Peirce's semiotic into a kind of structuralism *avant la lettre* are, as will be argued here, a paradoxical endeavor doomed to remain rather unconvincing[3].

Jakobson began drawing on Peirce's work in the middle of his intellectual career, at a time when his semiotic insights were already largely formed and formulated. As argued by Bruss (1978), Jakobson presented a version of Peirce which did not reflect the manifold, shifting, and yet consistent nature of Peirce's thought; rather, Jakobson availed himself of Peirce to strengthen the case of structuralism. This procedure was possibly in part a reflection on the heterogeneous and fragmentary nature of the almost collage-like text of the *Collected Papers of Charles S. Peirce*. That Jakobson read Peirce rather selectively, and gave his own interpretation of it rather than a balanced view, would appear, then, for instance, from his attempts to transpose the binary oppositions to Peirce.

As stated by Jakobson in 1974, Peirce's "triad is based on two binary oppositions: contiguous/similar and factual/imputed" (Jakobson 1987:451). In fact, the triadic paradigm, as proposed and elaborated by Peirce, is intrinsically

---

1988).

3 In his recent book, *Semiotics in the United States*, Sebeok (who was Jakobson's --as well as Charles Morris's-- semiotic student and friend) writes: "One of the remaining puzzles centers on the reconciliation of Jakobson's constant binarism --a cornerstone of all his pursuits, in and far beyond linguistics-- with Peirce's patent trinarism. . . Jakobson himself never came publicly to terms with this apparent contradiction, which since his death has been probed by several scholars . . . " (Sebeok 1991:79,cf.Sebeok 1991:128). See further Andrews (1990a) and, for a different view, Liszka (1981), who argues convincingly, though rather metaphysically, that a structuralist reconstruction of Peirce is possible, at least to some extent.

incompatible with structuralism's concentration upon binarism --which, I may add, is also the distinctive feature of the classical definition, *aliquid stat pro aliquo*. Even if the Saussurean concept of signifier be assimilated *grosso modo* to Peirce's concept of sign (or rather representamen), and even if Saussure's signified be made (by a logically audacious leap) to approach Peirce's interpretant, the third element, the object, is still missing. The Peircean object, which is no part of Saussure's twosided, yet nonrelational, notion of the sign, is in Peirce's philosophy of signs a crucial element in genuine (that is, triadic) sign action. Peirce himself addressed this radical difference, thus:

> It is important to understand what I mean by *semiosis*. All dynamical action, or action of brute force, physical or psychical, either takes place between two subjects... or at any rate is a resultant of such actions between pairs. But by "semiosis" I mean, on the contrary, an action, or influence, which is, or involves, a coöperation of *three* subjects, such as a sign, its object, and its interpretant, this tri-relative influence not being in any way resolvable into action between pairs. (*CP*:5.484,1907)

Jakobson's attempts were precisely directed, it would appear, at resolving Peirce's triadic structure of the sign relation, thereby reducing the scope of Peirce's semiosis to two-sided processes only. For the sake of analysis and discussion it is, of course, possible to break up triadic relations into dyadic ones --such as the relations between sign-object, sign-interpretant, and object-interpretant; but to blur the boundaries between the two notions of the sign, ignoring the details of their radically different logical properties, is to make a purely artificial construct. Triadic relations are for Peirce irreducible to dyadic ones.

To be sure, Peirce's triads include and build upon dyads and monads, so that Thirds build upon Seconds and Firsts. Peirce's thinking model is no rejection of the binary principle; it places it within a broader conceptual framework. This is argued by Peirce, thus:

> Now triads have at all times recommended themselves to all minds. There are psychological attractions for other number than three. Two is the number of hard common sense, of the stern moralist, of the practical man. "Yes or no? Answer me categorically," says such a man. Heaven and hell, right and wrong, truth and fiction, gain and loss, agent and patient, living or dead, --on such distinctions our practical life turns. The philosophy of two comes within my scheme. (*MS*907:2,n.d.)

Yet Peirce stated in his seminal essay, "A guess at the riddle":

> First and second, agent and patient, yes and no, are categories which enable us roughly to describe the facts of experience, and they satisfy the mind for a very long time. But at last they are found inadequate, and the third is the conception which is then called for.

> The third is that which bridges over the chasm between the absolute first and last, and brings them into relationship. (*CP*:1.359,1890-1891)

Peirce's theory of signs, including his concept of semiosis, is wholly an affair of triadicity and can therefore not be adequately explained in a structuralist framework.

Language and meaning

The two disciplines, semiology and linguistics, are in modern French structuralism two branches from one linguistic tree; and they are different only in a hierarchical manner of speaking[4]. Essential is that Saussure, the founder of modern linguistics, considered semiology to be the project of a future science of signs, under which linguistics was to be subsumed; while Barthes among later semiologists considered instead semiology to be subordinate to, and limited by, linguistics. Saussure had in fact acknowledged nonverbal sign-systems, but he underscored the privileged status of language as "a system of signs that express ideas, and is therefore comparable to a system of writing, the alphabet of deaf-mutes, symbolic rites, polite formulas, military signals, etc." (1966:16). To this Saussure immediately added: "But it [language] is the most important of these systems" (1966:16). Saussure's characterization of the hierarchical relation between language and semiology is further pursued and elaborated by Jakobson:

> The cardinal functions of language --referential, emotive, conative, phatic, poetic, metalingual-- and their different hierarchy in the diverse types of messages have been outlined and repeatedly discussed. This pragmatic approach to language must lead *mutatis mutandis* to an analogous study of the other sign systems. (Jakobson 1971b:703)[5]

The linguistic model and its conceptual tools are not only applied to linguistic objects of study but also, indirectly and by analogy, to objects belonging to other sign systems, or semiotic codes. This would then permit any object of research, language-based or not, to be considered as a text and to be analyzed "linguistically". Since culture is for semiologists identical to language, any cultural phenomenon can be studied semiologically, as a meaningful sign-structure. A typical example of this is Barthes's (1967) analysis of fashion. At the same time this concern with the interaction between verbal and nonverbal signs and sign systems explains and stimulates the interest in code-switching, or

---

4 See also Chapter 3.

5 As it stands, this statement is almost a truism and serves "as a lonely beacon and at that a weak one, since the *mutatis mutandis* remains unspecified" (Rauch 1986:916).

translation in the different modalities proposed by Jakobson, and which holds a central place in my argument in this essay.

By following Peirce, Jakobson rescued and, indeed, emphasized the meaning aspect of the (linguistic) sign, which has been systematically deemphasized, and even ignored, in the Saussurean tradition in which Jakobson must otherwise be placed[6]. In reference to Jakobson's vision on semantics (the standing-for aspect of the sign), Eco distinguishes a three-step chronological scenario which led Jakobson towards adopting an ostensibly Peirce-inspired view on the construction of meaning as a process of translation. In 1934, Jakobson stated that "there is a substantial difference between sense or meaning or signified and mere denotata" (quoted in Eco 1986a:407), thereby recognizing that signs are vehicles of sign-external meaning and refer back to this meaning-content. Subsequently, in 1952, Jakobson pointed towards Peirce's notion of interpretant, without which "the nature of the signified cannot be explained" (Eco 1986a:407). And finally, in the famous essay "On linguistic aspects of translation",

> . . . against the naive confusion between "interpretant" and "interpreter" Jakobson demonstrates that to interpret a semiotic item means to "translate" it into another item (maybe an entire discourse) and that this translation is always creatively enriching the first item (1959), this continuous creativity being the main result of Peirce's "unlimited semiosis." (Eco 1986a:407;1987:121)

Translation is, for Jakobson as well as for Peirce, the essence of semiosis, or triadic sign-action. In what follows, Jakobson's indebtedness to Peirce and his own original contributions to the discussion of translation will be dealt with in more detail; because inasmuch as Jakobson recovered the sign's meaning aspect and Peirce's notion of interpretant, he redefined the sign relation and its three terms in a way which is incommensurate with Peirce.

Translation

In Jakobson's formulation,

> One of the most felicitous, brilliant ideas which general linguistics and semiotics gained from the American thinker is his definition of meaning as "the translation of a sign into another system of signs" (4.127). How many fruitless discussions about mentalism and anti-mentalism would be avoided if one approached the notion of meaning in terms of

---

6 Eco has pointed out that "Jakobson has *always* refused to exclude the study of meaning from linguistics, according to his Husserlian inspiration and to the explicit assumption of the Prague Circle principles which he elaborated jointly with his Czech and Russian friends" (Eco 1986a:407;1987:121; emphasis added).

> translation... The problem of translation is indeed fundamental in Peirce's views and can and must be utilized systematically. (Jakobson 1977:1029)

It is crucial to underscore here that Peirce characteristically used "translation" and related terms in a very broad sense. For him, translation is the same as sign interpretation, and sign interpretation is translation[7]. Peirce's concept of translation being of a general sign-theoretical nature, it is wholly applicable to the different kinds of translation involving language, without however being identical with it. In the infinite process which Peirce commonly called semiosis, signs are being translated, or interpreted, thereby gradually becoming transparent in their material aspects (that is, as Firsts), while unfolding their meaning in successive interpretant-signs (Thirds), each of which interprets the previous sign. This is how signs, verbal and otherwise, reveal their (nonverbal) true object (Second).

The processuality of meaning implies that the latter can never be given once and for all, but needs to crystallize itself in increasingly firm and increasingly true beliefs about signs generated in a community of sign investigators, or sign translators. The truth of reality which is the ultimate goal of semiosis, is approached through what is an infinite series of translations, or interpretant-signs, one following the other and elaborating on it. For Peirce it is in this process of rule/habit-generating and rule/habit-generated continuity that signs establish their dynamic relation to other signs: "a sign is not a sign unless it translates itself into another sign in which it is more fully developed" (*CP*:5.594,1903). And the individual acts of making sense must be preceded by the possibility of giving a meaning in order to be followed by the translational praxis as a general. Thus, the translatability of signs comes first (and as a First interpretant); the actual translational events, second (and as Second interpretants); the law or habit of translating, third and (practically) last (and as a Third interpretant).

Jakobson agreed with the importance given by Peirce to the concept of translation. He stated unreservedly that "Beside encoding and decoding, also the procedure of recoding, briefly, the various facets of translation, is becoming one of the focal concerns of linguistics and of communication theory" (1971:576;1961a:250).[8] Yet Jakobson's re-formulation of Peirce points in some ways away from Peirce and towards structuralism. He saw in the (verbal) sign a dual incidence of translation, and repeatedly stressed that a sign, or *signum*, is composed of a perceptible, sensuous *signans* and an intelligible, translatable

---

7 For a discussion of Peirce's notions of translation, see Chapter 6.

8 See also, for instance, Jakobson's originally 1959 statement that translation is "eine der wesentlichen und immer wichtigeren sprachlichen Aktivitäten" (Jakobson 1971b:278-279).

signatum[9]. On the level of *signans*, signs organize themselves, in Liszka's interpretation of Jakobson,

> . . . from negative or non-meaningful units to meaningful complexes, i.e. for example, from the level of the phoneme and its distinctive features to the level of the most primitive meaning unit, the morpheme. (Liszka 1981:56)

Thus, phonemes are, in Jakobson's thought, "signs which are given *ad significandum* but which in themselves mean nothing" (Jakobson 1971b:9). Through this translational mode of encoding (and its reverse, decoding) words are formed out of phonemes, sentences out of words, and so on; and thus "translation is really a set of rules for combination and selection of elements into hierarchical wholes which, in turn, serve as combinative parts for more complex wholes" (Liszka 1981:57).

Verbal signs, simple and more complex, may be discriminated and explained because they refer to a set of learned linguistic and other, cultural codes. If they would not be ruled by a code, verbal signs would not signify; they would be meaningless. In Jakobson's definition, "code" may be taken both in its narrow sense, referred to the correlations between the elements of two different systems; or it may receive the broad definition of sign system as a culturally agreed entity. Coded rules determining the abstract meaning of verbal signs are at work in all signification through language; an uncoded verbal language, a language lacking rules and conventions, would be a glaring contradiction in terms.

---

9 Interpreting Peirce, but clearly departing from Peirce's theory of meaning, Greenlee distinguishes between two (not mutually exclusive) sorts of meaning: translational and articulational meaning: "Translational meaning requires an interpretant which is itself a sign --one that means what the sign interpreted means. 'Man' translates 'homme' because it is to be interpreted as standing for what 'homme' stands for. Translational interpretation preserves meaning, for it requires the interpretant-sign to have the same rule of interpretative response as the original sign had. Thus if one is to give the meaning, that is, interpret translationally, the command, 'Stop!', one must do so with another sign, perhaps a verbal one such as 'Halt!', perhaps with an entirely different sort of sign, such as a red light" (Greenlee 1981:144). While translational meaning seems to concentrate upon what Jakobson called the *signatum*, the concept signified, articulational meaning, which "does not, as such, admit of translation" (Greenlee 1981:144), seems to be concerned with Jakobson's *signans*, the material signifier. Here, "[i]n no way is the interpretant a replacement of the original meaning-vehicle . . . When a conductor tells a orchestra that he wants the fourth note of the opening of Beethoven's Fifth Symphony held just so long and no longer, he is interpreting that symphony, and he is doing so by shaping the musical structure or configuration of sounds and other musical elements (or, more technically, the order of musical elements), which is that symphony. His function is to clarify that order, or to treat it in a way that will reveal and express its properties as the musical order that it is. In short, his job as conductor is to articulate that order" (Greenlee 1981:144).

In addition to this Jakobson-based notion of back-translation there exists the mirroring procedure, which may be called, not only for the sake of symmetry, forward-translation. This metalinguistic operation occurs whenever a verbal sign requires higher explicitness in order to be adequately understood, and is for this purpose interpreted by some interpreter. Here the structural whole (that is, the verbal sign) receives an actual concrete meaning based upon the principle of customary, learned contiguity between the sign and what it is made to stand for.

Jakobson adopted Peirce's notion of the interpretant, which is (for Peirce) the meaning determined by the sign, which is in its turn determined by the object; but he modified its logical scope. While Peirce's notion implies a referential notion of meaning, Jakobson deemphasized reference to the object in Peirce's sense, thereby reapproaching a Saussurean view. In Jakobson's pragmatic concept of meaning reference lies in the situational correlation of the sign:

> To be operative the message requires a CONTEXT referred to ("referent" in another, somewhat ambiguous, nomenclature), seizable by the addressee, and either verbal or capable of being verbalized. (Jakobson 1960:353)

On Jakobson's view, context operates, in the broad sense, as the code in which the sign must be embedded, and in the narrow sense, as the sign's direct environment.

Jakobson's theory of translation --his idea of translational semiosis-- builds thus upon the factual elimination of Peirce's object, and its replacement by context. Elaborating on Saussure's theory of language as systematically structured into syntagms (linear sequences of verbal signs) and paradigms (different slots in otherwise identical syntagms), Sebeok describes context as follows:

> All signs enter into complex syntagmatic and paradigmatic contrasts and oppositions; therefore, their place in the web of a concrete text and the network of an abstract system is decisive as to which aspects will predominate in a given context at a particular moment, a fact which will lead directly to the problem of levels, so familiar to linguistics --being an absolute prerequisite for any typology. (Sebeok 1991:121)

The meaning of a sign (its interpretant) having thus become, for Jakobson, a function of its dual communicative context,--thereby resolving the question of the (un)translatability of the sign[10]--, Jakobson developed within this paradigm his

---

10 See also the following somewhat anecdotal quote from Jakobson (with, at the end, an implied, if somewhat revised, quote from Peirce): "Both the practice and the theory of translation abound with intricacies, and from time to time attempts are made to sever the Gordian knot by proclaiming the dogma of untranslatability. 'Mr. Everyman, the natural logician', vividly imagined by B.L. Whorf, is supposed to have arrived at the following bit of reasoning: 'Facts are unlike to speakers whose language background provides for unlike formulation of them'. In the first year of the

well-known typology of translations.

Through both interpretive instances in combination --back-translation conjointly with forward-translation, linked on the one hand to context and on the other to the entire system of which it is a part--, the signs and structured sequences of signs become meaningful by creating lingual equivalences, or (in a more Peircean terminology) "equational propositions" (Jakobson 1971:494). And thus, to use again Jakobson's own words, "diese Übersetzbarkeit enthüllt diejenige semantische Invariante, die wir im *signatum* suchen" (1971b:275).[11] This would imply that translational semiosis as Jakobson saw it, would serve first and foremost to reveal constants and invariants of informational content conveyed both within and across codes. An evaluation, in the final section of this paper, of whether this was actually what Jakobson meant to get across, will be preceded by a presentation, in the following sections, of Jakobson's translational types as they may be explained within the framework of Peirce's semiotics.

Three kinds of signs and translation

Jakobson pronounced himself most explicitly upon the subject of translation in his influential article, "On linguistic aspects of translation" (Jakobson 1959;1971b:260-266). In this essay Jakobson proposed his well-known three kinds of "interpreting a verbal sign". His distinction reads thus:

> (1) Intralingual translation or *rewording* is an interpretation of verbal signs by means of other signs of the same language.
> (2) Interlingual translation or *translation proper* is an interpretation of verbal signs by means of signs of some other language.

Russian revolution there were fanatic visionaries who argued in Soviet periodicals for a radical revision of traditional language and particularly for the welding out of such misleading expressions as 'sunrise' or 'sunset'. Yet we still use this Ptolomaic imagery without implying a rejection of Copernican doctrine, and we can easily transform our customary talk about the rising and setting sun into a picture of the earth's rotation simply because any sign is translatable into a sign in which it appears to us more fully developed and precise" (Jakobson 1959:23;1971b:262). Note that the meaning of the verbal signs mentioned by Jakobson, is determined by their contextualization. Note also Jakobson's relativistic "appears to us" as opposed to Peirce's original "is".

11 Jakobson identified the *signatum* with Peirce's immediate interpretant (in 1971b:346). It seems hard to believe that he hereby wished to limit the *signatum* to translatability, a mere potentiality, and from which Peirce's dynamical and logical interpretants would be excluded. Obviously, texts and, in general, all verbal signs must be interpretable by logical interpretants; but in order to establish their meaning, the immediate interpretant can only play a subsidiary role, insofar as it represents a doubly degenerate form of semiosic interpretation.

(3) Intersemiotic translation or *transmutation* is an interpretation of verbal signs by means of signs of nonverbal sign systems. (Jakobson 1959:233;1971b:261)[12]

If we follow Peirce's theory of signs and adopt the doctrine of the three categories on which it is based, his insights can be applied to Jakobson's three kinds of translation, thereby placing the latter in a broad epistemological framework and liberating them from the "tyranny" of what is language's Thirdness. Despite his profound interest in Peirce's work, Jakobson himself did, insofar as I am aware, not pursue such a line of thought, at least not in his writings[13]. This "neglect" may be due to the rather specific nature of Jakobson's interest in Peirce's works, signalled above; or it may have other reasons difficult to trace today. But to consider intralingual, interlingual, and intersemiotic translation as different configurations of Peirce's "genuine" vs. "degenerate" sign-activity is, I would suggest, an idea well worth exploring in some detail.

In earlier articles (Gorlée 1987,1990) I have discussed the notion of "degeneracy", particularly as it emerged in Peirce's earlier logic, in which he concentrated upon the sign-object relation and, concretely, upon Thirdness. The sign of Thirdness (the thought-sign or symbol) has an arbitrary, agreed connection with the object it is made to represent; it thus requires thought for its interpretation. The reason why Peirce in his earlier thought de-emphasized all signs except symbols is that only the latter are abstract and general and salient to his logic; the former (icons and indexes, representing Firstness and Secondness, respectively) lack these characteristics and are for this reason particularly unfit to be tools for intelligent reasoning. Later in his intellectual career, around 1885, Peirce would come to modify this generalization. He then acknowledged the necessity to include all three kinds of signs in the study of logical reasoning, thereby making his logic coterminous with semiotics.

As opposed to the conventional symbolic sign, an indexical sign has, for Peirce, a real existential connection with its object. The indexical sign is nothing by itself, without the object; it points towards the object, which is different from the sign but serves nonetheless as its natural complement. An iconic sign bears a qualitative or, more commonly, a structural likeness to its object, which makes that the one immediately evokes the other in the mind, without the mediation of reason. The similarity between the icon and its object may be in respect to, for instance, shape, color, or the mere relation of the parts to the whole. Firstness is the

12 A recent instructive study, "On Jakobson on Translation", is Sturrock 1991. Sturrock's methodological approach, though semiotic, is based upon Saussure, not Peirce.

13 See, however, the remarks on "The intrinsic nature of the signatum: translatability" by Jakobson's student and semiotic co-author, Waugh (1984:412-414), which point in a direction similar to my argument here.

category of pure potentiality; Secondness, of fact and brute reality; and Thirdness, of the mediating process introducing continuity and coherence. By the same token, indexes denote particular things, and anchor them in reality; icons describe things, both real and imaginary; and symbols establish logical relations between them, reason upon them, and, in general, draw conclusions from the things shown and pointed out.

The three categories, and thus the different sign-forms yielded by them, are not mutually exclusive but must be considered as co-present, interplaying, and interdependent agencies. Thinking never occurs without the presence in the mind of some feeling, image, conception, or other internal and/or visual quality which serves as a sign; nor can thought function without establishing a sign-external reference point in reality for such a representation. Thus in Peirce's semiotics a symbol must involve both an index and an icon; and an index in turn an icon. This makes a sign not into some kind of thing but into an event, a relation in which one of three elements plays a predominant role, thereby overshadowing the two others. In Peirce's terminology, genuine sign-action manifests Thirdness (that is, rationality, the symbolic) as its main governing element. This reduces sign-action where Secondness and/or Firstness have a strong impact, to degenerate forms of semiosis. In Peirce's parlance, the former is singly degenerate, or degenerate in the first degree; the latter is doubly degenerate, or degenerate in the second degree.

The relevance of this shifting concept of the sign as a dynamic process, for the different modes of translation involving language, should by now become clear. It is true that linguistic signs are general and conventional signs, and are therefore first and foremost symbols; yet as such they have implied iconic and indexical components. As Jakobson brought home as early as in 1963, "the pertinent role played in language by *iconic* and *indexical symbols* still awaits a thorough examination" (Jakobson 1971b:335); and in his 1965 essay "Quest for the essence of language", Jakobson stressed again that

> Peirce's graphic and palpable idea that "a symbol may have an icon or [let us rewrite in this conjunction in an up-to-date style: and/or] an index incorporated into it" opens new, urgent tasks and far-reaching vistas to the science of language. The precepts of this "backwoodsman in semiotic" are fraught with vital consequences for linguistic theory and praxis. The iconic and indexical constituents of verbal symbols have too often remained underestimated or even disregarded. (Jakobson 1971b:357)

If translation is taken more as a mainly cognitive activity than as a product of such activity, the actual translated thing *qua* artifact, it might serve as one exemplary instance of how in the different forms of manipulation of verbal language, which humans engage in, the symbolic, indexical, and iconic combine and shade in different meaningful and meaning-constructing ways into each other.

Returning to Jakobson's own trichotomy, his intralingual, interlingual, and intersemiotic translations may now be described and analyzed in a Peircean semiotic framework, as follows. Briefly, genuine semiosis is perhaps best manifested by intralingual translation; semiosis degenerate in the first degree, by interlingual translation; and semiosis degenerate in the second degree, by intersemiotic translation.

Intralingual translation

Intralingual translation consists in the translation of mental concepts (generals, signs of Thirdness) within one language. It directs itself wholly towards the creation of equivalences (in the Peircean sense of the term) on the abstract, symbolic level of the genuine sign, where the concern is not with delineating or indicating the object, but where the object is independent from the sign, and ever-new interpretations/translations must be made in order to cover all possible meanings of the sign. Here, the triadic sign relation operates

> . . . by virtue of a law, usually an association of general ideas, which operates to cause the Symbol to be interpreted as referring to that Object. It is thus itself a general type or law, that is, a Legisign. As such it acts through a Replica. Not only is it general itself, but the Object to which it refers is of a general nature. (*CP*:2.249,1903)

In actual language usage, sign and object are, as Peirce said, "thrown together" (*CP*:2.297,c.1895) voluntarily, but always by (social) agreement and to serve the purpose of efficient communication.

Intralingual translation is in fact made possible by the conventional but never static, nature of verbal language. It highlights the ability of one linguistic sign system to stand in more than one fashion for something else, to signify one, general (that is, non-specific) thing (the object) through various contextual forms alternatively. Peirce said that "the idea of a general involves the idea of possible variations which no multitude of existent things could exhaust" (*CP*5.103,1903).

Intralingual translation shows that in order to serve as an actual flexible instrument for communication, a language must have a strong element of negentropy; that is, it must have the tendency to take habits based upon social consensus; therefore choices must be made and rules and strategies established. But it shows at the same time that a linguistic code is a multi-purpose tool, and that habit-forming (negentropy) in language needs to alternate with entropy --that is, habit-breaking geared towards the creation of new and ideally better habits. That the new habits generated by intralingual translation improve the old ones, and are meant to be considered at least as strong as them, is manifested by the high truth-value which is claimed not only for the original sign but, *a fortiori*, for the "reworded" (in Jakobson's sense) sign, its logical interpretant. It is true that the latter is of the two the "more developed" sign (*CP*:2.228,c.1897), in the sense that it is supposed to be better equipped than the primary sign to fit a particular communicative purpose. But in principle the ideal aim of all intralingual translation is to provide a Peircean argument, or unfailing habit.

As instrumental in logical reasoning, and hence in translation, an argument is "an argumentation or statement expressly designed to lead to a given belief" (*MS*599:43,c.1902). An argument advances a definite conclusion meant to give the objective and final truth: it is a sign of law. Transposed to intralingual translation this is true on the lexical, sentential, and textual level, --whenever, in Jakobson's words, "a code-unit of the highest level" (1959:233;1971b:261), that is, one in which Thirdness is the preeminent aspect, is translated into a contextually more explicit (or, for that matter, a more elliptic) but always equivalent, genuine interpretant-sign through the instrumentalization of, particularly, language's Thirdness. Discourse referentiality (that is, meaning in discourse) having, for Jakobson, become an affair of twofold contextuality, intralingual translation is thus the variety of "interpreting a verbal sign" where no cross-systemic transfer takes place, but only intrasystemic substitution. Since one contextual pole remains untouched, and hence unchanged, this should enhance (at least in principle) the performance of the translator/interpreter.

Interlingual translation

Jakobson's "interlingual translation, or translation proper" (1959:233;1971b:261) is about two (or more) languages in contact. While intralingual translation concentrates upon genuine symbolicity, interlingual translation embodies indexical (that is, context-sensitive) symbolicity, or symbolicity degenerate in the first degree; because the Thirdness of genuine semiosis appears here overshadowed, as it were, by an prominent element of Secondness. Interlingual code-switching displays the two-sided experience of linguistic polarity, comparison, and struggle. It involves "two equivalent messages in two different codes" (Jakobson 1959:233;1971b:262); and as verbal facts are transcoded across language boundaries, the two linguistic codes involved are made to meet, interact, and (eventually and ideally) interconnect, creating a new contextual structure. This is how different languages demonstrate their similarities and, especially, how they aim to overcome their differences.

This exercise in "equivalence in difference" (Jakobson 1959:233;1971b:262) is inspired by the wish or need to increase communicational efficiency by deliberately modifying a verbal sign in order to make it fit an alternative linguistic code (and thereby make it intelligible to its users). Now it is, after the Sapir-Whorf hypothesis, a well-known fact that different languages verbalize and arrange things (i.e., semiotic objects, linguistic and extralinguistic) differently; and interlingual translation revolves precisely around finding a contextual form in the target language, which refers in more or less the same way to an object as does the sign in the source language. Interlingual translation is thus primarily concerned with breaking up and dislocating familiar sign-structures and relationships between signs, and with rearranging them meaningfully in the light of the new system. This makes interlingual translation into a semiotic encounter between two *Weltanschauungen*, an exercise in getting to terms, both in a non-empirical theoretical and in a practical problem-solving way, with alterity[14].

The original sign is informed by the object, and informs in its turn the interpretant. The latter is, however, determined by the sign only to a point: Peirce's indeterminacy always leaves a margin of liberty, which makes his meaning the outcome of a process of (logical) discovery. Transposed in Jakobson's interlingual translation the object (Peirce's object) can only be known under its newly-contextualized appearance, the new interpretant-sign, which is again determined by the verbal target-code as it appears from its encounter with the source code. This means that referentiality has, in the interlingual interpretation, crossed two contextual borders; though still predominantly a Third and encoded in verbal language (albeit a different language), it is twice removed from the original "reality" referred to.

The interpretant, then, lacks in interlingual translation the solid status of the Peircean argument. What is presented in the final interpretant is a truncated, once degenerate, argument, or Peircean proposition. Tuned in a lower and less ambitious key than the argument, the proposition is necessarily put forth with a more limited truth-value than the argument. The truth-value of a proposition is intersubjective rather than objective. A proposition gives information about the object of the sign; however, it is "not an assertion, but a sign capable of being asserted . . . One subjects oneself to the penalties visited on a liar if the proposition asserted is not true"(*CP*:8.337,1904). A proposition is, in Peirce's doctrine of signs, a practical solution, one which works more or less satisfactorily in a given situation, but one which is at constant risk of being superseded by a better or more workable proposition. This would explain why the new translations and re-translations which are constantly engendered worldwide, are no luxury, -- interesting and attractive phenomena, perhaps, but utterly disposable. These continuous acts of translating are in fact the signs of linguistic life. If the steady

14 Against the identification of language and culture, which is commonly practiced in structuralist research, a language is considered here as embedded in a culture, as well as an exponent of it. In accordance with this dual hierarchy, the concept of alterity is used here in the narrow sense of linguistic otherness, and in the broad sense of cultural otherness.

stream of interlingual interpretants would, for whatever reason, come to an end, all verbal activity --the life of language, no less-- would die.

Intersemiotic translation

Jakobson's third kind of translation, intersemiotic translation, is understood here to refer to the recodification of linguistic text-signs into nonlinguistic codes. Typical examples of this type of recoding are the translation from verbal language into visual languages (such as, in the plastic arts, architecture, painting, sculpture, and photography); into auditive languages (such as music and song); into kinesic languages (such as ballet and pantomime); and into multimedial languages (such as cinema and opera).[15]

What these modes of inter-code "transmutation" (in Jakobson's words) have in common is, firstly, that their source code is a verbal language, while the target code is a language only in a metaphorical manner of speaking. Our built environment, for instance, consists of architectural signs, simple and highly complex, which may be seen and studied as semiotic signs articulating and conveying a message; but this capacity must remain secondary, it would seem, to their primary function, which is purely utilitarian, and hence nonsemiotic. By the same token, if music may be considered as a language, it must consist of meaningful sounds and sound sequences corresponding to morphemes, words, sentences, and so forth in verbal language, thus enabling their transcodification.

The second common characteristic is that all nonverbal codes enumerated above are artistic codes --plastic, musical, and so forth. As opposed to language, in which Thirdness is preeminent and which requires intelligent interpretation, what is highlighted in art is Peirce's "quality of feelings" (*CP*:1.43,1896). Art consists primarily of signs of Firstness, self-evident, complete, and not needing rational explanation in order to be understood and interpreted. This should, however, not be interpreted to mean that the category of Thirdness --mediation, rules, codes-- is absent from art. Indeed, Peirce claimed that artists, in being primarily concerned with the category of Firstness, seek to articulate what is indefinite. This implies that some form of rationalization, in the form of rules and strategies, is a necessary ingredient of the creative act.

Firstness, the category governing iconic signs, and thus art, is the unanalyzed and immediate experience of pure sensorial emotion prior to any thought. It simply forces itself upon the mind and compels its total attention: one

---

15 The translation of verbal language into artificial languages, as epitomized by automatic (computerized or computer-aided) translation, is an operation involving units (in Martinet's terminology) with only one articulation (that is, in the strict sense, nonsigns), which lacks interpretive freedom on the part of the receptor/translator and thus falls outside the scope of intersemiotic translation as it is approached here.

cannot "think" a First. However, while pure Firstness is incompatible with thought, the work of art can be reflected upon and goes, for this reason, beyond Firstness. Peirce's own words go as follows:

> I venture to think that the esthetic state of mind is purest when perfectly naïve without any critical pronouncement, and that the esthetic critic founds his judgments upon the result of throwing himself back into such a naïve state --and the best critic is the man who has trained himself to do so the most perfectly. (*CP*:5.111,1903)

And two paragraphs later Peirce returned to the mixed nature of art, thus:

> . . . it seems to me that while in esthetic enjoyment we attend to the totality of Feeling -- and especially to the total resultant Quality of Feeling presented in the work of art we are contemplating-- yet it is a sort of intellectual sympathy, a sense that there is a Feeling that one can comprehend, a reasonable Feeeling. I do not succeed in saying exactly *what* it is, but it is a consciousness belonging to the category of Representation, though representing something in the Category of Quality of Feeling. (*CP*:5.113,1903)

This would imply that although artistic signs are meant to communicate privately rather than publicly, and although they are autonomous and self-sufficient -- untouchable, as it were--, yet they may be considered as embodying some form of knowledge, become the object of intellectual investigation and critique, be placed in theoretical frames of all sorts, and receive all kinds of interpretations. "Qualities of feeling show myriad-fold variety" Peirce said, "This variety however is in them only insofar as they are compared and gathered in collections. But as they are in their presentness, each is sole and unique; and all the others are absolute nothingness to it" (*CP*:5.44,1903). Intersemiotic translation is iconic symbolicity, or symbolicity degenerate in the second degree, the seemingly paradoxical juxtaposition and synthesis of Thirdness and Firstness, the problematic symbiosis of thought and instinct, mind and body.

Jakobson referred to the possibility and limitations of intersemiotic translation when he pointed out that

> We can refer to the possibility of transposing *Wuthering Heights* into a motion picture, medieval legends into frescoes and miniatures, or *L'après-midi d'un faune* into music, ballet, and graphic art. However ludicrous may appear the idea of the *Iliad* and *Odyssey* in comics, certain structural features of their plot are preserved despite the disappearance of their verbal shape. The question whether Blake's illustrations to the *Divina Commedia* are or are not adequate is a proof that different arts are comparable. . . In short, manypoetic features belong not only to the science of language but to the whole theory of signs, that is, to general semiotics. (Jakobson 1960:350-351)

In semiotic parlance this would mean that, as Jakobson also put it, "A symbol may be translated into an icon and vice versa, but of course only with a certain approximation" (Jakobson 1971b:268). Abstracted from the addendum, "and vice versa", the implication here is that source code and target code convey things (that is, they contextualize the object) in two entirely different but somehow still comparable ways: in intersemiotic translation mental facts, general concepts, signs of Thirdness, are replaced with sensorily perceived, precognitive qualities , which are equally general, but this time embodied in Firsts.

Intersemiotic translation is concerned with "the ludic informed by the ludic" (Plaza 1987a:209; my trans.); it substitutes unmotivated (or, at least, little-motivated) linguistic signs with their more directly motivated counterparts, namely, with signs which represent their object by virtue of their assumed similarity with it. Now it has often been argued that virtually anything may in fact be seen as being somehow like something else. This is *a fortiori* true in art, where likeness between the sign and what it represents, the object it is made to stand for, is a singularly selective and subjective affair; but likeness is always a relative notion, and can only make a slippery ground for transcoding, where equivalence is still somehow the primary requirement, yet much is left to the interpretive freedom on the part of the receptor in his/her multiple role of hearer/reader/interpreter/transcoder.[16]

If there exists, as argued by Toury, "no relation between codes, nor between codified parts/elements, it follows that innumerable different acts of translating may be performed on one source text, each yielding a different product" (Toury 1986:1119). Applied to the intersemiotic translation situation (which this argument seems tailored to suit), this means that in each of the series of possible interpretants, or artistic translations, the translated message is still somehow equivalent to the original message, but is unconcerned with both hard fact and rationality, and concentrates upon expressiveness, the beauty of pure emotion.

With Secondness and Thirdness being weakened or even removed, Peirce's "Pure Play of Musement" (*CP*:6.452ff,1908) takes center stage. This playful expression refers to the dreamlike state of mind which Peirce defined as "a certain agreeable occupation of mind" and

> The particular occupation I mean . . . may take either the form of aesthetic contemplation, or that of distant castle-building (whether in Spain or within one's own moral training), or that of considering some wonder in one of the Universes, or some connection between two of the three, with speculation concerning its cause. . . this last kind. . . I will call. . . "Musement" (*CP*:6.458,1908)

16 For a more detailed discussion of this assumed freedom, see Chapter 9, particularly the section on "The role of the translator"..

By "Universe" Peirce meant here "a receptacle or class of Subjects" (*CP*:4.545,1906), and he proceeded to identify the universes as familiar to us all: "The first comprises all mere Ideas, those airy nothings to which the mind of poet, pure mathematician, or another *might* give local habitation and a name within that mind" (*CP*:6.455,1908); "The second Universe is that of the Brute Actuality of things and facts" (*CP*:6.455,1908); whereas the "third Universe comprises everything whose being consists in active power to establish connections between different objects, especially between objects in different Universes" (*CP*:6.455,1908). Intersemiotic translation, *qua* "Pure Play" (*CP*:6.458,1908), would enable the interpreter to freely indulge his taste for recreative speculation and spontaneous associations-by-similarity, little clouds which lack a definite shape or form, equivalent (and not coincidentally so) to Jakobson's "subjective intangibles" (1971b:494).

Intersemiotic translation generates Peircean rhemes. A rhematic sign is a sign of possibility, that is not true nor false, gives no real information about the object, and can thus only have a very slight truth-value. Unconcerned, in and by itself, with truth and falsehood (though laying the foundation for future truth), intersemiotic translation is a rudimentary hypothetical argument, one which ventures a creative suggestion by showing it (rather than explicitly telling or explaining it). Intersemiotic translation receives its attractive force precisely herefrom: it "relies upon artistic force" (*MS*318:52,1907). The rhematic interpretant-sign is simply there, displayed but not pointed at and even less argued about. What is practiced here is the art of sensuous persuasion and even the art of seduction, but with no pretention of instructing nor of convincing. Art is not intended to be explained: it must first and foremost be felt.

An evolutionary view on information and translation

In his essay "On linguistic aspects of translation" Jakobson wrote:

> Because the information required by the English and Russian grammatical pattern is unlike, we face quite different sets of two-choice situations; therefore a chain of translations of one and the same isolated sentence from English into Russian and vice versa could entirely deprive such a message of its initial content. The Geneva linguist S. Karcevski used to compare such a gradual loss with a circular series of unfavorable currency transactions. But evidently the richer the context of a message, the smaller the loss of information. (Jakobson 1959:236;1971b:264)[17]

---

17 This is comparable to de Man's "economy of *loss*, a kind of political thermodynamics governed by a debilitating entropy" (de Man 1979:272).

This passage and Jakobson's conclusions, "Languages differ essentially in what they *must* convey and not in what they *may* convey" (1959:236;1971b:264) were written with particular reference to the interlingual transcoding situation, but there seems at first blush to be no reason why they may not be generalized to include intralingual and intersemiotic translation as well. Jakobson seems to argue that translation concentrates upon the transposition of the law-like, constants and invariants (Thirds) of informational content, and that consequently loss of information is an inevitable by-product of translational transactions.

This is, perhaps, a simplification of what Jakobson probably meant to say[18]. As an enthusiastic adherent to Peirce's ideas he no doubt appreciated Peirce's general evolutionist principle according to which Thirdness develops out of Secondness, and Secondness in turn out of Firstness. This means that invariance, within and outside verbal language, originates in variance, and that there is no invariance in which degrees of variance are not co-present as contributing components. By this token, intralingual translation presupposes and includes both interlingual and intersemiotic translation, and interlingual translation involves and builds upon intersemiotic translation. Interestingly, this makes intersemiotic translation, which is the most tentative and fragmentary of the three kinds of translation, into the very foundation of all translational operations, -- Peirce's "beginning and end of all conception" (*CP*:1.548,1867).

Translational semiosis is, in general terms, a teleological, truth-seeking process. Its purpose is to reveal the object (in the technical sense of whole meaning-content of the sign) through the generation of a series of interpretants. The hierarchical successivity which the Peircean paradigm establishes in the types of translation (interlingual translation in a higher place than intersemiotic translation, and intralingual translation in the highest place) is reflected in the three-step scale in which the types of translation are capable of fulfilling the purpose of revealing the object. In this endeavor, too, interlingual translation occupies a strategic middle position. Sandwiched between intralingual translation

---

18 In the 1950s, Jakobson had developed an interest in communication engineering, following Shannon and Weaver's (1949) mathematical theory of communication. According to Sebeok, "This induced him, in 1960, to become deeply involved in a 'Symposium on the Structure of Language and Its Mathematical Aspects', where he cited Shannon in support of his statement about the 'semiotic definition of a symbol's meaning as its translation into other symbols', referring to Shannon's definition of information as 'that which is invariant under all reversible encoding or translation operations", or briefly, "the equivalence class of all such translations" [Jakobson 1961b:251]. This was a neat way to bring under one umbrella Peirce's interpretant, Jakobson's translation theory, and Shannon's information theory. However, Jakobson's interest in information theory (as well as cybernetics) cooled considerably over time, and, except for remnants of fossilized terminology, it appeared to leave no permanent trace" (Sebeok 1991:77-78).

and intersemiotic translation, it includes and assumes, according to Peirce's evolutionist doctrine, the latter (intersemiotic translation) while itself being preceded, included, and assumed by the former (intralingual translation).

Intersemiotic translation epitomizes semiosic degeneracy as it concentrates on the creative transposition of the element of Firstness in the source-sign, itself a full Third. Yet the onesidedness of intersemiotic translation, its neglect of the "higher" dimensions of the sign, is destined to cause a strong informational loss, which can only to some degree be compensated by the added value, of an artistic nature, of the interpretant-sign. Its strong points are not information nor thought, but novelty and creativity, --in short, variance. Variance meaning openness and possibility, it permits, and even encourages, multiple interpretations.

Interlingual translation, or translation proper, is primarily concerned with the transfer of verbal facts, including their qualities. As a Second with an implied First, it does not achieve the synthesis of pure rationality, but must remain degenerate, stuck mid-way between irrationality and rationality, reason and instinct. As argued by Jakobson, in a sequence of interlingual translational events, some loss of meaning-content is inevitable, particularly if the object of investigation is a series (albeit a finite series) of successive translations.

Intralingual translation produces a Third (or "mind-set") involving a Second (or "fact-set"), interlingual translation, involving again a First (or "mood-set"), intersemiotic translation.

The triadic nature of translation

In the 1867 essay on "A new list of categories", Peirce put forth his theory of how ideas may be separated. According to this theory of experiential and logical abstraction, there are three grades of separability of one idea from another: (1) dissociation, (2) "prescission" or "precision", and (3) distinction. By dissociation Peirce meant that there may exist "consciousness of one thing, without the necessary simultaneous consciousness of the other" (*CP*:1.549; *W*2:50,1867), just as we can imagine the color red separate from the color blue. For Peirce, "prescission" occurs whenever it may be supposed that "in any possible universe" two closely connected ideas may be separated (*CP*:1.549,n.1; *W*2:50,1867). Thus color and space are commonly imagined together; but space can be supposed without, i.e., prescinded from, color --Peirce's "uncolored space" (*CP*1.549; *W*2:51,1867)-- , even though color cannot be supposed without (that is, prescinded from) space. By distinction Peirce meant simply that it is possible to discriminate between two ideas which cannot even be supposed one without the other, as for example, "open" and "closed", the meanings of which can be distinguished but not separated, because they are strictly relative to each other.

This trichotomy is indicative of how Peirce conceived the three elements of his categorial scheme to be related to one another. As mentioned above,

Peirce's categories are interdependent ideas. Accordingly, they cannot be dissociated in the mind from one another. Yet they may be prescinded from each other, albeit only in a specific order: Firstness may be prescinded from Secondness and Thirdness, Secondness may be prescinded from Thirdness, but Secondness may not be prescinded from Firstness, nor Thirdness from Secondness. It is unproblematic to make a logical distinction between the categories, Firstness, Secondness, and Thirdness[19] , as was actually argued by Peirce in his logic of relatives.

The relevance of this to the three kinds of translation should by now become clear. Mental concepts, such as the sign of Thirdness quoted by Peirce, "The dog is black" (*CP*:1.548ff;*W2*:50ff,1867)[20], are multiple impressions which must be processed both experientially and logically, in the order of prescission of the elements. This symbolic sign cannot be successfully (that is, in a semi-permanent way) transcoded into another, equivalent mental concept, unless the object in reality, as it is referred to ("the dog") is duly recognized, decoded, transcoded, and contextualized into an equivalent symbolized object, and unless, prior to this, the quality of the image-feeling underlying its verbalization and (con)textualization (blackness in "is black") has first been adequately attended to, decoded, and transcoded.

Once the threefold complexity of the translational operation has been duly dealt with, the danger of informational erosion will be successfully averted, and counteracted by the generative power, or "generacy", of semiosis. Consequently, informational loss must be highest in intersemiotic translation, in which the semiosis shows maximum degeneracy (and hence minimum generacy); and it must be lowest in intralingual translation, where the semiosis shows maximum generacy (and hence minimum degeneracy). In the final analysis it is therefore in intralingual translation, with its emphasis on the Thirdness of genuine semiosis, that the sign's meaning-potentialities are most accurately and fully explored and realized.

---

19 This logical distinction should not be confused with the far more complex, problematic, and indeed controversial, distinction between the multiple sign-forms which may be derived from the categories. For a discussion of this, see Gorlée 1990.

20 Peirce also used the deictically more emphatic form, "This dog is black" (*CP*:1.551 = *W2*:52,1867).

09. EQUIVALENCE, TRANSLATION, AND THE ROLE OF THE TRANSLATOR

"If we were to translate into English the traditional formula *Traduttore traditore* as 'the translator is a betrayer', we would deprive the Italian rhyming epigram of all its paronomastic value. Hence a cognitive attitude would compel us to change this aphorism into a more explicit statement and to answer the questions: translator of what messages? betrayer of what values?"

(Jakobson 1959:238)

Introductory remarks

Certain translation-theoretical key issues have loomed large in the preceding chapters, and deserve to be addressed at this point. Despite the longstanding discussions among translation theoreticians about precisely these issues, no agreement seems to be in view at this time. Yet it may be said without undue drama that proper and continued discussion of these controversial topics, from a variety of methodological angles, is critical to the harmonious evolution of the interdisciplinary (or better transdisciplinary) field of translation theory. If it can be shown --as I propose to do in these pages-- that Peirce's philosophy of signs throws new light upon these problems, my contribution here will be instrumental, albeit in a modest way, in bringing the discussion closer to a consensus, a "settlement of opinion" in Peirce's spirit.

Let me therefore next take up, as illustrative examples of the relevance of a Peircean semiotics to translation theory, the following issues: (1) equivalence between source text and target text, (2) the translation process and its phases, and (3) the role of the translator in the translation process.

Equivalence

By equivalence will be meant here the stipulation, recurrent in any text in the theory of translation, that there be between source text and target text identity[1] across codes. Firstly, different translation scholars use the notion of equivalence in different senses. Koller (1992:214-215) mentions, among others, Nida's "closest natural equivalent", Wilss's "möglichst äquivalenter zielsprachlicher Text", and Jäger's term, "kommunikativ äquivalent". The picture is further blurred by the manifold qualifications given the term, which is often used not in a merely descriptive (that is, value neutral) sense, but as an a priori requirement with which a text should comply in order to qualify as an adequate translation. The varieties of equivalence which have been put forth in translation criticism is indeed truly astonishing: besides "translation equivalence", the seemingly most general term[2], one finds "functional equivalence", "stylistic equivalence", "formal equivalence", "textual equivalence", "communicative equivalence", "linguistic equivalence", "pragmatic equivalence", "semantic equivalence", "dynamic equivalence", "ontological equivalence", and so forth; to say nothing of the ostensibly free use of related terms such as sameness, invariance, congruence, similarity, isomorphism, and analogy.

In this landscape of, it would seem, utter terminological and conceptual confusion, it is nevertheless clear that it is generally claimed that original text and translated text are ideally placed in a one-to-one correspondence, meaning by this that they are to be considered as codifications of one piece of information, as logically and/or situationally interchangeable, -- the "invariant core" being, of course, "a hypothetical construct only" (Toury 1978:93)[3]. However, from a semiotic viewpoint this would seem to be a misconception, or at least a gross simplification of the facts. One case in point is Jakobson's statement (1959:233): "Equivalence *in difference* is the cardinal problem of language and the pivotal concern of linguistics", and hence of translation. In general-semiotic parlance, one would say that both original and translation are

---

1 On identity vs. difference, see also Chapter 7. On the problem of translational equivalence, see also, for instance, van den Broeck 1978 and Wilss 1977:156-191.

2 The need to define, and thereby delimit, translation equivalence (both in theory and in practice) was emphasized in 1965 by Catford, thus: "The central problem of translation-practice is that of finding TL [target language] translation equivalents. A central task of translation-theory is that of defining the nature of conditions of translation equivalence" (Catford 1965:21).

3 Toury also speaks of "some informational core [which] is retained invariant under transformation" (Toury 1986:1112-1113) and, more specifically, of an invariant core which "may be *functional* (ad hoc, textual, or habitual, linguistic and/or text-typological)" or "*formal*, when . . . the invariant is the linguistic substance itself" (Toury 1986:1117).

signs forming part of a semiosic chain --a sequence of interpretive signs. Yet in contradistinction to the interchangeability claim, the translation follows from and is caused by (Peirce would obviously say "is determined by") the original; it is its interpretant-sign. If both signs are lifted out of the infinite semiosic sequence and studied in isolation, the original is of the two the primary sign, both temporally and logically. The interpretant is not an imitation of an immanent structure of the sign or the object, nor is it an arbitrary structure imposed on the object from the outside. It is the law or habit (weak or strong), through which sign and object become related so that an effect of the semiosis can occur. The mediating sign-action, once set into motion, is a recursive but irreversible process of sign translation. This implies that there is in the sense intended here no back-translation possible: the pre-semiosic situation cannot be restored. This turns the very idea of interchangeability between original and translation into a paradox. Indeed, the semiosis has not only dramatically changed the original sign; it also offers, perhaps, new knowledge of the dynamical object (in Peirce's sense) to which both signs, if still indirectly and incompletely, refer.

To reduce sign translation, linguistic or otherwise, to mimicry or to a mirroring procedure is to respond to nothing but the sign's Firstness, and thus to atrophy its full signifying potential. A translation is obviously more than a "hypoicon" --an iconic sinsign or otherwise degenerate Third (Gorlée 1990). From a semiosic standpoint, the zealously pursued preservation of any semiotic substance --be it meaning, information, ideas, or content (just to mention some of the commonly used terms)-- is more than irrelevant, counterproductive to what translation should be concerned with, namely the sign-and-code-enriching confrontation between sameness and otherness: "*du Même et de l'Autre*" (Ladmiral 1979:209)[4]. Genuine semiosis is non-mechanical engenderment and re-engenderment, and is for this reason the very opposite of mimesis: "Nay, exact conformity would be in downright conflict with the law [of habit]; since it would instantly crystallize thought and prevent all further formation of habit" (*CP*:6.23,1901).

4 In the translational-theoretical context, this is a conclusion also arrived at by Frawley (from a semiotic but non-Peircean point of view): "Thus, in an interlingual translation, for example, the matrix code provides the phonological information, the morphological information, the syntactic information, and so on, to be bound to different semiotic constraints. Hence the notion of identity is actually antithetical to the notion of translation. There is no meaningful (meaningful ≠ semantic) information except that it is coded, and the very fact of differential coding militates against 'exact translation' . . . [T]here is information only in *difference*, and the differential coding, the recoding, is what allows the interlingual translation to produce any information at all" (Frawley 1984a:168).

Mention of one tradition within linguistics --Humboldt's (1767-1835) linguistic relativism-- is in order here, because it opposed at an early date what may be called the received view (according to which fixed world-word connections are established), thereby foreshadowing Peirce's dynamic version of the indeterminacy of meaning, the Sapir-Whorf hypothesis, as well as some of Chomsky's concepts. I refer here to the

> adage of Wilhelm von Humboldt's, one that was later embraced (although never explained) by Chomsky --who called it in his early writings "creativity", or sometimes "open-endedness"-- about the capability of languages to "make infinite use of finite means". (Sebeok 1991:29)

Humboldt's "alternative" view is of particular interest in a discussion of translation, because it would later inspire, explicitly and/or implicitly, the "holistic" view on literary translation which was initiated by Holmes and further developed by Toury and others[5]. This approach would, despite its concentration upon one particular kind of translation --the translation of verbal art--, or perhaps because of it, breathe new life into what had become a rather unfruitful approach to it from traditional linguistics. According to the relativistic concept of verbal language, different languages correspond to different world-visions. From the viewpoint of the different languages, reality is not experienced as it "really" is, but as it is molded, reflected -- subjectively, homogeneously, but variously-- in and by the different languages.

Although Humboldt is frequently recognized as the founder of general linguistics, his pioneering role in linguistic semiotics has received scant recognition (Schmitter *et alii* 1986:317). This is perhaps due (as indicated by Trabant 1986) to Humboldt's language-orientedness which has turned problematic at a time when sign-theoretical discussions, following Peirce, are moving away from "linguistic imperialism" and towards a semiotic perspective which places the verbal and the non-verbal on a continuum, the former being superior to the latter, but nevertheless building upon it. Not coincidentally, Humboldt considered language to be not only a system of socially invented and intrinsically arbitrary signs, but also to have an iconic aspect to it[6].

---

5 See Chapter 2, especially the section on "Semiotics and translation studies: generalities".

6 Even Saussure, the champion of the arbitrary, conventional sign, recognized the existence of motivated (or, in his terminology, natural) signs. To address the form of language as having adopted, to some degree, the form of external reality, is particularly momentous for the study of literature, where a completely unmotivated sign concept would forbid all reference of the sign to its object. Interestingly, in this context, Humboldt also composed an art theory, which must fall outside the scope of the present discussion.

Prefiguring, it would seem, Saussure's *langue-parole* dichotomy, Humboldt distinguished between language as *ergon* (theory, a written or orally transmitted verbal corpus) and *energeia* (praxis, a verbal activity). While the latter builds and feeds the former, it --*energeia*-- is for Humboldt the essence of language itself. Language consists not only of a systematic, rule-bound whole, but of energies, and this dynamic interactive principle elevates language to the semiotic (or rather, semiosic) status of expression of thought. Humboldt's so-called "anti-semiotics" of language (Trabant 1986:69-90) was only opposed to a linguistic semiotics to the extent that the latter limits its considerations to the arbitrary and conventional nature of the signs of language, thereby "killing . . . all its spirit and sending all its life into exile " (Humboldt in Trabant 1986:72;my trans.). In fact, language is, for Humboldt (as it would later be, if in a more radically evolutionary paradigm, for Peirce) a living "organism" (Nöth 1990:201), an essentially semiotic sign-system, an irreversible processuality, in which man establishes shifting connections between language and the phenomena of the world surrounding him.

The relevance of this to translation/interpretation in Peirce's sense should be clear. Peirce himself used the term "equivalence" with special reference to the interpretant. This shows that for him equivalence was synonymous not with one-to-one correspondence, as in Firstness (iconicity) and, in a different modality, in Secondness, but with the kind of one-to-many correspondence that obtains whenever a sign "gives birth" to an interpretant (or rather a series of interpretants). Two signs which are thus dynamically equivalent[7] can be logically derived from one another. Peirce typically struggled with language trying to express exactly what he meant by his dynamic equivalence which takes place in the semiosis:

> A sign . . . is an object which is in relation to its object on the one hand and to an interpretant on the other in such a way as to bring the interpretant into a relation to the object corresponding to its own relation to the object. I might say "similar to its own"[,] for a correspondence consists in a similarity; but perhaps correspondence is narrower. (*PW*:32,1904)

In his much-quoted definition of a sign, Peirce said that the sign creates in the

---

7 This idea overlaps, at least to a certain point, with Nida's principle of "equivalent effect", which is "not so concerned with matching the receptor-language with the source-language message, but with the dynamic relationship between receptor and message [which] should be substantially the same as that which existed between the original receptors and the message" (Nida 1964:159). Upon this principle Nida based his well-known dynamic-equivalence (as opposed to formal-equivalence) model.

mind of the person it addresses an "equivalent sign, or perhaps a more developed sign" (*CP*:2.228,1897). Elsewhere he noted: "An equivalent of a proposition is the same proposition differently materialized. For the proposition consists in its meaning" (*MS*599:62,c.1902), which implies that it is not what language or code a text-sign is in, but what signification it has, which is to the interpretational (that is, the translational) point. That Peirce's concept of equivalence is teleological (that is, is governed by Thirdness) is further put into evidence by his statement that "two signs whose meanings are *for all possible purposes* equivalent are absolutely equivalent" (*CP*:5.448,n.1,1906; emphasis added).

Qualitative equivalence

Let us next take a closer look at Peirce's views on equivalence by approaching somewhat differently. It should by now be clear that translational equivalence cannot be identified, at least not wholly, with an algebraic equation or other sign of Firstness. Discussing different sets of diagrams, Peirce ascertained that "every algebraic equation is an icon, insofar as it exhibits by means of the algebraic signs (which are not themselves icons) the relations of the quantities concerned" (*CP*:2.282,c.1893). After giving this quote from Peirce, Jakobson added the following:

> Any algebraic formula appears to be an icon, "rendered such by the rules of communication, association, and distribution of the symbols". Thus "algebra is but a sort of diagram", and "language is but a kind of algebra". Peirce vividly conceived that "the arrangement of words in the sentence, for instance, must serve as *icons*, in order that the sentence may be understood". (Jakobson 1971b:350)

Now this is no doubt true for the physical construction of whole sentences and sets of sentences. And in this sense two linguistic signs, each one couched in a different code, can share the same overall external structure of their parts, and thus be derived from the same model, the common source which itself remains tacit. In this sense, too, a text and its translation (both composite linguistic signs), taken together, may be viewed as a self-reflexive dual construct; they do not need anything beyond themselves in order to be recognized and understood as signs sharing a number of significant qualities --sensory and/or material properties. It is easy to imagine that texts such as a sonnet, a marriage contract, and a court reporter's transcript share some significant physical features with their respective translated versions --sign-internal features which may even be appreciated without knowledge of the languages[8] involved. Such common features are abstracted from sign-external reality, and may occur, in some form or other, in all codes, linguistic and non-linguistic alike. For example, in the case of verbal text-signs, the primary text and its translation may show an equivalent length, distribution of paragraphs, rhyme structure, and/or use of punctuation[9]. Such features make them immediately recognizable as similar signs --similar, that is, in "feel", "tone", or other "quality of feeling" (as Peirce would say).

If both signs (the translated and the translating sign) are taken as being morphologically, syntactically, etc. symmetrical (in other words, as mutually convertible across code barriers) this is done without taking into due consideration that one is the antecedent and the other the consequent. Yet the essential hierarchical relation which determines the one to be the interpretant of the other, and not vice versa, cannot be denied. Translational equivalence must always be a diachronic affair (to use a term from Saussure). Moreover, various quasi-synonymous equivalents (with mutually inconsistent terms) may be obtained from one sign. This means that the sign and its equivalent interpretant-sign may only be considered as one another's counterparts to the extent that their signhood in its aspect of Firstness is under inquiry. I propose to call this equivalence referred to the signs-in-themselves "qualitative equivalence".

Referential equivalence

Having traced qualitative equivalence between a sign and its interpretant-sign, we may next consider equivalence originating from Peirce's other categories: Secondness, the category of the object, and Thirdness, the category of the

---

8 These remarks apply to the products of intralingual and interlingual, as well as intersemiotic translation; therefore it would be more adequate to use "codes" than "languages" here.

9 Jakobson argued that sequential use is made of equivalent units in two cases: "In poetry one syllable is equalized with any other syllable of the same sequence; word stress is assumed to equal word stress, as unstress equals unstress; prosodic long is matched with long, and short with short; word boundary equals word boundary, no boundary equals no boundary; syntactic pause equals syntactic pause, no pause equals no pause" (Jakobson 1971b:71). A translation of a poem must reproduce such equivalences across the language barrier. Yet Jakobson continued: "It may be objected that metalanguage also makes a sequential use of equivalent units when combining synonymic expressions into an equational sentence: $A = A$ ("*Mare* is *the female of the horse*"). Poetry and metalanguage, however, are in diametrical opposition to each other: in metalanguage the sequence is used to build an equation, whereas in poetry the equation is used to build a sequence" (Jakobson 1971b:71). Translation is, of course, a typical metalinguistic operation.

interpretant. The aspects of sign equivalence yielded by Secondness and Thirdness will be called respectively "referential equivalence" and "significational equivalence". The three aspects of equivalence together may then be named semiotic (or more accurately, semiosic) equivalence. This will be explained in adjacent paragraphs.

Concerning referential equivalence between sign and interpretant-sign, a distinction must be made between the standing-for relation on the level of the immediate object and on the level of the dynamical object[10]. The immediate object being the idea called up directly by a particular sign-use, is only knowable through the sign. As opposed to qualitative aspects of the sign (Firstness *sensu stricto*) the sign-immediate object relation represents the Firstness of Secondness; it concentrates on the sign's referent or referents on the code level. Of course, the sign may be placed in any code or sign-system, verbal or nonverbal; and its immediate object is given in the exhibitive, ostensive, or verbal (depending on the code) manifestation of the sign. The interpreter sees the object only insofar as the sign reflects it. Without previous acquaintance with the code the sign is in, it is not possible to gain knowledge of its immediate object, let alone to penetrate into the inner sanctum of its "deeper" signification.

Translation involves at least two codes: a source code and a target code. For a sign in one code to be a translation of a sign in a different code, the respective immediate objects need not be the same. Since the immediate object is "the idea which the sign is built upon" (*MS*318:70,1907), it is differently represented in each code. The immediate object will be subject to change in and through the intercode semiosis of translation. In tandem with equivalence on the level of the sign, here too sameness is no requirement, neither on the micro-level (such as, in language, word-to-word or sentence-to-sentence correspondence) nor on the macro-(i.e., textual) level; and here too equivalence must be understood in a broad sense, as the kind of "loose" sameness created through any kind of semiosic interpretation. This does not imply that it is not crucial for both signs (the primary sign and the translated sign) to give, through their immediate objects, "hints" (as Peirce called them), careful examination of which in their contexts must lead to the same underlying idea, --the common "real" or "dynamical" object, which stays itself outside the sign relation and is therefore not translated.

Let me give one example of this. To translate the Spanish expression, *cortar el bacalao*, by an expression which is identical on the immediate-objectual level creates equivalence if the expression occurs, for instance, in a

10 For details concerning Peirce's concepts, see Chapter 3.

fish recipe. But if the expression refers, in a figurative sense, to power structures, identity on the level of the immediate object would be a misinterpretation and distortion of the real facts pointed at by and in the code. The immediate object is therefore one referential meaning criterion, but one which needs to be supplemented by contextual information. A sign normally does not function in a vacuum, but is embedded in a communicational environment which supplies linguistic, referential, ideological, etc. indications to its right understanding. It is only within such a context that the interpreter can be led by the immediate object towards the dynamical object --the real feeling, thing, event, phenomenon, thought, or concept which causes the sign relation but remains itself independent from it.

The dynamical object is itself absent and remains outside the semiosic event. It is the Second under the aspect of Secondness; and as a "double Second" it is only knowable through the immediate object, which, as indicated, is the outward perceptible form in which the object manifests itself in the sign. In order to get to know the dynamical object of a sign one can only perceive, study, and try to understand what is implied by the immediate object. This requires, according to Peirce, "experience", "collateral observation" (real or imagined), and skills such as "imagination and thought" (*MS*318:77,1907). The dynamical object corresponds to the hypothetical sum total of all instances of the sign-bound immediate object, of which the primary sign and the translated sign are two instances couched in different (sub)codes and more often than not with different immediate object.

"No man can communicate any information to another without referring to some *experiences* to be shared by him and the person whom he addresses" (*NEM*3,2:770,1900). Like all other forms of communication, translation is sign-action within a physical universe of social interaction. The existence of a common experiential ground is a crucial element of communication: without it, access to knowledge of what the message really means (its dynamical object) is blocked. The more freely and directly collateral experience is shared with a partner in a communication situation, the more efficient the communication. Peirce wrote:

> I go into a furniture shop and say I want a "table". I rely upon my presumption that the shop-keeper and I have undergone reactional experiences which though different have been so connected by reactional experiences as to make them virtually the same, in consequence of which "table" suggests to him, as it does to me, a movable piece of furniture with a flat top of about such a height that one might conveniently sit down to work at it. (*NEM*4:259,c.1904)

In other words, "when there are both an utterer and an interpreter, the [dynamical object of the sign] is that which the former has in mind, but which it does not occur to him to express, because he well knows that the interpreter will understand that he refers to that, without his saying so" (*MS*318:69,1907). By this token, it is essential for intercode communication to successfully take place, that the communicational partners, though belonging to different codes, have acquired and possess, albeit implicitly, a shared knowledge of the phenomena of the world in their different semiotic expressions.

Obviously, it is easier to get to know a dynamical object which has an indexical relation to the sign than one which is an icon or a symbol[11]. What the latter have in common, and what distinguishes them from Seconds, is their generality. Iconic signs show possible attributes, yet unattached to any existent; symbolic signs give general rules, applicable but not yet applied to a particular case; while indexical signs are concrete sign-instances embodying icons and governed by symbols.

Now even if the primary sign and the translated interpretant-sign have different immediate objects, their dynamical objects will always need to be identically the same, at least ideally. Even their sameness is, however, relative, since it is to some degree always the result of an interpretation, of an inferential procedure. In other words, the relation between the two must be mediated by a semiosis which makes it possible for one to be a logical consequence of the other. Before embarking upon further analysis of this, I will try to explain from a slightly different angle how sign-representation is connected with sign-interpretation.

Breadth, depth, information

The sign's standing-for and standing-to relations must be taken together for a specific purpose: to introduce a group of concepts which, though still connected with the sign and the code it is in, pertain specifically to its external relations.

---

11 Since language is primarily a symbolic sign-system, this means that experiential knowledge is not only linguistic but may also be non-linguistic. For Jakobson, however, "The meaning of the word 'cheese' cannot be inferred from a nonlinguistic acquaintance with cheddar or with camembert without the assistance of the verbal code. An array of linguistic signs is needed to introduce an unfamiliar word. Mere pointing will not teach us whether *cheese* is the name of the given specimen, or of any box of camembert, or of camembert in general, or of any cheese, any milk product, any food, any refreshment, or perhaps any box irrespective of contents. Finally, does a word simply name the thing in question, or does it imply a meaning such as offering, sale, prohibition, or malediction?" (Jakobson 1971b:260-261). Jakobson's contention here would gain in clarity and scope by being placed in a broader framework --such as Peirce's philosophy of signs-- which does not separate linguistic sign from non-linguistic signs, but places the different kinds of mental processes in a continuum. This point is convincingly argued in Johansen (1993:235-244).

These concepts were addressed by Peirce as a young lecturer, most prominently in his paper "Upon logical comprehension and extension" (*W*1:454-471,1866[12]). I shall not attempt to give an exhaustive account of Peirce's thought here, but will limit myself to the ideas having a direct connection with my main theme.

Following a long-recognized tradition, Peirce argued in the above-mentioned Lowell Institute Lecture VII that a word (or any other symbol[13]) has two different logical dimensions which, as stated by Peirce in a later manuscript, "are equally applicable . . . to . . . all kinds of signs" (*MS*200:49,1907). One of these logical dimensions is "extension", "denotation", or "breadth"; the other is "comprehension", "connotation", or "depth". Despite the fact that these concepts have been standard expressions in logic since the Port Royalists, they have been lacking in precise designation. Peirce proposed to adopt as the most serviceable designations, logical breadth and depth.

The logical breadth, or denotation, of a term relates the term to the world. It indicates the (real) individuals or objects to which the term applies and which occasion its use. Logical depth, or connotation, refers to a term's meaning-content, the attributes or qualities that can be predicated to it, "the possibilities which are imagined or judged to be realized" in those individuals (*MS*200:49,1907). Not only does the word force an interpreting mind to recognize the thing, phenomenon, event, or relation which is indicated or designated by it; the word is also informed and influenced by its *designatum*, or object; and finally, "Everything must be comprehended or more strictly translated by something" (*W*1:333,1865). Note, however, that both aspects are not equally important: "Every symbol denotes by connoting" (*W*1:272,1865), Peirce wrote, and "Denotation is created by connotation" (*W*1:287,1865). Whereas both aspects of the word are essential, depth, as referring to sign-enriching action, thus has priority over breadth, the indicative aspect of the sign. As Peirce put it later (in an unpublished letter to his former student, Christine Ladd-Franklin), "The depth of the sign seems to be nothing but its better self. The sign is related to its depth . . . as an idea to an ideal, as memory to vivid hallucination . . ." (*MS*L237:187,1902).

Logical breadth refers backward to the object, and logical depth forward to the interpretant. The dual elements in the sign produce what Peirce called "information"[14]. Whenever a sign is interpreted, it "always results in an

---

12 An expanded version of this lecture has been published in *CP*:2.391-2.430,1866.

13 In his earlier period Peirce, the logician, identified "sign" with thought-sign, his "symbol". Following Peirce, I shall also use "term" in the general sense of "concept", unrelated to Peirce's specific understanding of it, as an alternative to "rheme".

14 Peirce used the term "information" as a measure of entropy --that is, similar to its modern use. He did this long before the recent development of information theory, of which he must

increase either of extension [denotation, breadth] or comprehension [connotation, depth] without a corresponding decrease in the other quantity" (*W*1:464,1866). By information Peirce meant the "amount of comprehension [connotation, depth] a symbol has over and above what limits its extension [denotation, breadth]" (*W*1:287,1865). And increase of information of a sign means "an addition to the number of terms equivalent to that term" (*W*1:465,1866). This occurs whenever a new equivalent is produced; in other words, in each act of sign interpretation/translation new knowledge (that is, Thirdness) is generated[15].

The following passage from Peirce, taken from a later work, may help to clarify the foregoing analysis:

> A symbol, once in being, spreads among the peoples. In use and in experience, its meaning grows. Such words as *force*, *law*, *wealth*, *marriage*, bear for us very different meanings from those they bore to our barbarous ancestors. (*CP*:2.302,c.1895)

Take, for instance, the occasion when, in common law, a judge makes a court decision which establishes a new precedent for a certain type of case; or when, in Roman law, a new law is added to the body of law. What transpires then is an increase of information. The term "law" can be applied to a new object, but its basic characters remain unchanged. Consequently, it has increased in breadth, but with no increase in depth. Or imagine a newly-married convert to Islam, locked up in a harem. Her concept of "marriage" has probably undergone a dramatic change. Though the marital institution itself is the same as she knew it previously, a series of new characters were added to it. The term "marriage" remained constant in breadth, but has increased in depth. In this case, too, information has increased. By "spreading among the peoples" (*CP*:2.302,c.1895) (that is, by being interpreted, translated), the semiotic features of symbols (words, concepts, etc.) are developed and enhanced.

Significational equivalence

Inspired by these and similar thoughts, Peirce "invented" the concept of the interpretant as he saw it, thus:

> Indeed, the process of getting an equivalent for a term, is an identification of two terms previously diverse. It is, in fact, the process of nutrition of terms by which they get all their life and vigor and by which they put forth an energy almost creative -- since

---

be considered a pioneer.

15 In reference to this, Peirce proposed three graded states of information, or knowledge, corresponding to the "essential", "informed", and "substantial" breadth and depth. See also Johansen 1993:147ff.

> it has the effect of reducing the chaos of ignorance to the cosmos of science. Each of these equivalents is the explication of what there is wrapt up in the primary -- they are the surrogates, the interpreters of the original term. They are new bodies, animated by that same soul. I call them the *interpretants* of the term. And the quantity of these *interpretants*, I term the *information* or *implication* of the term. (*W*1:464-465,1866)[16]

From the perspective of Peirce's evolutionary logic, each translation makes the implicit more explicit, thereby involving increased information. This is clearly expressed by Peirce's "a sign is something by knowing which we know something more" (*PW*:31-32,1904). The growth of knowledge is accompanied by an increase in either breadth or depth. It has no influence upon the signified facts themselves, nor the characters attributed to them, which may be either true or false (*NEM*4:241,c.1904). But when two signs are equivalent, they denote the same things and have the same logical breadth. They may depend, for their truth-value, upon a particular connotative depth (as obtained in interpretation) or they may depend only upon this denotative breadth.

The interpretant is supposed to indicate the same things or facts as the primary sign, and to signify these things, and assert these facts, in like manner. But both relations are unlikely to remain constant and unchanged in the course of time --in other words, in the course of a series of semiosic events of an inferential nature. Equivalence, in the strictest sense, between sign and interpretant is therefore logically impossible: it would stifle the growth of knowledge, which growth is exactly the point of sign production and sign use. Our whole human universe being, in Peirce's words, "perfused with signs, if it is not composed exclusively of signs" (*CP*:5.448,n.1,1905), we communicate by signs, of which we produce a constant stream of new interpretants, which we interpret again, and so on. During this never-ending inferential process, new significations (and thereby new truth-values) are constantly put forth, probed, weighed, accepted, negotiated, defended, ignored, held in reserve, rejected, etc.[17]. New knowledge is thereby accrued of the object. In accordance with Peirce's pragmatic maxim, the ultimate goal of this exercise remains, nonetheless, to achieve total knowledge of the meaning of a sign. To achieve this, one needs to persevere in making ever-new interpretations/translations of the sign, in order to gain access, via the sign and its immediate object, to the sign's *prima causa*, the dynamical object. In the final analysis, translation, linguistic and otherwise, is about our own life-world, real and imagined, and the

16 For a discussion of this crucial passage from a different perspective, see Chapter 5.

17 More on this in Chapter 10.

myriad ways in which we make sense of it by creating significational equivalents of it and its parts[18].

Translation process

Let us next take another example of an issue in translation theory for which a solution can be found by placing it into the framework of a Peircean theory of signs. The translation procedure itself has been commonly but arguably hypothesized as a chronological scenario involving variously three or four stages. It is tempting to view the nature and role of these stages in the light of Peirce's process of interpretation, which is systematically described by him as a threefold reasoning-process consisting in the production of three successive interpretants.

In reference to the study of the translation process in itself, Toury advances the following cautionary remarks:

> Since we know very little of the inner, psychological mechanisms involved in translating, any single act of this kind of activity is in the position of a "black box", that is, an open system whose internal structure can be guessed at, or tentatively reconstructed, only on the basis of the relationships between the entities established as its input and output. (Toury 1986:1114)

Now, rather than a sign of intellectual humility, the foregoing remarks appear to me to call for a Peircean approach to the phenomenon of translation. It is a well-known fact that Peirce, the logician, was radically opposed to psychologism --meaning by this the dependence of semiotics upon psychology. For him, the study of sign action does not require knowledge of the exact workings of the human mind. This is not to say that Peirce considered that the mind as a

---

18 Having discussed, in the foregoing, semiotic equivalence in terms of the three elements of the semiosic sign-relation --sign-related, or qualitative equivalence; object-related, or referential equivalence; interpretant-related, or significational equivalence--, I need to respond briefly to Johansen's view on this matter, since it differs somewhat from mine. Johansen (1988:26) includes in his list of partial equivalences, "extensional equivalence" and "significational (or intensional) equivalence", in addition to what he calls "intentional equivalence" and "rhetorical equivalence". That Johansen makes no explicit mention here of my qualitative equivalence, but includes instead the perspectives of respectively the utterer and the interpreter, is perhaps a reflection on the fact that he discusses one specific type of signs, namely literary signs. My own view on Johansen's extension of Peirce's triadic sign-relation, will become clear later in this Chapter. I may add here that, if I interpret Johansen's list of four equivalences rightly, his extensional equivalence and my referential equivalence overlap, his intensional (or significational) equivalence corresponds to my own significational equivalence, while my qualitative equivalence seems included in his rhetorical equivalence (but without being identical to it).

thinking (i.e., sign-processing) agency was irrelevant to his logic; rather, the reverse is actually true. "I am using *mind*", Peirce wrote half in jest,

> . . . as synonym of Representation; and mind that this mind is not the mind that the psychologists mind if they mind any mind. I think they mainly talk about consciousness, in the sense of the first category, and hypothetical arrangements in the brain. (*MS*478:157,1903)

Instead of Firstness, Peirce, the logician, studied Thirdness; "Not the psychological process, but the logical function" (*MS*L237:126,c.1900); not the contents of the "black box" itself, but the inferential processes leading from premisses to conclusions. These processes he called the "modes of action of the human soul" (*CP*:6.144,1892). All thought is, for Peirce, about showing how one sign leads rationally to another, thereby signifying growth and development. This being Peirce's main subject of inquiry, he would hardly have been inclined to embark upon a serious investigation of how mental processes may fail, derail, or get paralyzed, as would be the concern of the psychologist[19].

For the purpose of the argument here, it is critical to bear in mind that semiotics as Peirce conceived it is a query about the logical relationship between a particular sign on the one hand, and its interpretant or translated sign on the other; and also that this relationship can be defined as either abductive, inductive, or deductive. The translation process being a mental process not open to direct scrutiny, Toury seems to contend (at least in the above quotation) that it can only be explained by abduction. While this makes a perfectly valid statement, it would for Peirce probably have been a somewhat "pessimistic" way of dealing with the facts of the matter. Despite their reliance on guessing instinct, abductive hypotheses are often remarkably right in their explanations of the facts, so their truth-value should not be considered too lightly. Moreover, abductive leaps call for inductive testing, the search for facts by "experiments which bring to light the very facts to which the hypothesis had pointed" (*CP*:7.218,1901). Finally, induction again prepares the ground for deduction, the development of laws ruling the facts and giving them a "purpose or end" (*MS*292:13,c.1906). For the argument here, the questions raised by Toury are timely, because the three kinds of reasoning are directly dependent on the categories and must be considered as the equivalents, in the logical sign relation, of the three kinds of logical interpretants which correspond to the three stages

---

19 See also Chapter 10, particularly the section on "Utterer and interpreter in translational semiosis". For a detailed discussion of the relevance of Peirce's semiotics to psychology, see Colapietro 1989:49ff. and *passim*.

in the translation process. This shall be argued in subsequent paragraphs.

Let us first introduce, seriatim, some of the ideas as to the stages in translation, as profferred by different scholars. In a highly praxis-oriented spirit, Koller (1992:203-204) distinguishes between three "*Arbeitsstufen*": the "*Rohübersetzung*" or shortlived translation, the "*Arbeitsübersetzung*" or middlelived translation, and the "*druckreife Übersetzung*" or longlived translation. Koller's criteria are qualitative and correspond to a mounting scale of grammatical, lexical, stylistic, etc. "*Genauigkeit, Richtigkeit und Adäquatheit*", "accuracy, correctness, and adequacy" (Koller 1992:204). As explained by Koller, the first phase produces a draft translation of limited scope and usage. Its focus on "*Genauigkeit*", or accuracy, means that there must be "*Identität des Inhaltes*", but violations against morphological, syntactic, phraseological, lexical, stylistic, etc. rules are in this stage still accepted. In a second-phase translation, "*Genauigkeit und Richtigkeit*", accuracy and correctness, are required; it may contain no grammatical, lexical or stylistic errors. Finally, Koller's "print-ready" translation is characterized by the triad, "*Genauigkeit, Richtigkeit und Adäquatheit*" --accuracy, correctness, and adequacy. A product of solid research and serious reflection, it is intent on satisfying the highest norms and expectations. It must be noted, however, that the progression from, roughly, fidelity to source-fact, to agreement with target-code, and finally accordance with text-type between source-text and target-text, sets singularly relative priorities. The three steps advanced by Koller to describe the quality of the translator's performance can only be defined in relation to one another. External criteria of assessment are absent here. This greatly reduces the usefulness of Koller's three-step process outside pure translation practice and pedagogy.

With some necessary "theoretical speculation", Toury himself proposes a four-stage schematic representation of translation:

> (1) an indispensable *decomposition* of the initial entity up to a certain, varying level, and assigning its constituents at this level the status of "features";
> (2) a selection of features to be retained, that is, the assignment of *relevance* to some part of the initial entity's features, from one point of view or another;
> (3) the *transfer* of the selected, relevant features over (one or more than one) more or less defined semiotic border;
> (4) the *(re)composition* of a resultant entity around the transferred features, while assigning to them the same or another extent of relevancy. (Toury 1986:1114)

In contradistinction to Koller's practical proposal describing the quality of the end-product, Toury's program is highly theoretical and process-oriented. A prerequisite for it is that the text *ab quo* can be divided into discrete units, some of which may then be considered as relevant "from one point of view or another" (as signifying, in semiotic parlance) and others as irrelevant (as non-signifying). Only the former are then transcoded, while the fate of the latter, evidently disposable, units remains rather unclear in Toury's proposal.

It would seem to me that no parts of a text-sign may be concealed by camouflage without practicing some form of erosion, whereby the semiotic substance is thinned in the successive semioses it undergoes, instead of becoming progressively richer in content, as Peirce would have it. The notion of relevancy brandished by Toury is really a dangerous and indiscriminate weapon. Due to the fact that it may have either an ideological or an intuitive bias, or both, Toury's scenario here seems more tailored to suit rhetorical needs than to lead to the *summum bonum*, the truth in the way Peirce saw it[20].

In *After Babel*, Steiner proposes a fourfold "hermeneutic motion, the act of elicitation and appropriative transfer of meaning" (Steiner 1975:296), which in his description really consists of three stages and an illusory fourth. In the first stage there is, according to Steiner, "initiative trust" in the meaningfulness of the "'other' as yet untried, unmapped alterity of statement" (Steiner 1975:296) in the text-to-be-translated. This trust "will ordinarily be instantaneous and unexamined, but it has a complex base" (Steiner 1975:296). After what looks like a description of Peirce's Firstness, Steiner proceeds to the second stage of translation, where the initial trust is put to the test of confrontation, and the "manoeuvre of comprehension [becomes] explicitly invasive and exhaustive' (Steiner 1975:298). The text is now attacked, as it were, in its "otherness", in an act of aggression in which we "'break' [its] code . . . leaving the shell smashed and the vital layers stripped" (Steiner 1975:298). Now, this is remarkably similar to Peirce's Secondness. "The third movement", Steiner continues, "is incorporative, in the strong sense of the word . . . embodiment . . . [W]e come to incarnate alternative energies and resources of feeling" (Steiner 1975:298-299). This last process, of "comprehensive appropriation", may result in a "complete domestication, an at-homeness" of the translation in its new situation; or the translation may have acquired a "permanent strangeness and marginality" in it (Steiner 1975:298). The fact that

20 See also Holmes 1988:89. Given the general and rather indeterminate character of Toury's representation of the translation process here, I may perhaps venture an alternative interpretive suggestion. If by relevancy is (implicitly) meant the opposite of redundancy in the information-theoretical sense, this makes the "irrelevant" units the non-informative relative waste of the message *qua* content. Seen from the point of typology, this would then refer to the invariants in the semiotic process --repeatable and thus superfluous. This reductionist approach creates more problems than it solves, because in a semiotic context, invariance is not identical with insignificance, nor is variance the same as significance.

a translation may work either like "sacramental intake" or like its opposite, an "infection" (Steiner 1975:299), means, for this critic, that it still lacks

> . . . its fourth stage, the piston-stroke, as it were, which completes the cycle. The a-prioristic movement of trust puts us off balance. We "lean towards" the confronting text . . . We encircle and invade cognitively. We come home laden, thus again off-balance, having caused disequilibrium throughout the system by taking away from "the other" and by adding, though possibly with ambiguous consequence, to our own. The system is now off-tilt. The hermeneutic act must compensate. If it is to be authentic, it must mediate into exchange and restored parity. (Steiner 1975:300)

By reaching this new state of synthesis, Steiner's model has come full circle. Though Steiner would surely never place himself under the banner of semiotics --any semiotic banner-- , yet his "hermeneutic motion" closely resembles semiosis, and his stepwise scenario described above is interestingly reminiscent, conceptually and otherwise, of Peirce's succession of three interpretive moments as manifested in the first (immediate/emotional), second (dynamical/energetic), and third (final/logical interpretants) --the latter again subdivided, according to Short (1986a:115), in a "non-ultimate" and an ultimate logical interpretant[21].

Translation, at least in its lingual varieties, deals with signs interpretable by logical interpretants; it is a "pragmatic" process of making sense of intellectual concepts, or signs of Thirdness. The solution of mental problems, of which translation would be one exemplary instance, occurs for Peirce in three, perhaps partly overlapping, inferentially-reached developmental stages showing an increasing degree of "hardness" or solidity of belief[22]. When embodied in an actual (and thus observable) tangible (and thus testable) translation, this concept may serve as a quality norm roughly similar to Koller's above-mentioned three grades of "accuracy, correctness, and adequacy" (Koller 1979:94). This is hardly coincidental, because Peirce's logic is a normative science (Ransdell 1981:201-202n;Fisch 1986:269ff.) --albeit in a more "technical" sense than meant by Koller-- and translation taken in its non-

---

21 For Peirce's different interpretants see also Chapter 3. Robinson's (1991:294-296,n.24) criticism of Steiner contains an interesting point: Steiner is accused of "unwillingness to take a stand on the theoretical status of his movements", of not stating clearly "whether they are psychohistorical phases in every translator's approach to a text, sociohistorical phases in a culture's approach to foreign texts . . . or static logical categories into which specific translations can be classified" (Robinson 1991:295,n.24).

22 Peirce himself referred to "three grades of clearness" in *CP*:3.456ff.,1897. See also his essay on "How to make your ideas clear" (*W*3:257-276,1878).Following Fisch (1986:290,327-329), the three grades of clarity are interpreted as connected with the categories.

descriptive performance-directed aspects is equally processual and, at the same time, norm-governed.

First, second, and third logical interpretants

The first in the series of logical interpretants emerges when we are faced with problematic situations of an intellectual nature, as a fleeting belief, a mere set of feelings arising

> . . . when upon a strong, but more or less vague, sense of need is superinduced some involuntary experience of a suggestive nature; that being suggestive which has a certain occult relation to the build of the mind. We may assume that it is the same with the instinctive ideas of animals; and man's ideas are quite as miraculous as those of the bird, the beaver, and the ant. For a not insignificant percentage of them have turned out to be the keys of great secrets. (*CP*:5.480,c.1905).

To solve or explain the problem a conjecture, or hypothesis, is formulated. Peirce drew a felicitous parallel between this initial, heuristic stage of scientific inquiry and the "Pure Play of Musement", or intellectual reverie (*CP*:6.452ff.,1908). In the translation process this would correspond to the more instinctive than rational phase when the text-sign first enters a receptive mind. A trained translator's mind will then, spontaneously and with practiced ease, start generating a flow of ideas. This impromptu translation may be a fragmentary and tentative draft, perhaps; it is nevertheless a new sign susceptible of serving as a point of departure in the next semiosis.

Whereas with animals "conditions are comparatively unchanging, and there is no further progress" (*CP*:5.480,c.1905), with humans the first conjectural interpretants can be further developed, introducing a process of growth of ideas. The next logical interpretant is a product of what Peirce called "the dash of cold doubt that awakens the sane judgment of the muser" (*CP*:5.480,c.1905), and expresses itself in experimentation, in weighing pros and cons. The working hypotheses are at this stage put to the test and verified by solid judgment. In the translation situation the more or less lucky guesses are now put on the dissecting table and analyzed with a clear head. The result is "a" translation which provides "a" solution to the problem. It offers at best a successful solution, one which works in the intended communicational situation and one which makes sense (that is, is significant) in the target culture. But it may at worst be received in it with mixed feelings, shock, or even rejection.

Given time and hard work, a practiced mind is bound to produce a third logical interpretant as the near-perfect solution with which semiosis to all intents and purposes may come to a (possibly temporary) logical standstill. Such an ideal translation will have found its natural habitat in the recipient situation, thereby losing its acute "percussivity" (*NEM*4:318,c.1906). The new configuration having thus become unproblematic and more or less harmonious, the mind ceases to be in the "state [of] activity . . . mingled with curiosity" (*NEM*4:318,c.1906) by which it is stimulated to put out further interpretant-signs.

This ideal *status quo* should, nevertheless, never become a taking refuge in some artificial fixity. The third logical interpretant does express a firm belief, but it is still a thought-sign; and its primary goal is therefore to remain alive and communicative throughout time. To ignore its need to grow would be an antiquarianism. The judge of any interpretant's finality must always be the social community, or *communis opinio*, the norms of which are naturally changeable. Although the semiosis at this point may have lost its edge, yet the translation process has reached a still non-ultimate moment. Its apparent finality is no more than a resting-point.

For this reason it is possible, and even essential, to take the semiosic process one crucial step further, and to consider that the semiosic fire is susceptible of rekindling at any future moment, however distant or utopian. The sign would then be called upon to fulfill the explosive task of generating the one single unfailing habit with which the semiosis would definitively come to its end. This ultimate logical interpretant would embody the final truth-norm and would therefore no longer be placed in the triadic relation which characterizes the Peircean sign. A translation which would pretend to give final answers is, however, an alarming oxymoron, a sure sign that culture itself has, for instance by some irreversible catastrophic final event, come to an end[23]. This would make the actual production of a truly final ultimate translation a terminal matter, or sign of the death of the sign (*CP*:5.284=*W*2:224,1868).

The role of the translator

The next and last point that will be raised here is the role of the translator in the translation process. Alternatively criticized and ridiculed, enhanced and romanticized, the translator has frequently been taken out of proportion to the job he or she really does. The technical translator has essentially been seen as a craftsman (or craftswoman), and his or her work as a form of expertise -- difficult, perhaps, but not an impossible skill to master. At the other end of the

23 Eco's semiosic concept of culture as translation or an ongoing process of generating new interpretants by a society of interpreters (Eco 1979:71) is incompatible with the idea of an ultimate logical interpretant. I am indebted to Professor Eco for some of the stimulating ideas he put forward during his lecture on "Drift and unlimited semiosis" at the Institute for Advanced Studies of Indiana University at Bloomington on July 19,1989. A version of his lecture has been published in *The Limits of Interpretation* (Eco 1990:23-43).

scale, the literary translator, and in particular the poetic translator, has been elevated (or has elevated him- or herself) to the interesting status of creative artist in his or her own right. This dichotomy has created a potent mythology around the figure of the translator, who has been invested, and indeed infested, with such images as the copyist, the acolyte, the slave, the amanuensis, the *bricoleur*, the re-creator, the mediator, or other metaphors serving to either efface or aggrandize the translator's personal performance.

In the face of such ambiguous assessment of the professional *persona* and talents of the translator, and of his or her role in the translation process, I would like to construe the translator in terms of Peirce's semiotics, in order to argue that on the whole, the personal impact of the translator on the translating procedure seems perhaps to have been subject to indue inflation --both "upward" and "downward" inflation. This is at least the (hopefully more realistic) direction in which Peirce's doctrine of signs would point us.

The translator as communicator has a dual role. He or she embodies both the addressee (or one of the addressees) of the original message, and the addresser of the translated message; both interpreter and utterer; both the patient interpreting the primary sign, and the agent uttering the translated meta-sign. In semiotic terms, the translator is charged with both the standing-for and the standing-to relation, and thus he or she monopolizes the whole sign-manipulative process in which translation consists. The following statements, from Peirce, seem to point by implication to the translator's situation: ". . . two separate minds are not requisite for the operation of a sign . . . [T]wo minds in communication are, insofar, 'at one', that is, are properly one mind in that part of them" (*MS*283:107,1905-1906); "In the Sign they are, so to say, *welded*" (*CP*:4.551,1906).

Now it is a notorious fact that Peirce considered that "neither an utterer, nor even, perhaps, an interpreter, is essential to a sign, characteristic of signs as they both are" (*MS*318:58,1907). Although semiosis is for Peirce triadic action and he did not explicitly include any such fourth or fifth component, in addition to the sign, its object, and the interpretant[24], this is not to say that Peirce did not recognize the existence of either. In fact, he did so repeatedly, for instance, when he stated that when a (verbal) sign is made, "there really is some speaker, writer, or other sign-maker who delivers it; and he supposes there is, or will be, some hearer, reader, or other interpreter who will receive it" (*CP*:3.433,1896); or in his often-cited definition of the sign as "something which stands to

24 It was not Peirce but Charles W. Morris who first spoke (1938:3) of the interpreter as a fourth element of semiosis (which for Morris was a relation between "sign", "signification", and "interpretant").

somebody for something . . . It addresses somebody, that is, creates in the mind of that person an equivalent sign . . . " (*CP*:2.228,1897); or when Peirce referred to "the Utterer's (i.e. the speaker's, writer's, thinker's or other symbolizer's) total knowledge" (*CP*:5.455,1905).

Some caveats are in order. Firstly, Peirce did not have in mind, it would seem, that the utterer and the interpreter were human individuals or even specific minds[25]. "A sign is whatever there may be whose intent is to *mediate between* an *utterer* of it and an *interpreter* of it, both being *repositories of thought*" Peirce wrote (MS318:206,1907;Peirce's emphasis). He was rather thinking, in an abstract way, of what he called "theatres of consciousness" (*MS*318:55,1907) or "quasi-minds": "Signs require at least two Quasi-minds; a Quasi-utterer and a Quasi-interpreter" (*CP*:4.551,1906). Peirce argued as a central piece of his theory of signs that semiosis "not only happens in the cortex of the human brain, but must plainly happen in every Quasi-mind in which Signs of all kinds have a vitality of their own" (*NEM*4:318,c.1906). Secondly, the interpreter seems to be more essential for sign-action than the utterer. Many signs have no utterer, or at least they do not emanate from any personalized and conscious sign-maker. To illustrate this, Peirce mentioned "such signs as symptoms of disease, signs of the weather, groups of experiences serving as premisses, etc." (*MS*318:56-57,1907). But a sign is no sign unless there is some interpreter interpreting it as such --"capable of somehow 'catching on'" (*MS*318:205,1907)-- if not really then at least potentially. A sign which for whatever reason is unable ever to be interpreted can not really be considered a sign in the semiotic sense. Thirdly, the utterer and the interpreter inside the translator's mind are engaged in a dialectic relation evolving over time, a dialogue, half internal and half external, in which the translator/utterer is subordinate to the translator/interpreter; yet the performance of both "roles" by the one translator is clearly dominated by that of the interpretant-sign --that is, the interpretant turning again sign, or the sign as it is being transformed into an interpretant.

As opposed to Saussurean-based linguistic semiotics, with its emphasis on sign production, pragmatic semiotics (that is, semiotics in the Peircean tradition) proceeds to the contrary and manifests itself first and foremost as a theory of sign interpretation. The sign as Peirce conceived it is, in contradistinction to its Saussurean counterpart, not defined in terms of an utterer and/or interpreter, but in terms of its relations --with itself, with its object, with its interpretant. Through semiosis, the sign deploys its meaning; its full

---

25 This is also demonstrated by Peirce's repeated remarks on the "sop to Cerberus" (see, for example, *PW*:81,1908). This issue is also discussed in Chapter 10.

meaning is thus knowable, "although it may lie only at the ideal and infinitely distant terminus of inquiry" (Savan 1983:6). Sign action and sign interpretation are not necessarily determined by a human utterer or interpreter: Peirce's semiosis is self-generating triadic action. As all semiotic signs, the text-sign is a living agency actively seeking to realize itself through some interpreting mind rather than passively waiting to be realized by it, as is the case in linguistic semiotics. One reason why the Peircean concept of text-sign may at first seem fanciful is that it diminishes the significance of the reader/interpreter/translator. In a Saussurean-inspired text-semiotics, the latter is customarily looked upon as the sole discourse-producing subject, as the one agency giving the text-sign its meaning by matching signifier with signified. By moving instead to a pragmatic, Peircean paradigm, the presence of an interpreter is somehow subsumed but at the same time de-emphasized.

This means that the active mediating role in the kind of semiosic action ordinarily called translation is played not by the translator, as is commonly thought, but by the autonomous action itself through which the sign gets to realize its meaning. Peirce wrote about thought and the thinking person that thought thinks in man rather than man in it (*CP*:5.289,n.1=*W2*:227,n.4,1868), and

> [T]he idea does not belong to the soul; it is the soul that belongs to the idea. The soul does for the idea just what cellulose does for the beauty of the rose; that is to say, it [the cellulose] affords it [beauty] opportunity. (*CP*:1.216,1902)[26]

Applied to the translation situation this means that the translator is merely instrumental in making sign-action possible; he or she is used (that is, acted upon, influenced) by the sign. Therefore it would be a misconstrual of the facts to hold, as is generally done, that the sign is translated by the translator, because it really translates itself[27]. The translator does not address the text-sign; the

---

26 Liszka (1981:47) affirms that "for Peirce, unlike Kant, the mind is not primarily synthetic, but analytic (1.384), i.e., mind does not constitute experience, but merely analyzes it. The mind gets synthesized rather than serving as the synthesizing agent: 'Real synthesis occurs when we are carried in spite of ourselves from one thought to another' (1.384)".

27 Eastern martial arts, in which Zen-Buddhist and other meditation systems are an integral part, build upon similar ideas. The art of archery, for instance, is wholly an affair of "finding one's cosmic center". Paradoxically to the Western mind, it is not the archer who shoots the arrow: once the "tao", or moment of inner balance, has been found, the arrow is simply shot from the bow. As the metaphor goes, it leaves the bow as the ripe fruit falls from the tree. Coincidentally or not, Peirce used the same image when he described "that ultimate . . . , definitive, and final interpretant" as "the ripe fruit of thought", "attaining the purpose" (*MS*298:24,1906). And he added: "But this perfect fruit of thought can hardly itself be called

text-sign addresses the translator. And the translator is not addressed as a flesh-and-blood person but as a mind (that is, as a sign). The sign addresses, in the interpreter's memory, "a particular remembrance or image" which is "the mental equivalent" of that sign --in short, its interpretant (*W*1:466,1866). "The whole function of the mind is to make a sign interpret itself in another sign" (*MS*1334:44,1905). Of course, the translator may be a Marxist, a woman, an Italian; but at the moment of translating one is, if not simply the "site being traversed by words" which Barthes postulated, certainly not a calculus of ideological or sexual or national sentiments. The text-sign must be seen as a living organism requiring translation for its survival and actively seeking a receptive mind capable of generating interpretants; without interpretive response the text-sign would die and disappear.

The relevance of this semiotic transaction to machine translation is obvious. To be sure, Peirce envisioned, in 1905, the possibility of translation by a mechanical device --non-human but programmed by a human mind. He wrote:

> . . . if we had the necessary machinery to do it [translation], which we perhaps never shall have, but which is quite conceivable, an English book might be translated into French or German without the intervention of translation into the imaginary signs of human thought . . . Supposing there were a machine or even a growing tree which, without the interpolation of any imagination were to go on translating and translating from one possible language to a new one, . . . (*MS*283:97-98,1905)

The translator is thus for Peirce essentially a passive medium in the translational business, which he or she (like Peirce's "growing tree") can influence only peripherally.

Embodying the (above-mentioned) idea that thought thinks in man rather than man in it (*CP*:5.289,n.1=*W*2:227,n.4,1868), the translator is "carried in spite of [him- or herself] from one thought to another" (*CP*:1.384,1890-1891). Peirce's deemphasis of the personal interpreter bears on his (still somewhat mysterious) "man is a sign" equation (*CP*:5.314=*W*2:241,1868). In Peirce's semiotic aphorism, man is considered as much as a symbol, a process of communicating, knowing, and learning, as is the sign itself; consequently, all terms involved in the semiosic process are signs. Neither the utterer nor the interpreter can function as autonomous agencies under the umbrella of semiosis.

---

thought, since it has no signification and does not belong to the faculty of cognition at all; but rather to the *character*" (*MS*298:24,1906). Transposed to a different artistic key, the music is in the instrument, and the player needs only to make him- or herself available to it, for the music to come out.

They are as much signs convertible into one another within this communicative relationship, as the sign uttered and/or interpreted somehow needs them for its existence. By this token, signs of all kinds interpret themselves by themselves, man interprets man, man interprets signs, and signs man, all in an irreversible self-organizing generative system which constantly renews itself[28]. This makes the pragmatic process of carrying ideas (that is, thought-signs), as opposed to being carried by them, into a sort of contractual relationship[29] in which

> . . . men and words reciprocally educate each other; each increase of a man's information involves and is involved by, a corresponding increase of a word's information. (*CP*:5.313=*W2*:241,1868)[30]

While "[e]very utterance naturally leaves the right of further exposition in the utterer" (*CP*:5.447,1905), at the same time the interpreter enjoys what Peirce significatively called the "privilege of carrying its [the sign's] determination further" (*CP*:5.447,1905). Being a term subsumed by the triadic sign-process, the translator-sign is only given a limited freedom of interpretive action. As Peirce stated, "a sign which should make its interpreter its deputy to determine its signification at his pleasure would not signify anything, unless *nothing* be its significate" (*CP*:5.448,n.1,1906). By this shrewd but slightly malicious observation Peirce obviously meant more than that interpreters/translators, when left to their own resources, are capable of, and indeed prone to, producing non-sense. Peirce's remark that "the barbaric conception of personal identity must be broadened" drives home the fact that

> All communication from mind to mind is through continuity of being. A man is capable of having assigned to him a *rôle* --no matter how humble it may be, --so far he identifies himself with its Author. (*CP*:7.572,c.1892)

A translator in Peirce's intellectual spirit leads therefore a "problematic existence" (*CP*:2.334,c.1895): he or she is not so much an individual expert who may pretend to know all the answers, as he or she needs to be a dedicated

---

28 For a particularly lucid, learned, and provocative study of this, see Merrell 1991.

29 See Chapter 10.

30 The same idea, viewed from the side of man as interpreter, is implied in the following quotation: "In any case, such a Sign [Pheme] is intended to have some sort of compulsive effect on the Interpreter of it. . . It [The Delome] is a Sign which has the Form of tending to act upon the Interpreter through his own self-control, representing a process of change in thoughts or signs, as if to include this change in the Interpreter" (*CP*:4.538,1906). Note, however, Peirce's "as if" in the last sentence, which, again, seems to limit the active role of the interpreter in semiosis.

student of what transpires in the semioses in which he or she participates. The truly Peircean translator is intrigued, fascinated, or puzzled by the sign in front of him or her, even in love with it. By the same token, the translator's mind needs to be open and subject to semiosis --that is, committed to growth and engaged in an ongoing learning-process. It must submit itself unreservedly to the sign's attractive force, inspired by what can rightly be called "creative Love", as opposed to self-love (Henry James, William James's father, quoted in Murphey 1961:351;see also *CP*:6.287,1893).

The erotic overtones of this imagery are hardly coincidental. They serve to highlight the fact that the translator is to some degree a devotee of the sign, one whose desire consists in unconditional surrender to *its* needs and desires, rather than looking in the text-sign for opportunities to show off his or her own skills and talents. Whereas love of self is, for Peirce, a mere euphemism for greed (*CP*:6.291,1893), creative love is, in accordance with Peirce's agapastic theory of evolution with its roots in the gospel of St. John, the same as his "evolutionary love",

> . . . which teaches that growth comes only from love, from I will not say self-*sacrifice*, but from the ardent impulse to fulfill another's highest impulse. Suppose, for example, that I have an idea that interests me. It is my creation. It is my creature; . . . it is a little person. I love it; and I will sink myself in perfecting it. It is not by dealing out cold justice to the circle of my ideas that I can make them grow, but by cherishing and tending them as I would the flowers in my garden. The philosophy we draw from John's gospel is that this is the way mind develops . . . (*CP*:6.289,1893)[31]

This, too, is synechism, the evolutionary principle of inquiry, which, applied to the translator's (or any other investigator's) mental attitude, concentrates upon facts not as isolated phenomena, but as embodying "a true continuum . . . whose possibilities of determination no multitude of individuals can exhaust" (*CP*:6.170,1902). In this fashion, then, the translator partakes of a metaphysical cosmology in which meaning-potentialities, relationships, and generalities informing the sign are established which would escape the atomically-oriented mind.

I hope to have made clear that in tandem with this conception of the role of the translator as disinterestedly performing a labor of love, translation as semiosis finds a whole new and exciting expression[32].

---

31 In a previous article (Gorlée 1987) I addressed more specifically the meaning of Peirce's horticultural metaphors.

32 This concept of the translator displays a striking similarity to the purport of Walter

Concluding remarks

A turn away from the linguistic approach to translation, and a return (following Peirce and in the company of Jakobson, Steiner, and others) to a philosophical perspective on the phenomenon of translation, makes the whole perennial discussion regarding the "fidelity" or "infidelity" of a translation (as it is often called with a moralizing flavor) redundant, and sheds a wholly new light upon the epistemology of its "truth". These ideas are no longer in order in a theory of translation which aims not at the reproduction of meaning (without, however, losing its normative and purposive character) but at the embodiment and deployment of a sign's meaning-potential.

Translators shall accept the compliant role and be considered as bare and anonymous minds. In the epigraph of this chapter I mentioned the old cliché, *traduttore traditore*, and Jakobson's timely remarks upon it. Perhaps *traditore* may be taken here positively, in its etymological sense --which would make the translator a neutral transmitter of the message. Perhaps also, translators should be able and willing to sabotage their "traditional" duties, to display deviant behavior, and to engage in the creative, or simply deceptive, "paradox of betrayal by augment" (Steiner 1975:298), and also betrayal by reduction or distortion. Otherwise what they may produce are transliterations, dead replicas of the original. To the degree that a translation is a mere simulacrum it only serves to stifle semiosis, because it weaves patterns in which likeness, or even sameness, is a recurrent motif. Modelling in translation needs to be speculative, by suggesting a hypothesis. It makes its start from facts, but without, at the outset, having any particular theory in view. It aims to propose the construction of a prognostic model, but it must do so guided by instinctive "reason". This is not the oxymoron it looks like at first blush. Let me therefore propose *traduttore abduttore* as a new adage suited to reflect what should, in a Peircean philosophy of signs, be the primary concerns of the translator. This makes semiosis, translational or otherwise, perhaps a risky game, but never a trivial pursuit. For the translation of texts, it is the breath of life.

Benjamin's essay on "The task of the translator": see Chapter 7. For a full, if more "conservative" discussion of the role of the translator in the translation process, see Wilss 1988:41-59. Finally, Bellett (1978) places "translation as personal mode" *vis-à-vis* "the translator as nobody in particular": "Both are ploys, impersonations, heuristic deceptions", this writer argues (Bellett 1978:30), and "The operative word is *faith* and not *fidelity*" (Bellett 1978:39). Although these statements sound remarkably Peircean, Bellett refers here to the (un)faithfulness of the translator to the author of the original, not to the translator's relation to the original text, nor to the translation process --as Peirce would have it.

10. QUID PRO QUO: CONTRACTUAL SEMIOSIS AND TRANSLATION

". . . the Greeks used 'throw together' (συμβάλλειν) very frequently to signify the making of a contract, or convention. Now, we do find symbol (σύμβολον) early and often used to mean a convention or contract"
(*CP*:2.297,c.1895)

Introductory remarks

Peirce offered the contract as the paradigm of triadic sign-processes. In this Chapter I intend to analyze contract and contractual semiosis, and to apply the outcome of this analysis to the phenomenon of translation, which can be seen as one, specific kind of contractual transaction. By juxtaposing these three notions (contract, semiosis, translation), taken from three different spheres of intellectual life, a semiotic approach presents the possibility of seeing new and meaningful relationships between diverse entities. Concretely, the convergence of contract and semiosis will throw new light upon translation[1].

A contract is expressed as a conventional, primarily verbal promissory act by which a legally binding nexus is established between parties, with consequences for future behavior. The central idea of contract in law involves further a series of elements (such as intention, future action, and responsibility) which in their co-presence and interaction equally pertain to the symbolic action which Peirce called genuine semiosis. By deemphasizing, as Peirce usually did, the personal performance of the utterer and the interpreter, semiosis becomes a formal logical relation between a sign, its object, and the interpretant, in which

1 For an account of Derrida's deconstructionist concept of translation as a contract, see van den Broeck 1988.

meaning is negotiated in the conditional mode, i.e., relayed to the future; and the same thing happens in translation.

Finally, I will show that translation is a communicative act which possesses a contractual nature and must be considered as a degenerately semiosic act. Here, promisor and promisee have lost their performative individuality vis-à-vis one another and the promise intended. They converge into one mind, the translator's mind. Consequently, the promissory act is debilitated by the private, non-enforceable basis of the contract of translation. Genuine semiosis has thus degenerated into a dyadic or even a monadic affair.

Contract

A contract, basically, is an agreement between two (or more) persons, creating mutual legal obligations between them[2]. In its essence, it is a legally and morally binding promise[3] to do something or refrain from doing something. The "something" is called the subject matter of the contract, which must be legal. It is illegal to contract against good morals or national security, for example.

There is no set (verbal) formula to enter into a contract. Written contracts are as a rule supposed to set out what the parties actually intend, while the intent of orally-made and other informal agreements is, from a legal standpoint, not definitely fixed. Interpretation may there be necessary in order to clarify parties' intentions. It is the task of the trial judge to make the implicit explicit by inference from the evidence available to him or her (the written and/or oral agreement corroborated by conduct by parties).

The consensual basis of contract, its first formal requirement, implies that parties (called promisor and promisee) agree voluntarily and in good faith to enter into a common enterprise involving future actions, thereby yielding some portion of their freedom of behavior in the future. The will of parties is, in law, considered to be manifested in the fact that, to the effect of the contract, a definite offer or proposal from one party has been consciously and willingly accepted, without new terms, by the other party. An offer not clearly and explicitly put forth and/or not freely and knowingly accepted makes no contract, --or better, it makes a defective contract. Thus, if A asks B to promise some future performance, and B makes no answer indicating his (present) willingness to do so at some (future) time, B has made no promise.

---

2 For this and adjacent paragraphs on contract in law, I have drawn on Fuller and Eisenberg 1981, Eisenberg 1984, and the more popularizing Wincor 1970.

3 On the legal implications of this equation, see Fried 1981.

To qualify as a valid and legally binding contract, there must be mutuality, or exchange of promises. Under a contract, one party undertakes an obligation, thereby giving the other, to whom the obligation is owed, a claim against him, her, or itself, which consists in the right to have a performance of the terms of the contract. By this token, parties do not share benefits and burdens, but each party has his, her, or its definite privileges and responsibilities arising from the contract.

Contracting parties must further be competent, that is, they must have the proper legal capacity to enter into a contractual agreement. As a case in point, a contract entered into by a minor (or a mentally disabled person) is a defective, and hence voidable, transaction. It is not void, and therefore still creates legally binding obligations on a competent party, unless the minor (or mentally disabled person) repudiates it. This may happen in person or through a guardian acting on his or her behalf.

However, a contract is not binding, and therefore void (and not merely voidable), if it is lacking what is called, in legal jargon, "consideration". A bare and gratuitous promise is generally insufficient ground to create, for the one party, an enforceable duty to deliver any (material or immaterial) goods, nor for the other, to take and pay for them. The obligation resting upon each party only exists "in consideration of" the act or promise of the other, --meaning that neither is bound unless both are bound. Consideration is, in the Anglo-American legal system (the so-called common law), the essence and backbone of legal contract. It is also known as the *quid pro quo* ("what for what"; "something for something") mentioned in the title of this Chapter because of the analogy to the scholastic *aliquid stat pro aliquo*, which exemplifies the semiotic sign relation and is (like *quid pro quo*) rooted in equivalence. *Quid pro quo* indicates that something must be given in return for the promise; that there must be some bargain; that a responsibility incurred by the one party must be matched by a corresponding benefit gained by the other. Consideration pits the promise to give (often, to pay) against the promise to do, thereby highlighting the thing of value each party agrees to give in exchange for what he or she receives by the bargain. This thing of value, or consideration, is the reason for which the contract is made.

Semiotics being, essentially, the study of how verbal and nonverbal messages are created, sent, received, understood, interpreted, and otherwise used, it is clearly the case that contract is a semiotic problem. Here we must distinguish a contract as a written document from contract as a communicative act or event. Though different, both are facts of law and both are semiotic signs.

The written document, or contract form, is an object which is a sign because of the verbal signs (signs of Thirdness) it is codified in. When filled out and signed, it serves as a genuine Third, or sign of law. In accordance with Peirce's classification of signs, it must be characterized as a symbolic sign[4] strongly tinged with indexicality. More specifically, it is a proposition, or dicent symbolic legisign[5] which on being signed by parties (and, if necessary, co-signed by one or more witnesses, an attorney, and/or notary public) will acquire the status of an argument, or argumentative symbolic legisign[6]. The mixed, symbolic-indexical nature of the contract is signified in the appearance of the formal, written contract but can also be recognized (though perhaps in a less explicit form) in informal contracts --agreements, that is, which may result from an exchange of letters or even from casual acts.

The written contract is a verbal text, and language is the obvious example of a system of Thirds. The use of the linguistic signs in contract forms is stipulated by convention and consists substantially of a succession of formal recitations, of which the following are supposed to serve as typical examples:

> Agreement made in ------------ on ------------, between ------------, residing at ------------ (hereinafter called the Owner) and ------------, copartners trading and doing business under the firm name of ------------, and having its place of business at ------------ (hereinafter called the Contractor),
> WHEREIN it is mutually agreed as follows:..........
>
> WITNESSETH:
>
> WHEREAS, the Seller is engaged in the sale and distribution of ------------ among its customers; and WHEREAS, the Purchaser desires to purchase the ------------ business, the good will of said business and the route and list of customers of the Seller pertaining to said business.
>
> NOW THEREFORE, in consideration of the sum of ------------ DOLLARS, each to the other in hand paid, and of the mutual covenants and conditions hereinafter contained, it is agreed as follows:
>
> IN WITNESS WHEREOF, the parties have executed this agreement.

These and other formulaic expressions specify contractual essentials such

---

4 A contract was for Peirce definitely a sign: "The dictionary is rich in words waiting to receive technical definitions as varieties of signs", he wrote (*PW*:194,1905), and in his long and rather intriguing list of examples of this, Peirce included "oath, vow, promise, contract, deed" (*PW*:194:1905).

5 Also called by Peirce a dicent symbol or dicisignificant symbol. According to the qualification rule, every symbol is a legisign. More on this in Chapter 3.

6 According to the qualification rule, every argument is a symbol. See also n. 5 above.

as consideration, subject matter, purpose, agreement of will, and future performance. They are formulated in the typical language of law, the language of authority and time-honored tradition, which means that its vocabulary is

> . . . governed by doctrines of memory, recognition and usage, defined in turn by reference to extensive and obscure etymologies, in the last resort, of "sources" of law in which words are transmitted by a dogmatics of quotation, reference, citation and specialised and restricted commentary: . . . (Goodrich 1987:178)

Determined by diachronic and synchronic intertextuality, the meaning of this language can only be apparently precise, because the complexities of legalese (such as is used in the law of contract) are instrumental in covering layer with layer, thereby obscuring meaning instead of clarifying it:

> Far from being expressly bound by any extra-linguistic content or denotative meaning, the terms are connotative and symbolic; they lend themselves to an obfuscating, rhetorical or symbolic usage, to figurative and analogical manipulations within which their actual meaning or referent is obscure. In any given instance the mobilisation of the vocabulary of contract is both a semantic and a symbolic adventure in its own right, and equally the beginning of a professional or judicial utterance which is predominantly defined by the latitude of freedom which it allows the authorised speaker. Lacking any clear denotation, the legal lexicon facilitates the directly intentional possibilities of the language it uses, its concrete instancing is intentionally rather than lexically determined. (Goodrich 1987:179-180).

This author argues that the same point can be made about legal syntax. The features enumerated in the above passage link legal language again with the category of Thirdness, in which signs are always generally applicable (i.e., usable for various purposes) and susceptible of at any time being provided with a new meaning, thereby creating a new habit. This is made possible by the arbitrary nature of the (linguistic) sign which, lacking a direct connection with the object referred to, may consequently be used to refer to any object. Thirds are non-natural and must be learned. They address themselves to the "expert" and make little or no sense to the uninitiated. This is *a fortiori* true for legal texts.

To supplement the generic nature of legal language and counteract the manifold special purposes it can be made to serve in the hands of legal experts, written contracts must anchor themselves in extralinguistic reality (legal reality and general social reality), where the origin, motive, purpose, and execution of contracts must lie. On the textual level this anchoring function is fulfilled by inserting on the blank spaces a series of necessary deictic features[7]. By this token, a proposition is, on the one hand, a truncated argument (it lacks a definite conclusion and can be contradicted) and, on the other, it may be transformed into a rheme by removing the deictic, that is indexical, entities which give it a here-and-now, a subject, and hence a coherent story-line. In a contract, the indexical features make the text applicable to a particular situation involving particular subjects. These features include place and date of the agreement, performance, etc.; names, addresses, etc. of parties; full details of duties to be performed; and penalties. Pointing to discrete spatio-temporal units in the external physical world (persons, objects, events), these indexical features serve to indicate exactly who promises whom to do what, when, and in return for what[8].

As described so far, the written contract is a concrete proposition with a built-in rheme. It offers a blueprint for future action, but gives itself no security. It builds upon the possibility in the appearance of a promise, where the quality of Firstness must remain general, that is, vague and non-committal. That this is the case was experienced by Peirce himself, as he authored a piece of embryonic contractual writing. In one of the drafts of his elaborate, but tragically and undeservedly failed, application to the then newly founded Carnegie Institution of Washington, DC, for a grant to enable him to complete the treatise on logic (scheduled by Peirce to consist of a series of thirty-six memoirs) which he had been writing for thirty years, Peirce wrote:

> As an additional or alternative security, I should suggest, supposing that other security were desired by the Executive Committee, that a contract be executed between the Carnegie Institution and me by which I should be bound to send in the memoirs with no interval between any successive two exceeding three months, unless some visitation of providence (say, a five month's illness, a conflagration, or a domestic calamity) should intervene, and even then not exceeding five months. Otherwise, I falling in this, should be bound to repay to the Carnegie Institution all money up to that time paid to me, while losing the copyrights of the printed memoirs. I would yearly furnish bonds that such money should be refunded, if failure should occur within one year. I should secure my bondsman by putting into his hands first draughts of the memoirs for the ensuing year, which though they would not be satisfactory to me, would, nevertheless, *à la rigueur* conform to the agreement. Of course, this would be but partial security. . . . Of course, in case any contract were made, the Carnegie Institution would by its

7 The reader is referred again to the text of Chapter 3, particularly to the section on Peirce's interpretant.

8 By implication, they also make clear to which persons, etc. the terms and conditions of the agreement are not applicable. On text-internal referential-cohesive features (as is the use of demonstrative pronouns), see Kurzon 1986:49-56.

> terms become bound to persist in the arrangement to the end, and to publish each memoir within, say, one year of the date of its approval. (*MS*L75A:76-78,1902).

And Peirce added here:

> I have a reputation of not finishing things. I suppose there is some basis of truth beneath it. But it has been, like every evil reputation, exaggerated out of all semblance to truth by calumny. It should be remembered that I was connected for a long time with the Coast Survey; and it will be easy for members of the committee to ascertain that office has been, at times, a veritable hot-bed of intrigue, and that I, in particular, have some times suffered great injustice there. Voluminous volumes were prepared by me for publication which I never could get printed; and then I was accused, vaguely and in intangible forms, of not getting my work ready for publication. For the truth of this (except that the accusations were made) I stand responsible. I have often made this statement. If it is not true, why am I not called upon to go ahead with the printing? (*MS*L75A:78-79,1902)

This text is certainly a human document (and a very poignant one at that), but as Peirce himself was no doubt acutely aware, it was, and still is, highly inadequate as a legal document. In fact, it is as rudimentary a contract as its truth value is weak. It is a mere rhematic indexical legisign, or rhematic symbol[9]. Of this, Peirce gave as a prototypical example the demonstrative pronoun (Peirce 1953:51;also quoted in *PW*:161), thereby indicating that it is intended to stand for and point to something more tangible. In the case of contract, it suggests and prefigures an eventual synergetic relation in the form of a real exchange of promises. As a case in point, Peirce's letter certainly said something, it expressed an intention. But it was as yet a mere suggestive idea without *quid pro quo*, a one-sided promise without legal (and, more importantly for Peirce, without economic) consequences.

The plaintive and apologetic overtones of the monologue here reflect the desperate attempt by Peirce to achieve something from the Carnegie Institution, any offer it would be able and willing to make him. As it stands, it is an attempt which is all subjective feeling and, as judgment, germinal possibility. From there to a signed real-world contract by which Peirce would actually be offered and given the desired grant, was apparently too bold a leap. Peirce's proposal was unfit to persuade the Carnegie Institution of the necessity that his project be financed: all its doubt would have to be removed and hardened into pure rationality. Peirce was unable to engage his potential sponsor into a genuine dialogue, in which his rhematic symbol could have grown to an

9 See Chapter 3 and previous notes in this Chapter.

argument --that is, the ripe judgment or assertive sign (*CP*:5.546,c.1908) prescribing rules of future conduct. Unfortunately for Peirce, a one-sided promise is nothing but a contract *manqué*.

A full-blown contractual relationship is typically not identical to a written document. While the latter serves as material evidence of the existence of the former, is its outward manifestation or, in other words, its translation, the former is the communicative act through which a legally binding contract is created. To translate an action (or rather series of actions) into a series of written signs is of course an everyday phenomenon within any verbal culture. The constant stream of printed matter which is a "natural" part of modern life, provides a running commentary upon all current events, big and small, public and private. These commentaries can in turn be commented upon "and so on *ad infinitum*" (*CP*:2.303,1901). Kevelson writes on semiosis and legal facts:

> A continuity of inquiry requires that any judgment become the ground from which further investigation may begin. Such ground may be abstracted from still further judgments, such that the initial concept in question --the law in relation to the case at hand-- may be further defined and refined. The rhetorical evidence provides a new quality, in turn to become a new fact, and in its turn, to become a new sign or representation, an interpretant of its object. The final interpretant concludes a complete process of inquiry. These brief explanatory remarks may be useful for further discussion of semiotics and contract in law. (Kevelson 1988:140)

In contract, a specific kind of semiosis is at work: one motivated and governed by the conventions of a legal system wary of anecdotal evidence (both of Firstness and Secondness) and requiring hard and reliable (that is, formal and written) proof. The law calls for Thirdness. For all its apparent finality, the written contract is, however, still one interpretant of the actual agreement, or meeting of the minds, preceding it. It is in turn a two-faced phenomenon: it is both a trimmed version of the previous consensus, stripped of the emotional and factual sideshows which may accompany bargains between flesh-and-blood (as well as institutional) partners, and inevitably stripped of some informational content; and, at the same time, it is also a version burdened with the legal clichés and other code-related niceties which make it fit into the pre-established doctrinal grid of the law[10]. This is one important reason why the law requires

---

10 See further Fisch's Chapter on "Justice Holmes, the prediction theory of law, and pragmatism", in which Fisch quotes the following pragmatically-inspired remark on contract, by the famous American legal theoretician: "You see how the vague circumference of the notion of duty shrinks and at the same time grows more precise when we wash it with cynical acid and expel everything except the object of our study, the operations of the law" (Fisch 1986:8). In a note, Fisch clarifies this sentence by saying that it is "in the astringent tradition of Hobbes,

that transactions, particularly business contracts, be conducted in good faith (*bona fide*) and according to standards of fair dealing. No linguistic sign can be wholly determinate as to its meaning; and to counteract indeterminacy of meaning a fundamental requirement is, on Peirce's view, honesty:

> . . . honest people, when not joking, intend to make the meaning of their words determinate, so that there shall be no latitude of interpretation at all. That is to say, the character of their meaning consists in the implications and non-implications of their words; and they intend to fix what is implied and what is not implied. They believe that they succeed in doing so, and if their chat is about the theory of numbers, perhaps they may. But the further their topics are from such presciss, or "abstract", subjects, the less possibility is there of such precision of speech. (*CP*:5.447,1905)

The kind of translation described above is the reverse of what Jakobson called "intersemiotic translation, or *transmutation*" and which he defined as "an interpretation of verbal signs by means of signs of nonverbal sign systems" (Jakobson 1959:233;1971b:261)[11]. A proviso for making this analogy is that the actions causing the verbal translation form a coherent sign system; in so far as this is considered to be true, the analogy works. However, it is only true from the vantage point of the formal addresser of the message in the written interpretant-sign. And the voice (or better, voiceover) we hear in the written contract is the voice of Authority, the voice of the Law. From the perspective of the other, explicit parties involved, the message may therefore come across as an oblique, distorted, or otherwise overcoded version of the actual agreement of the minds.

Jakobson's intersemiotic translation is by its very nature imprecise and impressionistic; from linguistic signs, Thirds, it produces rhematic signs, i.e., Thirds in their aspect of Firstness, a slackened, softer version of language's primary Thirdness. This corresponds to Peirce's degeneracy[12]. In the case of contract, almost the reverse is true. While pretending to express the intention of the parties and manifesting the will on which it is based, the written contract tends to take advantage of the interpretational latitude of both the nonverbal code (in this case a sign of Secondness) and of the verbal code. To translate what is originally a Second into a (verbal) sign of Thirdness belonging to a

---

Bentham, and Austin, who were Holmes's trinity. 'The light of human minds is perspicuous words, but by exact definitions first *snuffed* and *purged* from ambiguity.' Cf. Chauncey Wright's nihilism --'an *exorcism* of the vague'-- and especially James's 1898 lecture on the '*shrinkage*' that follows application of the principle of pragmatism" (Fisch 1986:13,n.5).

11 See Chapter 8, for a fuller discussion of Jakobson's views on intersemiotic translation as seen from a Peircean viewpoint.

12 More on this in Merrell 1991:76-79 and Gorlée 1990.

legal subcode, means to impose additional constraints upon parties, thereby hardening their original positions. Not only does the written contract formalize past and present events: it also gives binding rules for conduct in the future. This is generacy, the opposite of degeneracy.

The projection into the future implies that the written contract, as compared to the primary agreement, is a forward-translation, --in Peirce's terminology, "an equivalent sign, or perhaps a more developed sign" (*CP*:2.228,c.1897). To the degree that it is an extrapolation from the actual will of the parties (albeit, it is hoped, a fair and reasonable extrapolation from it), a written contract is an equivalent[13] interpretant-sign. But in terms of the two codes involved, it must be understood as a clarified if possibly biased translation of it. And it is definitely still a non-ultimate, evolving, and fallible interpretant-sign, another fact of law capable of being again interpreted. The translation from (forms of) degeneracy into (forms of) generacy is a pragmatic phenomenon which will return throughout this Chapter. It will manifest itself in all its many contractual guises as translation from (mostly precontractual) subjective feeling, Firstness, via intersubjectively acting Secondness to objective, rational Thirdness.

Contract as speech-act

In order to have force of law, a contract needs to be ratified. Ratification or, in Peirce's terms, assertion of a proposition, is a semiotic act in which parties make themselves responsible for the terms of the agreement. This form of guarantee serves to "distinguish promises from firm statements of intention and emphatic predictions" (Searle 1969:46). All three are verbal acts creating expectations; but a contractual promise is by far the firmest assertion, the one with the highest truth-value; because in it the promisor intentionally invokes a convention whose function it is to give moral and legal grounds for another to expect the promised performance. To see the contract as rooted in promise has led language-philosophers to regard the act of promising as a speech-act.

Peirce's one-sided, and therefore inchoate and abortive, contractual act, discussed above, was infected by what speech-act theoreticians call an "infelicity"[14], one which can affect all "illocutionary acts". In speech-act theory, "locutionary acts" (such as saying or writing "It's raining") limit themselves to the mere uttering of a verbal message, regardless of whether it produces an intended effect upon the (possible) receiver of the message or not. "Perlocutionary acts" (such as commands, promises, and questions) aim at

---

13 More on equivalence in Chapter 9.

14 Austin dubbed this kind of infelicity a "hitch". See Austin 1962:36-37.

causing any contingent practical consequence of the message, in the form of an action or reaction by the speaker or hearer. Last in this division come illocutionary acts (for instance, "Hereby I baptize you in the name of the Father, the Son, and the Holy Spirit", "This is to appoint you as sales manager of our Amsterdam branch office"), which communicate the special intention underlying the utterance and are aimed at making the hearer recognize this intention.

The triad of speech-acts fits the various configurations of Peirce's theory of signs, and is prefigured in Peirce's own application of it to linguistic signs[15]. The simple declaration or spontaneous utterance would then, in its sign-interpretant relation, correspond to a rhematic sign, representing the Firstness of Thirdness. The two-sided directive speech-act, focused on the immediate effect it produces upon the hearer, would correspond to a proposition, or Secondness of Thirdness. And the cooperative language-act through which the hearer is made to perceive and believe the purpose or mediate effect with which the speaker has endowed the utterance, would correspond to a Peircean argument, or genuine Third.

A contract must be understood as a relational speech-act; consequently, it can never be a mere locutionary act. Now a promise, in its simplest form, is a perlocutionary act in which a speaker manifests his or her intention, based upon his or her volition, to perform some act in the future. This would make a contract a dual promise from some speaker to some hearer and vice versa, a double perlocutionary act. However, a contractual promise is more than two promises amalgamated. While the performance in the future is no doubt a perlocutionary effect of at least one promise, contractual acts are themselves illocutionary acts in which a future exchange is foreshadowed, almost magically[16], by a present, symbolic exchange. What makes the contractual promise special, what gives it legal consequences, is the third element carried by it --the clue for its correct interpretation. It consists in the joint declaration's special purpose, the legal consequences that enhance what would otherwise be a trivial and inconsequential transaction.

Following Searle's (1976) canonical classification of illocutionary acts, but refining and redefining it, Hancher[17] (1979) offers a comprehensive

15 For Peirce as a precursor of speech-act theory, see Brock 1981a and 1981b, Hilpinen 1982, and Ferriani 1987, on whose insights I have, when necessary, drawn.

16 See Hancher 1979:3. On the magical aspects of the contract model of cultural psychology, see Lotman 1990:254ff.

17 Hancher notes (1979:2,n.2) that Searle's 1976 article was also published elsewhere two other times, in slightly different forms.

revision of it, which considers contracting as a reciprocal illocutionary act, one requiring two (or more) participants instead of one[18]. Hancher concludes that

> . . . many important performative speech acts are not, as Searle would have it, simple declarations. Some, like offering and nondirective appointing, are commissive directives --that is, precooperative speech acts. Others are cooperative speech acts -- cooperative declarations, as in the case of gifts, or cooperative commissives, as in the case of bilateral contracts. (Hancher 1979:12)

The cooperative commissive act of contracting is a joint venture preceded by, and containing, precooperative commissive directive acts of offering and accepting[19]. In other words: the first, initiating party cannot reasonably expect the second party to commit him-, her-, or itself to a contract until the first party has advanced a promise setting out his, her, or its own obligations. If nothing is offered in exchange, the essence of a *quid pro quo* or consideration, the bargain by which both parties agree to limit their choice of future behavior, is lacking, and there is no legal contract. Each contractual speech-act contains really two prior speech-acts in which speaker and hearer assume alternating roles of promisor and promisee[20].

From proposition to assertion

As already seen[21], in Peirce's terminology a contract must be referred to as a declarative proposition or dicent symbol[22] which, through the act of assertion, is upgraded to an argument or argumentative symbolic legisign.

A linguistic proposition can be a sentence or any combination of

---

18 Searle (1976) previously identified five basic kinds of illocutionary acts: "representatives", "directives", "commissives", "expressives", and "declarations", besides a subclass, "representative declarations". All of these speech-acts involve one speaker.

19 Directives are, according to Searle (1976:11), attempts "by the speaker to get the hearer to do something". This includes suggesting, proposing, ordering, and commanding to do something. Commissives are "those illocutionary acts whose point is to commit the speaker . . . to some future course of action" (Searle 1976:11). This includes promising, guaranteeing, and solemnly vowing to do something.

20 In Jakobson's semiotic terminology (as put forth in his famous 1960 essay), a contract would be a form of verbal communication involving an addresser and an addressee who exchange a message in which the primary functions are referential (emphasizing the cognitive, informational aspect of language) and conative (oriented toward the addressee, indicating what he or she must do).

21 See notes 5 and 6 above.

22 Also called by Peirce dicisignificant symbol. See Chapter 3. Without making any attempt to reconstruct and analyze here Peirce's theory of propositions, which is not so clear as could be wished, I may instead refer the reader to Brock 1981b.

sentences functioning as a meaningful whole, commonly called "text"[23]. Accordingly, a contract as a written document is, on Peirce's view, a proposition, a "Dicisign that is a Symbol" (*CP*:2.320,c.1902), a "Third attached to a Second" (*MS*L75:324,1902). Despite its dual nature, its "essence does not lie in its being compound, but on the contrary upon its being asserted or at least conceived to be asserted" (*MS*499:29,1906); and according to one of Peirce's many other definitions, a proposition is "A sign which though *calculated* to produce belief, that is, though it has the character of a *possible* assertion, is nevertheless not necessarily so *intended*, not necessarily *used* toward that end" (*MS*200:51,1907). Peirce underscored that a sharp distinction be made between the two: a proposition is not an assertion[24] but it is "assertible", a sign "capable of being asserted" (*CP*:8.337,1904). While, in semiotic terms, a proposition, "separately, or independently, indicates its object", an assertion is "a sign which separately shows what interpretant it is intended to determine" (*NEM*4:242,c.1904), thereby giving it a particular reference to Thirdness. In this process what was originally a sign of fact "capable of truth or falsehood" (*CP*:8.337,1904) is transmogrified into a "rationally persuasive sign" (*CP*:2.309,c.1902), one that has acquired, besides "a degree of energy" (*MS*L75:324,1902) (its Secondness), logical status (Thirdness). Peirce made it clear that "It is not *words* that are "asserted", but *facts*" (*MS*699:3,1911); and by being asserted, the factual proposition, which Peirce regarded as empirically verifiable, becomes a sign of truth.

While Peirce wrote that "the assertion is made by the utterer in a living effort to make its interpreter believe it true" (*MS*646:16,1910), he also made it clear that an assertion is "no *thought* but is an *act* related to the thought" (*MS*499:30,1906). Peirce's prototype of the assertion is the syllogism. In order to create it, the proposition must be placed in a particular assertory mood or mode of assertion, which gives its content a particular force with public (i.e., social and, in the case of contract, legal) repercussions. In a letter of January 22, 1905 to his friend William James, Peirce offered the following analogy, his favorite one:

> Now an assertion belongs to the class of phenomena like going before a notary and making an affidavit, executing a deed, signing a note, of which the essence is that one

23 In my project *Reading the Signs: A Peirce-Based Text Semiotics* (in progress) I examine the concept of text in detail.

24 Every assertion includes, of course, a proposition.

> voluntarily puts oneself into a situation in which penalties will be incurred unless some proposition is true. (*CP*:8.313,1905)[25]

To assert a proposition means "a voluntary self-subjection to penalties" (*NEM*4:249,c.1904); in more generic terms, it is

> . . . an exhibition of the fact that one subjects oneself to the penalties visited on a liar if the proposition asserted is not true. An act of judgment is the self-recognition of a belief; and a belief consists in the acceptance of a proposition as a basis of conduct deliberately. (*PW*:34,1904)

What binds together the act of assertion and the act of contracting is, first, the assumption of responsibility and, second, the idea of promise made against a background of shared beliefs and intentions. To assert a proposition is to make oneself responsible for it (vs. to command a proposition, which is to make the interlocutor responsible for it), and to sign a contract is to enter into a relation involving mutual rights and responsibilities. Peirce wrote that

> To make yourself responsible means that if on a certain defined occasion a certain definitely described phenomenon does not emerge then you confer upon somebody a right which he otherwise would not have. (*MS*499:30,1906)

Now this is a remark upon the assertive act; but it could equally be a description of the idea governing contract. To assume responsibility is to make a public promise in the present, a promise to do (or refrain from doing) something in the future. This pertains to the part of the contract that is future-oriented; and in so far it may perhaps be called its forward-translation. At the same time, however, a contract needs to be rooted in a "past" of shared purposes and experiences, norms and values, and even a shared theory of the world, --unexpressed in the text of the contract, but presupposed in it. In a manner of speaking, a contract must be susceptible of being back-translated into this more general cultural context[26]. Without such a common (or at least

---

25 See also, e.g., the following quotation: "If a man desires to assert anything very solemnly, he takes such steps as will enable him to go before a magistrate or notary and take a binding oath to it. Taking an oath is not mainly an event of the nature of a setting forth, *Vorstellung*, or representing. It is not merely saying, but is *doing*. The law, I believe, calls it an 'act'. At any rate, it would be followed by very real effects, in case the substance of what is asserted should be proved untrue" (*CP*:5.546,c.1908).

26 This corresponds to Wittgenstein's notion of "forms of life". See for this Chapter 5, especially the section on "Culture".

partly common) background no meaningful social interaction is possible. Mutual comprehension is the "implicit contract" (Greimas and Courtés 1982:59) which must precede any successful contract and is crucial to the whole doctrine of good faith[27].

The similarities between Peirce's theory of the proposition (or, to put it more broadly, Peirce's linguistics[28]) and speech-act theory are clear. See, for instance, the following typical quotations from Peirce, which highlight his pragmatic approach to linguistic signs --the Wittgensteinian ways in which they can be used as tools, without losing their basic identity:

> A proposition may be stated [expressed] without being asserted. I may state it to myself and worry as to whether I shall embrace or reject it, being dissatisfied with the idea of doing either. In that case, I doubt the proposition. I may state the proposition to you and endeavor to stimulate you to advise me whether to accept or reject it: in which case I put it interrogatively. I may state it to myself; and be deliberately satisfied to base my action on it whenever occasion may arise: in which case I judge it. I may state it to you: and assume a responsibility for it: in which case I assert it. I may impose the responsibility of its agreeing with the truth upon you: in which case I command it. All of these are different moods in which that same proposition may be stated. (*NEM*4:39,1902)

> One and the same proposition may be affirmed, denied, judged, doubted, inwardly inquired into, put as a question, wished, asked for, effectively commanded, taught or merely expressed, and does not thereby become a different proposition. (*NEM*4:248,c.1904)

> . . . the meaning of a sentence . . . not only remains the same in whatever language it is expressed, but is also the same whether it be believed or doubted, asserted (by somebody's making himself responsible for it,) commanded (by somebody's expressing that he holds another responsible for it,) or just as a question (when somebody

---

27 In conversation, acoustic and optic messages (such as eye contact and verbal forms of feedback) broadcast wittingly or unwittingly, allow the interlocutors to monitor whether communication is succeeding or not. In written communication such direct clues about mutual agreement are largely absent; consequently, misunderstandings and conflicts can easily arise. Following Greimas and Courtés (1979:70; here quoted from the English translation, 1982:59) (who again apply Jakobson's well-known 1960 notion), '[i]t is indeed necessary to recognize, hidden under the contract, this 'phatic communication' which constitutes the necessary and preliminary undergirding for any communication and which seems to involve both a tension (a well-disposed or a mistrustful expectation) and a relaxing (as a kind of response to the expectation)".

28 Only in recent years have Peirce's numerous but largely unknown writings on general-linguistic topics become the object of serious study. See Rauch and Carr (eds.) 1980, Shapiro 1983, Pharies 1985, Rauch 1986, and Rethoré 1988.

> expresses an attempt to induce another to make himself responsible for it.) . . . (*MS*L75b:396,1902)

Apropos of the assertive sign (i.e., the assertible sign as it is asserted), Peirce stated that "it is to be understood that proposition, judgment, and belief are logically equivalent (though in other respects different)" (*MS*789:2,n.d.)[29], thereby implying they can be logically derived from one another and must be considered as successive stages in a semiosic chain:

> . . . an assertion involves an endless series of enunciations, or at any rate, two; namely, the assertion involves the enunciation asserted and also the enunciation asserting it. And this asserting enunciation is itself asserted. (*MS*599:18,c.1902)

In fact, there exists, at least potentially, an endless series, and an endless variety, of propositions asserted[30]. Assertive acts generate different signs; but their meaning or informational content (Peirce's dynamical object) remains in essence unchanged. Each of them acts as interpretant, or translation, for the one preceding it, for the utterance to which it gives a special purpose. Taken together, they show the multiple ways in which one and the same utterance can be intended to signify. This (self-)generative complex of speech events amounts to semiosis.

Contractual semiosis

In his essay on "The classification of cooperative illocutionary acts", which supported my argument on the contract as speech-act, Hancher makes a distinction which is also central to the semiotic view on contract which was advanced by Peirce. Hancher writes:

> It is necessary to distinguish *cooperative* acts from *multiple* speech acts and *collective* speech acts. If two persons simultaneously pledge allegiance to the flag, there are two different speech acts under way --here called "multiple" speech acts. If one person speaks on another's behalf as well as on his own (e.g., "We accept your invitation"), or if two persons sign the same letter, the speech act is a "collective" one. . . . There are multiple speech acts when a congregation sings a hymn or says a prayer that is cast, explicitly or implicitly, in the first person singular; there is a collective speech act when it sings a hymn or says a prayer cast in the first person plural. In all of these cases the fact that there is more than one speaker does not matter to the nature of the speech

---

29 Chapter 9 contains a more detailed account of Peirce's view on equivalence.

30 Analogously, there exists an infinite number of language-games. The three-way affinities between Wittgenstein's doctrine of language-games, speech-act theory, and Peirce's theory of signs can only be cursorily touched upon here. For the similarities between Peirce and Wittgenstein, see Chapter 5, as well as Gorlée 1989a,1989b.

> actbeing performed, whether it be pledging, asserting, petitioning, or whatever. But when two or more persons join in a cooperative speech act, such as contracting or voting, the fact that there is more than one speaker is not accidental but essential to the very nature of the act. (Hancher 1979:12)

The point which Hancher makes here squares nicely with Peirce's explicit mention of the contract as a schematic example of the Thirdness of triadic processes. Peirce argued that in genuine Thirdness the three elements, or terms, must be intrinsically connected:

> Now let us consider the triad, A makes a contract with C. To say that A signs the document D and C signs the document D, no matter what the contents of that document, does not make a contract. The contract lies in the intent. And what is the intent? It is that certain conditional rules shall govern the conduct of A and of C. There is no positive fact in this; it is only conditional and intentional. Still less, if possible, is there any mere monadic quality. It has reference to conditions of experience, involving existence, involving dyadic fact. It may be said that it is a psychical fact. This is in so far true, that a psychical fact is involved; but there is no intent unless something be intended; and that which is intended cannot be covered by any facts; it goes beyond anything that can ever be done or have happened, because it extends over the whole breath of a general condition; and a complete list of the possible cases is absurd. From its very nature, no matter how far specification has gone, it can be carried further; and the general condition covers all that completable possibility. (*CP*:1.475,c.1896)

Peirce touched in this passage upon several aspects of the genuinely triadic sign-relation. First, that it is irreducible. Second, that the intent is the third element of the triad. Third, that it is characterized by conditional futurity. Fourth, that it aims at determination. Fifth, that it is in principle infinite. Let us briefly consider these features of semiosis, taking them more or less *seriatim*.

As opposed to Peirce's example of the thoughtless flipping of a stone and that stone's striking some other person (*CP*:1.366,1890-1891) and other degenerate phenomena[31], a genuinely triadic relation can, on Peirce's view, not be broken into dyads or monads without losing an essential, namely the mind or third element connecting the sign with its object. Analogously, a contract comes into existence through a meeting of the minds (called, in legal terms, *consensus ad idem*) resulting from some *quid pro quo* maneuvering and again resulting in the intent of the contracting parties. They infuse this element into the respective triadic sub-relations of which they are terms; and together they infuse it in the actual contracting relation. This rational, cognitive intent (or intention) acts both as a Third (built upon the Secondness of willing and the

---

31 See my article on degeneracy, Gorlée 1990.

Firstness of feeling) and as the third element of the contractual sign-relation, where it indicates the common purpose, design, or resolve with which parties have agreed to act. At the outset this common purpose is still a general, a vague idea[32], but it is susceptible of being determined in the course of the different semioses in which it engages. Starting from its translation into the making of an explicit offer and subsequently into a written form, this idea undergoes a series of semiosic transformations, necessary for its further development into a genuine sign of law.

For the harmonious evolvement of the content of the contract *qua* sign, the intentional agency needs to be translated into future action[33]. This necessity is one implication of the pragmatic maxim[34]: the "effects that might conceivably have practical bearings" (*CP*:5.402;*W*3:266,1878) mean, in the case of contract, that its effects must be connected to the real world, where they manifest themselves in actions. The meaning-potentiality carried by the contract is actualized and deployed through controlled sign-action in the future. Hence Peirce's empiricism allows for verification. In 1905, Peirce reworded his pragmatic maxim in semiotic language, thus:

> The entire intellectual purport of any symbol consists in the total of all general modes of rational conduct which, conditionally upon all the possible different circumstances and desires, would ensue upon the acceptance of the symbol. (*CP*:5.438,1905)

Applied to the contractual situation, this means that the (symbolic) contract, once "accepted" (that is, duly signed, and its truth in the future asserted, affirmed) is intended by the parties to reproduce and translate itself in forms of

---

32 Fried states that : "It is a truism in the philosophy of language that in interpreting a person's words we are not guessing at the hidden but determined content of some list of meanings in the speaker's head. Rather our concerns particularize, render concrete, inchoate meanings. . . Similarly in contract law there is a vaguely marked boundary between interpreting what was agreed to and interpolating terms to which the parties in all probability would have agreed but did not" (Fried 1980:60). This author traces this idea back to Wittgenstein *PI*:1:138-326, its "fons et origo" (Fried 1980:145,n.12). For one instance, see Wittgenstein's remarks upon the "connexion between the act of intending and the thing intended" (*PI*:1:197).

33 In reference to futurity, in his essay on "Practical and theoretical beliefs", Peirce drew an interesting analogy between constitutional law, the law of contract, and the scope of human thought-action: "Now an ex post facto law is forbidden by the Constitution of the United States of America, but an ex post facto contract is forbidden by the constitution of things. A man cannot promise what the past shall have been, if he tries" (*CP*:5.543,c.1902).

34 See Chapter 3, particularly the section on Peirce's pragmati(ci)sm. The pragmatic maxim, in its early (1878) formulation, goes as follows: "Consider what effects that might conceivably have practical bearings, we conceive the object of our conception to have. Then, our conception of these effects is the whole of our conception of the object" (*CP*:5.402;*W*3:266,1878).

rule-bound behavior. This behavior consists in a series of dynamical interpretants, each of which is a (still partial) realization of its terms. Directed, in a conditional way, toward some future time, and guided by the principle of "fixation of belief", the contract will eventually achieve its point of fulfillment, at which time the abstract facts, promised and thus expected, are supposed to have materialized in factual ones, bringing relaxation to the contractual relation. The ultimate (or, more realistically, still non-ultimate) logical interpretant then produced is the *moment suprême* when contractual performance is due, the orgastic moment when all intentions must be realized and all purposes attained. Once all obligations have been discharged, all tasks performed, and all debts canceled, the *summum bonum* of law and generality has been achieved. At the same time, however, through the "execution" of the contract --both its completion and its death-- , an Edenic situation is restored: precontractual, pristine, unburdened, free[35] --and open to assuming new responsibilities, if so desired.

Utterer and interpreter in translational semiosis

> . . . signs require at least two *Quasi-minds*: a *Quasi-utterer* and a *Quasi-interpreter*; and although these two are at one (*i.e.*, *are* one mind) in the sign itself, they must nevertheless be distinct. In the sign they are, so to say, *welded*. Accordingly, it is not merely a fact of human Psychology, but a necessity of Logic, that every logical evolution of thought should be dialogic. (*CP*:4.551,1906)[36]

Peirce, the anti-psychological and anti-individualistic logician, expressly de-emphasized a personal utterer and/or interpreter in semiosis of all kinds, and preferred to see them as non-individual minds or, in his terminology, quasi-

---

35 Compare this to: "What the world was to Adam on the day he opened his eyes to it, before he had drawn any distinctions, or had become conscious of his own existence --that is first, present, immediate, fresh, new, initiative, original, spontaneous, free, vivid, conscious, and evanescent" (*CP*:1.357,1890-1891)

36 On Peirce's dialogic concept of thought and language, see, e.g., *MS*1334:45,1905, *MS*292:11,c.1906, *MS*498:25,1906, and *CP*:6.338,c.1909.

minds[37]. There is no place for a specific utterer nor for a specific interpreter in what is a triadic (sign-object-interpretant) structure. Peirce acknowledged their existence, considered them as necessary features, but he placed them on the periphery of semiosis. This idea seems to have slowly crystallized in his mind and only became unambiguously clear in his later, mature thought. On December 23, 1908, Peirce wrote to Lady Welby:

> I define a Sign as anything which is so determined by something else, called its Object, and so determines an effect upon a person, which effect I call its Interpretant, that the latter is thereby mediately determined by the former. My insertion of "upon a person" is a sop to Cerberus, because I despair of making my own broader conception understood. (*PW*:80-81,1908)[38]

This point (Peirce's "sop to Cerberus") is also nicely illustrated in the following quotation from the important *MS*318:

> The action of a sign generally takes place between two parties, the *utterer* and the *interpreter*. They need not be persons; for a chamelion and many kinds of insects and even plants make their livings by uttering signs, and lying signs at that. Who is the utterer of signs of the weather, which are not remarkably veracious, always? However, every sign certainly conveys something of the general nature of thought, if not from a mind, yet from some repository of ideas, or significant forms, and if not to a person, yet to something capable of somehow "catching on" . . . : that is of receiving not merely a physical, nor even merely a psychical dose of energy, but a significant meaning. (*MS*318:205-206,1907)[39]

---

37 See, for the basics of this, Chapter 3 (particularly the section on "Semiosis"); and also, for the consequences of this for translation, Chapter 9 (particularly the section on "The role of the translator").

38 For the "sop to Cerberus" as a sign of the general nature of Peirce's theory of signs, see Fisch 1986:342-344.

39 Despite appearances to the contrary, Peirce's mentalistic terminology does not contradict his repeated statements that his doctrine of signs is not psychologically based; nor is it at variance with Peirce's own early work in experimental psychology. This point is driven home by Ransdell: "Peirce's use of mentalistic terminology does not usually indicate a shift to a psychological perspective, because these terms did not bear the meaning for him that they usually bear for the contemporary reader. In his later writings, when psychology was beginning to flourish, Peirce sometimes uses such terms with the awareness that they might be misconstrued, but with the idea that others probably will grasp little of his meaning unless they first understand him psychologistically. The purpose of his special semiotic terminology was that of making it possible to break out of a psychologistic stance toward meaning-phenomena. His dilemma --on the horns of which he impaled himself repeatedly-- was that if he defined his terms in a non-psychologistic way no one would understand him at all because his approach was too alien to the prevailing ways of thinking; whereas if he defined them psychologistically his

In Peirce's de-individualized universe of signs, human mind-activity has a reduced impact. To distinguish between Peirce's quasi-minds and to give them distinct roles in the formal sign-relation, the utterer must be considered as closely linked to, and determined by, the object, and the interpreter, by the interpretant. The former, or sign-maker, itself a sign, is one presemiosic (or better, extrasemiosic) connection between the sign and its object; the latter, or sign-user, also a sign, connects the sign and the interpretant-sign. In this quality utterer and interpreter are allowed to play secondary, though implicit and abstract, roles in what Peirce saw as a self-generative processuality independent of the human mind.

Semiosis, then, would operate as follows. Chronologically and logically, its "first" instance would take place between an object (with implied utterer 1), a sign signifying the object, and the interpretant (with implied interpreter 1) bringing the sign and its object into a meaningful relation. The object informs and influences (determines, in Peirce's terminology) the sign, through the utterer, and the sign determines again the interpretant through the interpreter. Next, the interpretant (or rather, one of the interpretants) would again become a sign and set into motion the "second" semiosis, where it (the semioticized sign) would be placed in a relation with the object (with implied utterer 2). The object here is also semioticized, but refers back to the same, "first" object. This produces the "second" interpretant (with implied interpreter 2), and so on, until sign and object would be identical, and all semiosis would come to a standstill. The sign would at that time have become a transparent vehicle of meaning, which would enable the object to be known unmediated. Indeed, with the terms of a formal-logical sign relation taking central stage, utterer and interpreter would become largely redundant entities. They are acted upon by the object and the sign, respectively; they act upon the sign and the interpretant-sign, respectively; but they are themselves unable to directly influence the threefold sign-object-interpretant sign relation. Were this not so, their mental activity would impair the efficiency of sign activity rather than help it achieve its ultimate goal[40].

---

readers might gain *some* idea, but a badly distorted one. One cannot read Peirce with any real understanding without a grasp of the desperate communicational situation he was in and the effect this had on how he expressed his ideas" (Ransdell 1980:183-184,n.12).

40 Ransdell describes the role (or better, attitude) of what he calls the sign observer in semiosis thus: ". . . the sign-interpretant process, construed as one in which the observer is trying to observe intelligently, is one which involves *strategies* and *techniques* of observation of the signs and their sign actions, and the symbolic sign in particular has to be understood in terms of the appropriate strategy for the observation of it. In fact, it can only be differentiated from nonsymbolic signs with reference to that strategy. Thus while an iconic sign can be

Both an utterer and an interpreter must be somehow subsumed under the semiosic act of (human) translation (in its three Jakobsonian guises involving language, that is symbolic signs). In translation they participate conjointly, if in reversed order (first the interpreter, then the utterer), as the two sides of one and the same translator. To further complicate the situation (or, in Peirce's view, to simplify it) there are, in tandem with this translator (both utterer and interpreter), at least two additional agents at work: one utterer and one interpreter. Their influence is camouflaged, perhaps, but undeniable:

> We may say that the *sign* is *moulded* to the *meaning* in the *quasi-mind* that *utters* it, where it was, *virtually* at least, . . . already an ingredient of *thought*. But *thought* being itself a *sign* the *meaning* must have been *conveyed* to that *quasi-mind*, from some anterior *utterer* of the *thought*, of which the *utterer* of the *moulded sign* had been the interpreter. The *meaning* of the *moulded sign* being *conveyed* to its *interpreter*, became the *meaning* of a *thought* in that *quasi-mind*; and as there *conveyed* in a *thought-sign* requires an *interpreter* of the *moulded sign* becoming the *utterer* of this new thought-sign. (*MS*318:206-207,1907)[41]

It is no doubt true that, in translation *sensu stricto*, the interpretation of the primary sign precedes the uttering of a translated version, so that an interpreter must have done his or her work before an utterer can start doing his or hers. Yet logically, the interpreter of the primary sign is again preceded by the utterer, if any, of it; and the utterer of the translated sign is in turn followed by some interpreter of it; and so on, both backward and forward[42]. Though the "added" utterer and interpreter are, in translational semiosis, bracketed and reduced to backstage status, they are nevertheless logical elements in successive semiosic events, and they help create hierarchical relations between them.

Translation as contractual semiosis

In the above pages, the phenomenon of contract in law has been analyzed

---

defined in terms of de facto qualitative likeness to its object, and an indexical sign in terms of the de facto power of presencing another phenomenal object, the symbolic sign can be defined only relative to how it is to be treated or regarded by the sign observer (interpreter, reader, audience). Its unique sign value as symbolic is wholly dependent upon its being treated in a certain way by the intelligent sign observer in the observational process. (This is a shorthand way of speaking: it does *not* mean that we must introduce an external mind as an independent factor; it means rather that a certain reflexive operation must be introduced into the analysis of the sign-interpretation sequence whenever a symbolic sign as such is supposed to occur" (Ransdell 1980:175)

41 On the hand-written manuscript page, this is immediately followed by Peirce's exclamation, "Enough of the italics!" (*MS*318:207,1907).

42 These terms are used here metaphorically, both in a temporal and a logical sense.

semiotically, as a series of translations, as different but equivalent interpretive events. Also, the reduced role Peirce gave to utterer and interpreter in the sign-process has been touched upon in its consequences for translational semiosis. These considerations have, in the previous section, led to a description of the process of semiosis, in which the communicative parties were subsumed under the terms of the sign-action. This model is wholly applicable to the process of translation in the more specific, Jakobsonian sense, which presupposes a translating mind functioning both as receiver of the primary sign and as emitter of the translated sign, the end and beginning of two separate but linked chains of semiosis. Pursuing this line of thought, in the last part of this Chapter I propose to complement my analysis with some remarks upon translation as a semiosic activity with markedly contractual features[43].

Regarded contractually (and thus, as shown above, semiosically), translation is a self-imposed, well-described duty for the future, a promise to perform a task, that is, to do something, and to do it "together". The two sides of the translator's professional self must be *ad idem*, prepared to unreservedly engage themselves in what is a joint and not an individual enterprise. In the division of labor, which must be (implicitly) agreed upon here, each of the translator's *personae* must do half (or rather "half") of the same job. Both have different contracts to respect, different skills and competences, different missions to fulfill. This creates between them, and between both of them and the "obstacle" facing them, an indexical relationship, of physical and logical contiguity, which implies that the element of symbolic equivalence --the *quid pro quo* which is an essential feature of contract-- is weakened. In translation real exchange "degenerates" into complementarity.

In such cooperative-contractual activity as is translation, no (hypothetical) nonperformance claim against the other can be raised *a posteriori*. In the actual performance they take turns instead of having separate shares. But not only must they physically and mentally operate in one spatiotemporal context; also, linked by a feedback mechanism, they are almost forced to continuously interact and make themselves conjointly responsible for the work done. The patient translator (the interpreter of the primary sign) is an exponent of (determined by) the object, the agent translator (the utterer of the translated sign) enjoys a margin of indeterminacy, of "poetic" freedom, in the interpretant. At the same time the work of the translator *sensu stricto* (the translator-utterer in the terminology used above) must build, logically and temporally, upon that of the translator-interpreter, which is again followed by a performance of the

43 The subject of translation as a perlocutionary and/or illocutionary speech-act is addressed in van den Broeck 1989.

former, and so on (at least ideally[44]) until the translation has been completed.

The agreement between the two "halves" within the same translator is typically created in a strictly nonformulaic and even nonformal fashion. Far from being reduced into writing, with no oral manifestation and not even an informal act which can be deemed to document the existence of a contract between the translational partners, the agreement must be considered as not intended by them to be complete, explicit, and operative as such. If there is a proposal made by the one party and accepted by the other, it is neither clear nor unambiguous. In fact, its very vagueness underscores that the translational contract is, in essence, formless and depends, for its realization, upon the private desire of the parties; and desire, if not expressed in spontaneous action, cannot be enforced.

Like the contractual relation, the semiotic structure of translational phenomena is rooted in a form of social organization, namely in dialogue. To be sure, translation implies a rather rudimentary dialogue, namely the inner dialogue of self with self, the ongoing dialogic interaction, within the translator, between the interpreter (receiver, sign-user) and the utterer (emitter, sign-maker). Peirce said that "all deliberate meditation, or thinking proper, takes the form of a dialogue. The person divides himself into two parties which endeavour to persuade each other" (*MS*498:25,1906). In the same paragraph he also quoted the "vernacular phrase . . . 'I says to myself, says I'" (*CP*:5.546,c.1908) in order to illustrate that "solitary dialectic is still of the nature of dialogue", meaning that "here too there is contained an element of assuming responsibility, of 'taking the consequences'" (*CP*:5.546,c.1908). By the same token, translation somehow involves "an element closely analogous to *assertion*" (*CP*:5.46,c.1908), although here the assertion typically lacks the outward social dimension which is its leading feature in genuine contractual relations. The agreement in translation is not publicized and has no legal consequences.

Back to translation as semiosis. Translation is mainly concentrated upon the second semiosic instance in the more complex (and in fact endless) process analyzed in the previous section of this Chapter. However, for a correct perspective upon its possible implications and extrapolations, it is crucial to situate translation upon an ongoing continuum of meaning-producing events, a chain of successive semioses (strictly translational and otherwise) from which one or more episodes may be set apart to be studied in isolation. Ransdell stresses this point, thus: "There are [in semiosis] only signs produced by signs and producing signs, with no absolute starting point and no absolute stopping

44 In actual translation practice there will be a great deal of overlapping.

point" (Ransdell 1980:165). Ransdell's remarks are equally true for translation. A text-sign does not appear *ex nihilo*, but is the result of other, previous signs. And complementary to this backward-intertextuality (infinite regress toward the object), the actual living text-sign produces in its turn interpretant upon interpretant, translation upon translation without end, each of them updating the available information upon the object, but sooner or later becoming itself outdated. This is forward-intertextuality --the infinite, creative, multidimensional, and labyrinthine progress toward the final interpretation:

> The sign-interpretant series is not a simple linear chain. It is rather to be thought of as a complex of initially independent sequences which join with one another, branch, join with still others, branch, and so on, such that by the end of the process all have ultimately contributed (like contributory rivers) to a final resultant interpretant. (Ransdell 1980:175)[45]

The fate of the primary, secondary, etc. signs, once they have produced a translation (or a whole network of translations), is often as "tragic" as it is unescapable. Following the inexorable course of time, Peirce wrote, "The future grows into accomplished fact by a gradual unrolling. The new becomes gradually old. Its effects remain, but they dwindle in importance toward utter oblivion" (*NEM*4:52,1902). Unless the translated sign succeeds at some point in again finding and appealing to some mind willing and able to continue the process of its translation, it becomes dormant and its meaning becomes ossified, like "a law which has operated for the last time has ceased to exist as a law, except as a mere empty formula which it may be convenient to allow to remain" (*CP*:5.545,c.1902). Just as "all this Universe is perfused with signs" (*CP*:5.448,n.1,1905), it is perfused with translations --living agencies, that is, some of them active and full of energy, others not yet discredited, perhaps, but distinctly becoming outmoded. The translated signs populating our entire life-world, permeating it, are in different stages of either growth, vitality, and development, or of stagnancy, obsolescence, and finally death.

It has already been shown above that in translation the utterer (as a function of the object) and the interpreter (as a function of the interpretant) must not only be considered marginal to the action of the sign; more characteristically, in translation they are conflated into one, the translator's mind, who fulfills both functions alternately. This is, Peirce wrote, "the mind

---

45 See also Chapter 4, particularly its section on "Decision-tree vs. associative network". I also address this issue in my article on "Symbolic argument and beyond: A Peircean view on structuralist thought" (Gorlée 1992b).

into which the minds of utterer and interpreter have to be fused in order that any communication should take place. This mind may be called the commens" (*PW*:196-197,1906). The way in which the sign-making and the sign-using minds observe and experience the power of the sign is expressed in what Peirce called the "Intentional Interpretant" (Firstness of Thirdness) and "Effectual Interpretant" (Secondness of Thirdness), respectively; but not until both minds act together (i.e., not until there is a common intent) can a genuine Third or "Communicational Interpretant, or say the Cominterpretant" (*PW*:196,1906) be produced. In the kind of semiosis under investigation here, the product of this joint venture is the special (idealized and authorized) translation; but it is also the contract, the symbolic action in which the minds of promisor and promisee manifest their common purpose in the form of a rational, public, and conventional sign of law. This is a state of perfection which translations cannot normally attain.

The anatomy of semiosis is like the anatomy of a contract in which parties subordinate their personal needs and desires to a *quid pro quo* imposed entirely by the sign-in-action. Translation is analogous to both semiosis and contract --without, however, ever achieving the status of genuine Thirdness which is common to both genuine semiosis and the full-blown legal contract. The reason for the degenerate nature of translation is that the contracting parties not only lack individuality and performative power: also, there is no real bargain, no economic aspect, no exchange in which things of value are being put at stake, no gain or loss of capital (material and/or spiritual), and hence no penalties in case of default. In the absence of a *quid pro quo*, translation must be thought of as a truncated contract, one in which the translator makes a promise to him- or herself: a promise to oneself to do something (to produce an interpretant) not by acting (i.e., by interfering with the action of the power of the acting sign) but by letting the sign's intended meaning be transferred through his or her skillful mind. Pragmatically, translation is a private, non-enforceable promise[46]; and to assert it is an inconsequential affair, because

---

46 This is a unilateral promise, not a unilateral contract (such as a gift or a will). While all contracts are rooted in promise, the reverse is not true. See also the interesting parallelism with Wittgenstein's example of private experience: "Why can't my right hand give my left hand money? -- My right hand can put it into my left hand. My right hand can write a deed of gift and my left hand a receipt. -- But the further practical consequences would not be those of a gift. When the left hand has taken the money from the right, etc., we shall ask: 'Well, and what of it?'" (*PI*:1:268). Not coincidentally, Wittgenstein's "further practical consequences" correspond to the "effects that might conceivably have practical bearings" (*CP*:5.402;*W*3:266,1878) in Peirce's pragmatic maxim (discussed earlier in this Chapter, as well as in Chapter 3).

there is no point in making oneself believe what is asserted, and there is no penalty for breaking a promise to oneself[47]. The contract in translation is self-reflexive and specular. This means that its intentional component[48] (its Thirdness) is underdeveloped. It is, insofar as it is turned within itself, a recursive, self-sufficient system.

Concluding remarks

Translation lacks a proper *quid pro quo* (the sign of contractual agreement), because it lacks a full precontractual "trialogue" (object-utterer-sign) as well as a genuine contractual "trialogue" (sign-interpreter-interpretant). As a consequence, if it has a semiosic structure, it is definitely a degenerate semiosis, one in which the interacting elements (sign, object, interpretant) lack the Thirdness of explicit combined will, purpose, and intention. The threefold contractual nexus in translation shows clear signs of Firstness and, especially, Secondness. It is thus a semiotic activity based upon observation and experience and motivated by desire and feeling. If it must at the same time be considered a learning process in which the translator acquires knowledge about which mental attitude most efficiently brings out the power of the sign, final generalization (the creation of truly "hard" laws and their logical application or, in contractual terms, enforcement on particular cases) will remain forever out of reach. In contradistinction to the security provided through full contractual semiosis, translation is fallible: it engenders a series of evolving, revisable signs. Transposed into a logical key, translation is governed by (speculative) abduction and (experimental) induction, rather than by a (fully rational) deduction dominating and giving a special purpose to the other two, "lower" modes of reasoning. The final translation, equivalent to a full-blown contractual argument as well as genuine semiosis, is destined to remain an idealized model.

---

47 The translational contract is as much a pseudocontract as the following: "You say to yourself with great force, feeling, and seriousness that you commit yourself to make a thousand-dollar donation to your local classical music station. Surely there is something odd in saying that you have *promised* to do that. To whom have you promised? Perhaps to God --but this just makes the point that a personal promisee must be posited, a promisee who holds the reins of the obligation. Have you promised to yourself then? If to yourself, then you are free to release yourself in the same way that any other promisee may. When it comes time for performance you may release yourself on whatever grounds would have been morally sufficient for not making a contribution at that (later) time in the absence of a promise. A promise to oneself adds nothing to the moral grounds for making the contribution absent the promise" (Fried 1981:42).

48 As regards this, see Ransdell's cautionary remark, "Do not construe the term *intentional* as equivalent to or as implying *reflective* or *selfconscious*" (Ransdell 1980:151).

11. CONCLUSION AND RECOMMENDATIONS

"So then, the writer . . . feels that it is time to kiss this child good-by and relinquish it to its higher destiny . . .
(*CP*:5.414,1905)

Introductory remarks

For a book on translation written from a relational-semiotic viewpoint, the reader may still find its separate Chapters disjointed and contrived. For example, it may not be easy to understand what I conclude from my account of translation as semiosis, the latter a little-used but frequently-implied (both by Peirce) concept which may have remained overly general here; the Chapters discussing Wittgenstein's as well as (Walter) Benjamin's pseudosemiotic ideas on translation may be viewed as floating somewhat free from the rest of the book; learning about the scope and usage of the interpretant in its terminological and conceptual intricacies has not led to clear conclusions. And the numerous references to translation as a cosmic perspective, a holistic experience, sprinkled about the book, may be considered interesting but perhaps fanciful, or even vague, in a work on translation.

However, the generality of the argument here --the lack of practicality of its ideas and proposals-- is a reflection of the theoretical complexity of the sign-theoretical paradigm which has served as my guide. In contradistinction to the more concrete (and thus more readily applicable) theory of signs in Saussure's tradition, Peirce's semiotics works on a level of abstraction which is as intellectually stimulating as it is relatively inaccessible to practical application. It would therefore be unfair to hold forth simple usefulness and workability as criteria of its merits and claim to attention.

The goodness of scholarly argument depends on the unity of its logical texture. Peirce wrote that this implies that it should

> . . . trust rather to the multitude and variety of its arguments than to the conclusiveness of any one. Its reasoning should not form a chain which is no stronger than its weakest link, but a cable whose fibers may be ever so slender, provided they are sufficiently numerous and intimately connected. (*CP*:5.265,1893)[1]

Let me therefore conclude this book by knitting the threads of my argument together and weaving a logical cable out of the various idea-fibers, some still tenuous, some strong, which have so far been severally spun, and which cooperate in favor of some conclusions.

My pretensions are, and only can be, limited at this point. In accordance with Peirce's pragmati(ci)sm, a "scientific proposition", such as the one developed throughout this book, is

> . . . merely something you take up provisionally as being the proper hypothesis to try first and endeavor to refute. The only belief you --as a purely scientific man-- have about it is that it is adopted in accordance with a method which must lead to the truth in the long run. (*CP*:6.216,1898)

What I offer here to the community of scholars in terms of translational semiosis (which I will now rename "semiotranslation"), is a reasoned but strictly non-doctrinaire view[2]; no dogma but a an idealized model capable of yielding and accommodating, in present, past, as well as future, as many different programs and scenarios as there may be (proto)theories of translation conceived by any thinking mind.

Semiotranslation

My central premise has been that a Peircean semiotics provides crucial insights that may enrich both our theoretical accounts of translational phenomena and our observation of the phenomena themselves. Two themes run throughout: first, that we should consider seriously the logical implications of semiosis as a paradigm for (sign) translation (of which interlingual translation is only one ramification); second, that translation (in its manifold varieties, but concentrating

1 The metaphor is felicitous. Elsewhere Peirce wrote that pragmatic thought means "to perform the reflexion necessary to the straightening out the threads of thought and laying them orderly and parallel" (*MS*478:159,1903).

2 As Sebeok has often repeated, a doctrine implies the *generalized* acceptance of a principle as taught by a (limited) community of believers.

on Jakobson's language-based distinction, with particular emphasis on interlingual translation) exemplifies in its turn semiosis.

The decentering of language and linguistics within semiotics should, in my view, be interpreted positively, meaning that verbal signs are accompanied by, and build upon, nonverbal ones, so that a constant interaction takes place between them. This aspectual differentiation has important consequences for the varieties of translation between them. Jakobson's still relatively narrow concept of intersemiotic processes has been stretched to include not only the transmutation of verbal signs into nonverbal sign systems, but also the reverse operations. More recent advances into semiotics have made possible intersemioses of all kinds, not automatically involving language (Lawendowski 1978:280-281). The horizons of intersemiotic processes have thereby been so dramatically broadened that "We could be on the verge of a new era of freedom in intersemiotic studies, the opening of direct analytic relations between semiotic systems" (MacCannell and MacCannell 1982:153). In the pages of this book, no attempt has been made to deal systematically with nonverbal sign-processes. Although the discussions on sign degeneracy point, at least theoretically, into this direction, to study fully such processes in their mutual interactions with verbal sign-systems within the arts and the sciences is one task within semiotranslation which deserves to be carried out in the future. This project represents an enormous undertaking, the execution of which this study is not designed to accomplish. It would involve the classification, organization, and hierarchization (in a Peircean terminology: the categorization and semiotization) of the possible intersemioses. This sort of evaluation would also enable us to anticipate and plan the future behavior of these intersemioses vis-à-vis one another and the natural/cultural context in which they operate.

The implicit assumption in the game metaphor was that semiotranslation had a definite number of players as well as a well-defined beginning and end. As happens in any analogy, this one does not solve the entire range of problems implied. In fact, a Peircean player/translator appears to have resources which enable him or her to indefinitely continue the game. The contractual model has been additionally instrumental in showing that Peirce assimilated his game model of semiosis to the sort of open, self-generating system of which life on earth is the ultimate example. No one individual can realistically have the kind of unlimited resources enabling him or her to engage him- or herself in a play without end. This is one reason why it has been argued in these pages that, from a logical viewpoint, we do not deal here with a real person but with a (not necessarily human) mind; logically thinking but without being individualized; sporting special skills yet replaceable at any time by another mind better equipped to favor those strategies which stabilize a desired result while also allowing the trained player to give free play to the aspect of creativity. In semiotranslation we deal with a processuality in which creative feeling (Peirce's term for the chance element in any form of inquiry) is gradually integrated into the course of action by controlling it (that is, by experimenting with it and rationalizing it):

> The main element of habit is the tendency to repeat any action which has been performed before. It is a phenomenon at least coëxtensive with life, and may cover a still wider real realm. Imagine a large number of systems in some of which there is a decided tendency toward doing again what has once been done, in others a tendency against doing what has once been done, in others elements having one tendency and elements having the other. Let us consider the effects of chance upon these different systems. To fix our ideas suppose players playing with dice, some of their dice are worn down in such a way that the act of losing tends to make them lose again, others in such a way that the act of losing tends to make them win. The latter will lose much more slowly, yet after a sufficient length of time they will be in danger of being ruined and if the game is quite even, they will eventually be ruined and destroyed. Those whose dice are so worn as to reproduce the same effects, will be divided into two parts, one of which will quickly be destroyed, the other made stronger and stronger. For every kind of an organism, system, form, or compound, there is an absolute limit to a weakening process. It ends in destruction; there is no limit to strength. The result is that chance in its action tends to destroy the weak & increase the average strength of the objects remaining. Systems or compounds which have bad habits are quickly destroyed, those which have no habits follow the same course; only those which have good habits tend to survive. (*W*4:553,1883-1884;see also *CP*:2.653=*W*3:282-283,1878))

Semiosis explains and exemplifies the cumulative effect of the development of habits, rules, and strategies, embodied in interpretants; thereby strengthening the acquisition of habits and the force of their dynamic, and making it predictable. It also shows that this happens at the expense of other habits, which do not survive. The same is true for semiotranslation. By this post-Darwinian, normative token, "bad" translations (translations with Peirce's bad habits) represent falsity and will be lost in the game; while "good" translations (translations with good habits) will engender other, "better" translations which will again engender other translations, with better habits, and in the long run what shall ideally emerge from this stream of semioses is a translation fulfilling the conditions of truth. In logic (which is, for Peirce, coterminous with semiotics) truth is the final norm, the final cause.

From the Chapters of this book it has become clear that for Peirce sign translation was to be studied most fruitfully within the framework of pragmaticism, his version of pragmatism. This is why Peirce's thoughts on the pragmatic principle, particularly the later versions of it, are wholly and unreservedly applicable to the identification, description, and analysis of translation as a meaning-generating thought experiment in which a hypothesis is severally tested. The essence of Peirce's conception of sign translation is therefore reflected in his mature writings. To illustrate this, quotation of one especially revealing passage, from Peirce's article on "What pragmatism is" (published in 1905 in *The Monist*), is in order here:

> The rational meaning of every proposition lies in the future. How so? The meaning of a proposition is itself a proposition. Indeed, it is no other than the very proposition of which it is the meaning: it is a translation of it. But of the myriads of forms into which a proposition may be translated, what is that one which is to be called its very meaning? It is, according to the pragmaticist, that form in which the proposition becomes applicable to human conduct, not in these or those special circumstances, nor when one entertains this or that special design, but that form which is most directly applicable to self-control under every situation, and to every purpose. This is why he locates the meaning in future time; for future conduct is the only conduct that is subject to self-control. But in order that that form of the proposition which is to be taken as its meaning should be applicable to every situation and to every purpose upon which the proposition has any bearing, it must be simply the general description of all the experimental phenomena which the assertion of the proposition virtually predicts, For an experimental phenomenon is the fact asserted by the proposition that action of a certain description will have a certain kind of experimental result; and experimental results are the only results that can affect human conduct. No doubt, some unchanging idea may come to influence a man more than it had done; but only because some experience equivalent to an experiment has brought its truth home to him more intimately than before. Whenever a man acts purposively, he acts under a belief in some experimental phenomenon. Consequently, the sum of the experimental phenomena that a proposition implies makes up its entire bearing upon human conduct. (*CP*:5.427,1905)

This passage is crucial for a conception of sign translation addressing grades of clarity, evolving into a theory of meaning and consequently into a theory of truth. It eloquently reflects Peirce's pragmatic view of sign translation as a proposition-based (not a word-based!) processuality rooted in Thirdness: its futurity, rationality, multiplicity, infinity, generality, evolutionism, and logical practicality.

Contrary to Descartes and the Cartesian tradition, in which thought proceeds unrepresented (that is, without signs or metaphors), Peirce held that knowledge can only be accumulated through the triadic sign-relation and is grounded in the notion of the interpretant-sign:

> Since then its interpretant is itself a representation, it must have its own interpretant and there must be a series which cannot be completed by successive accretions of units. Yet the entire series must be represented and therefore its limit . . . Consequently, a representation can only have its being in a continuum. (*MS*478:147-148,1903)

Knowledge increases because of the goodness and liveliness (in Darwinian parlance: the fitness, hence the survival) of some habits of interpretation (interpretants) and the sterility of others. As demonstrated throughout the pages of this book, the generation of active interpretants is the very essence of semiosis, and hence of semiotranslation.

Peirce connected this with a formal definition of the sign:

> A sign is anything, A, in a relation, *r*, to something, B, its *object*, this relation, *r*, consisting in fitness to determine something so as to produce something, C, the *interpretant* of the sign, which shall be in the relation *r* to B, or at least in some analogous relation. Thus, the sign involves the idea of a possible endless series of interpretations. (*MS*107:25-26,1904)

In the sign relation, the sign is wholly determined by the object, while the interpretant is determined by the sign only to a point. The sign's meaning is thus, on the one hand, bound to remain, at least partly, indeterminate, and, on the other, thanks to this indeterminacy the threefold sign-relation becomes a process of inquiry and discovery, in which the shifting scope of precisely the "space between" the interpretant (or translation) and the object (or real state of affairs) via the sign is experimented with. It has been shown in this book that Peirce's idea of "some analogous relation" also squares nicely with the ideas of the later Wittgenstein and those of Benjamin, thereby resolving (within two entirely different frameworks: the socalled linguistic turn in analytic philosophy, and the cultural-romantic tradition in literary studies) the bipolar concept of translation as oscillating between "fidelity" and "infidelity".

The pseudo-contradictory nature of Peirce's account of the interpretant as a mercurial sign (goal-directed yet infinite, serial yet structural, diachronic yet synchronic, continuous yet incomplete, objective yet subjective, explicit yet implicit; in brief, generate yet degenerate) forbids that a univocal study of its role in translation be given. The picture is blurred if we add to this Peirce's outline of the variety of first and second objects and of the various, possibly overlapping or complementary, first, second, and third interpretants. The former distinction is clear-cut and has received ample attention here. The latter is an issue which could barely be touched upon in this book. A more thoroughgoing study of its theory and application to the translation phenomenon will have to wait until the present controversy among Peirce scholars about this key concept in Peirce's philosophy of signs, will have reached more of a consensus. The importance of this debate for a harmonious evolution of a future theory of semiotranslation should not be underestimated.

Emphasis has been placed, throughout the pages of this book, upon the idea of growth through sign-based translation. It is an exponent of the centerpiece of Peirce's theory of meaning, his pragmatic maxim, which is colored by a post-Darwinian evolutionary optimism. Indeed, the image of translation that emerges from a Peircean semiotics is one of change and growth, of expansion through transformation. Peirce wrote: "The third and noblest function of a Representation is Growth. . . [T]he process of growth is the *summum bonum*" (*MS*478:158,1903), and this is perhaps why equivalence (a central topic in any book on translation, including this one) was treated rather cursorily by Peirce. Now, again according to Peirce, "things grow all one way and none in the reverse sequence of states. It is easy to see that no conservative force can be the cause of that" (*MS*478:156,1903). On this view, semiotranslation is a unidirectional, future-oriented, cumulative, and irreversible process, one which advances, in successive instances, toward higher rationality, complexity, coherence, clarity, and determination, while progressively harmonizing chaotic, unorganized, and problematic translations (and elements and/or aspects of translations), as well as neutralizing dubious, misleading, and false ones. By steadily integrating new pieces of information on what Liszka (1990:52-53) calls "the indexical anchor of the process", the dynamical object, the sign's translations make its real meaning more complete, detailed, and continuous. Yet there will always remain informational lacunae. In like manner, a translation (that is, the rule of translation between sign and object as it crystallizes itself) is never finished and can always, however minimally, be improved upon.

Growth comes from change. The Peircean claim that this change is both teleological and non-conservative has been developed with particular imaginative power by Walter Benjamin, the theoretist of literary translation. Translations in Peirce's sense are elements in a series of interpretants, built up out of sign-internal and -external differences. Responsive to evolutionary theory, Peirce's view seems to be that the sign relation and all the elements which compose it (as well as those subsumed in it), are subject to constant change. Nothing is fixed in sign translation: the translating text-sign, the translated text-sign, the (non)linguistic codes, the translator, the translational and general-cultural norms, all are subject to continual interaction and change, even to a minute degree. And outside semiosis, the dynamical object is (as everything in lived and imagined reality) also evolving. If the world man experiences and the world he creates are both constantly expanding, man's knowledge of the world in all its manifestations, will not only be fallible but it will lag behind, requiring continuous criticism, improvement, and correction. Speculative though these ideas may appear, they are certainly relevant to a Peircean semiotranslation, and should be interesting topics for further research in this field.

One final point: Semiotranslation is also a kinetic situation (I borrow this term from Holmes) in a different sense. As often worded and reworded by this shrewd and pioneering scholar (a case in point is his paper on "The future of translation theory: A handful of theses", first presented in Moscow in 1978),

> No adequate general theory of translation can be developed before scholars have turned from a sentence-restricted linguistics to produce a full theory of the nature of texts. (Holmes 1988:100)

Mindful of Holmes's reasoned theses on this crucial (for translation theory, linguistics, and text theory) point and particularly inspired by Merrell's lucid and insightful work in the field of a semiotic text-theory[3], I would like to argue that a (Peircean) theory of texts should precede the development of a full and coherent translation-semiotics. From Peirce's point of view, written texts are organic (that is, growing) wholes characterized by the dynamic interdependence of, and interaction between, their parts. Not surprisingly, therefore, to develop a "text semiotics" based upon Peirce will be the object of my next research project[4].

Concluding remarks

This book reflects the state of my ideas on semiotranslation. For discussion in its separate Chapters I have chosen those features of Peirce's thought and those of translation theory, which opened up valuable possible directions of research in this combined field. My proposals here are tentative. They share the lot of all speculative theorizing: of trying to turn the shifting "airy-nothingness"[5] (*CP*:6.455,1908) of sheer word-clouds into a solid argument. A good deal more than this can (and should) be said about the semiotics of translation. Therefore, I devoutly hope my proposals will prove to be stimuli for future research.

---

3 See especially Merrell 1982.

4 See my *Reading the Signs: A Peirce-Based Text Semiotics* (Gorlée [in progress]).

5 Peirce constructed this noun from "airy nothings", which he borrowed from Shakespeare's *A Midsummer Night's Dream* (V,i,7).

12. BIBLIOGRAPHY

"A book may have three kinds of value. First, it may enrich your ideas with the mere possibilities, the mere ideas, that it suggests. Secondly, it may inform you of facts. Thirdly, it may submit, for your approbation, lines of thought and evidences of the reasonable connection of possibilities and facts"
(*CP*:4.597,1908)

Aguirre, Manuel (1981). A matter of choice. *Restant* 9-4:191-206.

Anderson, Myrdene, and Floyd Merrell (eds.) (1991). *On Semiotic Modeling* (=Approaches to Semiotics 97). Berlin and New York: Mouton de Gruyter.

Andrews, Edna (1990a). A dialogue on the sign: Can Peirce and Jakobson be reconciled? *Semiotica* 82-1/2:1-13.

Andrews, Edna (1990b). *Markedness Theory: The Union of Assymetry and Semiosis in Language* (=Sound and Meaning: The Roman Jakobson Series in Linguistics and Poetics). Durham, NC and London: Duke University Press.

Anspach, Silvia Simone (1987). Verbal-pictoric translation in Steinberg's labyrinth: Uniqueness, freedom and coercion. Deely and Evans (eds.) 1987:170-178.

Apter, Ronnie (1989). The impossible takes a little longer: Translating opera into English. *Translation Review* 31:27-37.

Arendt, Hannah (ed. and intro.) (1968). *Illuminations*. Trans. Harry Zohn. New York: Harcourt, Brace, and Jovanovich.

Artosi, Alberto (1981). Significato, giochi e traduzione. *Lingua e stile* 16-3:457-469.

Austin, J. L. (1962). *How To Do Things with Words*. Cambridge, MA: Harvard University Press.

Bailey, R. W., L. Matejka, and P. Steiner (eds.) (1978). *The Sign Around the World* (=Michigan Slavic Publications 9). Ann Arbor: University of Michigan Press.

Barthes, Roland (1964). *Le degré zéro de l'écriture, suivi de: Elements de sémiologie*. Paris: Gonthier.

Barthes, Roland (1967). *Le système de la mode*. Paris: Seuil.

Barthes, Roland (1985). *The Grain of the Voice: Interviews 1962-1980*. Trans. Linda Coverdale. London: Jonathan Cape.

Barthes, Roland ([1967]1986). *Elements of Semiology*. Rprt. Trans. Annette Lavers and Colin Smith. New York: Hill and Wang.

de Beaugrande, Robert (1978). *Factors in a Theory of Poetic Translating* (=Approaches to Translation Studies 5). Assen and Amsterdam: Van Gorcum.

Bellett, Ben (1978). *Adam's Dream: A Preface to Translation*. New York: Grove Press.

Benjamin, Andrew (1989). *Translation and the Nature of Philosophy: A New Theory of Words*. London and New York: Routledge.

Benjamin, Walter (1968). The task of the translator. Arendt (ed.) 1968:69-82.

Benveniste, Emile (1947). Le jeu comme structure. *Deucalion* 2:161-167.

Brent, Joseph (1993). *Charles Sanders Peirce: A Life*. Bloomington and Indianapolis: Indiana University Press.

Brock, Jarrett E. (1981a). An introduction to Peirce's theory of speech acts. *Transactions of the Charles S. Peirce Society* 18-4:319-326.

Brock, Jarrett E. (1981b). Peirce and Searle on assertion. Ketner, Ransdell, Eisele, Fisch, and Hardwick (eds.) 1981:281-287.

van den Broeck, Raymond (1978). The concept of equivalence in translation theory: Some critical reflections. Holmes, Lambert, and van den Broeck 1978:29-47.

van den Broeck, Raymond (1984-1985). Verschuivingen in de stilistiek van vertaalde literaire teksten: een semiotische benadering. *Linguistica Antverpiensia* 18-19:111-146.

van den Broeck, Raymond (1987). Jacques Derrida en de toren van Babel: deconstructie en vertaling. *Linguistica Antverpiensia* 21:127-148.

van den Broeck, Raymond (1988). Translation theory and deconstruction. *Linguistica Antverpiensia* 22:266-288.

van den Broeck, Raymond (1989). Literary conventions and translated literature. D'haen, Grübel, and Lethen (eds.) 1989:57-75.

Brower, Reuben A. (ed.) (1959). *On Translation* (=Harvard Studies in Comparative Literature 23). Cambridge, MA: Harvard University Press.

Bruss, Elizabeth W. (1978). Peirce and Jakobson on the nature of the sign. Bailey, Matejka, and Steiner (eds.) 1978:81-98.

Bunn, James H. (1981). *The Dimensionality of Signs, Tools and Models* (=Advances in Semiotics). Bloomington, IN: Indiana University Press.

Buzetti, Dino, and Maurizio Ferriani (eds.) (1987). *Speculative Grammar, Universal Grammar and Philosophical Analysis of Language* (=Amsterdam Studies in the Theory and History of Linguistic Science, Series 3: Studies in the History of the Language Sciences 42). Amsterdam and Philadelphia: John Benjamins.

Caillois, Roger (1961). *Man, Play, and Games.* Trans. Meyer Barash. New York: The Free Press of Glencoe.

Callaghan, W. J. (1986). Peirce's general theory of signs. *Semiotica* 61-1/2:123-161.

de Campos, Haroldo (1970). *Metalinguagem: Ensaios de Teoria e Crítica Literária* (=Nosso Tempo 5). Petrópolis: Editora Vozes.

de Campos, Haroldo (1981). *Deus e o Diabo no Fausto de Goethe: Marginália Fáustica* (=Colecao Signos). Sao Paulo: Perspectiva.

de Campos, Haroldo (1987a). Más allá del principio de la nostalgia (Sehnsucht). Trans. Néstor Perlongher. Derrida, Rodríguez Monegal, Campos, *et alii* 1987:135-146.

de Campos, Haroldo (1987b). Transblanco: Reflexión sobre la transcreación de "Blanco" de Octavio Paz, con una digresión sobre la teoría de la traducción del poeta mexicano. Trans. Carlos Pellegrino. Derrida, Rodríguez Monegal, Campos, *et alii* 1987:147-156.

Capra, Fritjof (1976). *The Tao of Physics: An Exploration of the Parallels between Modern Physics and Eastern Mysticism.* New York: Fontana/Collins.

Carlson, Lauri (1983). *Dialogue Games* (=Synthese Language Library 17). Dordrecht and London: Reidel.

Carroll, Michael (1980). A structuralist looks at chess. *Semiotica* 31-3/4:273-287.

Catford, J[ohn] C[unnison] (1965). *A Linguistic Theory of Translation: An Essay in Applied Linguistics.* London: Oxford University Press.

Cesarini, Remo, Donatella Ferrari Bravo, Paola Pugliatti, and Henri Quéré (1988). *Semiotica del frammento* (=Documenti di Lavoro e prepubblicazioni 170-171-172, serie B). Urbino: Centro Internazionale di Semiotica e di Linguistica.

Chatterjee, Ranjit (1986). Wittgenstein. Sebeok (gen.ed.) 1986:1162-1164.

Colapietro, Vincent M. (1989). *Peirce's Approach to the Self: A Semiotic Perspective on Human Subjectivity.* Albany, NY: State University of New York Press.

Day-Lewis, C. (1970). *On Translating Poetry* (=Jackson Knight Memorial Lecture 2). Abingdon-on-Thames: Abbey Press.

Deely, John, Brooke Williams, and Felicia Kruse (eds.) (1986). *Frontiers in Semiotics* (=Advances in Semiotics). Bloomington, IN: Indiana University Press.

Deely, John, and Jonathan Evans (eds.) (1987). *Semiotics 1986*. Lanham, New York, and London: University Press of America.

Deledalle, Gérard (1988). Épistémologie, logique et sémiotique. *Cruzeiro Semiótico* 8:13-21.

Deledalle-Rhodes, Janice (1991). Translation: The transposition of signs. *Cruzeiro Semiótico* 15:101-110.

Derrida, Jacques (1985). Des Tours de Babel. Graham (ed.) 1985:165-207.

Derrida, Jacques, Emir Rodríguez Monegal, Haroldo de Campos, *et alii* (1987). *Diseminario. La desconstrucción: otro descubrimiento de América*. Lisa Block de Behar (intro.). Montevideo: XYZ Editores.

D'haen, Theo, Rainer Grübel, and Helmut Lethen (eds.) (1989). *Convention and Innovation in Literature* (=Utrecht Publications in General and Comparative Literature 24). Amsterdam and Philadelphia: John Benjamins.

van Dijk, Teun A. (1978). *Tekstwetenschap: een interdisciplinaire inleiding* (=Aula 633). Utrecht and Antwerp: Spectrum.

Dil, Anwar S. (ed.) (1971). *Language, Culture, and Communication*. Stanford, CA: Stanford University Press.

Eco, Umberto (1976). Peirce's notion of interpretant. *Modern Language Notes* 91-6:1457-1472.

Eco, Umberto (1979). *A Theory of Semiotics* (=Advances in Semiotics 1). Rprt. Bloomington, IN: Indiana University Press.

Eco, Umberto (1984a). *Semiotics and the Philosophy of Language*. London and Basingstoke: MacMillan.

Eco, Umberto (1984b). The frames of comic "freedom". Eco, Ivanov, and Rector 1984:1-9.

Eco, Umberto (1986a). Roman Jakobson. Sebeok (gen. ed.) 1986:1:402-408.

Eco, Umberto (1986b). Dictionary vs. encyclopedia. Sebeok (gen. ed.) 1986:1:201-206.

Eco, Umberto (1987). The influence of Roman Jakobson on the development of semiotics. Krampen *et alii* (eds.) 1987:109-127.

Eco, Umberto (1990). *The Limits of Interpretation* (=Advances in Semiotics). Bloomington, IN: Indiana University Press.

Eco, Umberto, V. V. Ivanov, and Monica Rector (1984). *Carnival!*, Thomas A. Sebeok (ed.) (=Approaches to Semiotics 64). Berlin: Mouton de Gruyter.

Eco,Umberto, and Thomas A. Sebeok (eds.) (1983). *The Sign of Three: Dupin, Holmes, Peirce* (=Advances in Semiotics). Bloomington, IN: Indiana University Press.

Eisele, Carolyn (1979). *Studies in the Scientific and Mathematical Philosophy of Charles S. Peirce* (=Studies in Philosophy 29), R. M. Martin (ed). The Hague, Paris, and New York: Mouton.

Eisenberg, Malvin A[ron] (1984-1985). *Contracts* (=Gilbert Law Summaries). 11th ed. Chicago, IL: Harcourt Brace Jovanovich Legal and Professional Publications Inc.

Eschbach, Achim, and Wendelin Rader (eds.) (1980). *Literatursemiotik* (=Kodikas, Code; suppl.1). Tübingen: Günther Narr.

Esposito, Joseph L. (1980). *Evolutionary Metaphysics: The Development of Peirce's Theory of Categories*. Athens, OH: Ohio University Press.

Even-Zohar (ed.) (1990). Polysystem studies. *Poetics Today* 11-1.

Ferriani, Maurizio (1987). Peirce's analysis of the proposition: Grammatical and logical aspects. Buzetti and Ferriani (eds.) 1987:149-172.

Finch, Henry Leroy (1971). *Wittgenstein --The Early Philosophy: An Exposition of the "Tractatus"*. New York: Humanities Press.

Finch, Henry Leroy (1977). *Wittgenstein --The Later Philosophy: An Exposition of the "Philosophical Investigations"*. New York: Humanities Press.

Findler, Nicholas V. (1978). Computer poker. *Scientific American* 239-1:112-119.

Fisch, Max H. (1986). *Peirce, Semeiotic, and Pragmatism*, Kenneth Laine Ketner and Christian J. W. Kloesel (eds.). Bloomington, IN: Indiana University Press.

Fischer-Lichte, Erika (1986). Walter Benjamin's "Allegory." *American Journal of Semiotics* 4,1-2:151-168.

Fitzgerald, John J. (1966). *Peirce's Theory of Signs as Foundation for Pragmatism* (=Studies in Philosophy 1). The Hague and Paris: Mouton.

Fogelin, Robert J. (1976). *Wittgenstein* (=The Arguments of the Philosophers). London and Boston: Routledge and Kegan Paul.

Føllesdal, Dagfinn (1973). Indeterminacy of translation and the underdetermination of the theory of nature. *Dialectica* 27-3/4:289-301.

Frawley, William (1984a). Prolegomenon to a theory of translation. Frawley (ed.) 1984b:159-175.

Frawley, William (ed.) (1984b). *Translation: Literary, Linguistic, and Philosophical Perspectives*. Newark: University of Delaware Press *and* London and Toronto: Associate University Presses.

Fried, Charles (1981). *Contract as Promise: A Theory of Contractual Obligation*. Cambridge, MA: Harvard University Press.

Fuller, Lon L., and Melvin Aron Eisenberg (1981). *Basic Contract Law* (=American Casebook Series). 4th ed. St. Paul, MN: West Publishing Company.

Gardin, Jean-Claude (1974). *Les analyses de discours* (=Collection Zethos). Neuchâtel: Delachaux et Niestlé.

Gardner, Martin (1978). On Charles Sanders Peirce: Philosopher and gamesman. *Scientific American* 239-1:18-21.

de George, Richard T. (ed.) (1981). *Semiotic Themes* (=University of Kansas Humanistic Studies 53). Lawrence, KA: University of Kansas Publications.

Goodman, Nelson ([1968]1985). *Languages of Art: An Approach to a Theory of Symbols*. Indianapolis, IN: Hackett.

Goodrich, Peter (1987). *Legal Discourse: Studies in Linguistics, Rhetoric and Legal Analysis* (=Language, Discourse, Society). Houndmills and London: Macmillan.

Gorlée, Dinda L. (1986). Translation theory and the semiotics of games and decisions. Wollin and Lindquist (ed.) 1986:96-104.

Gorlée, Dinda L. (1987). Firstness, Secondness, Thirdness, and Cha(u)nciness. *Semiotica* 65-1/2:45-55.

Gorlée, Dinda L. (1989a). Wittgenstein, translation, and semiotics. *Target* 1/1:69-94.

Gorlée, Dinda L. (1989b). Wittgenstein et Peirce: Le jeu de langage. *Semiotica* 73-3/4:219-231.

Gorlée, Dinda L. (1990). Degeneracy: A reading of Peirce's writing. *Semiotica* 81-1/2:71-92.

Gorlée, Dinda L. (1991). "Traduttore traditore"?; Semiotic musings on translation. Grzybek (ed.) 1991:21-43.

Gorlée, Dinda L. (1992). Translation after Jakobson after Peirce. Tarasti (ed.) 1992:55-82.

Gorlée, Dinda L. (1992a). Fundamentals of the semiotics of Charles S. Peirce. *Livstegn* 8/1:74-117.

Gorlée, Dinda L. (1992b). Symbolic argument and beyond: A Peircean view on structuralist reasoning. *Poetics Today* 13-3:407-423.

Gorlée, Dinda L. (1992c). La semiótica triádica de Peirce y su aplicación a los géneros literarios. *Signa* 1:13-51.

Gorlée, Dinda L. (1993). *Semiotics and the Problem of Translation: With Special Reference to the Semiotics of Charles S. Peirce* (Doctoral Thesis, University of Amsterdam, 1993)

Gorlée, Dinda L. (in progress). *Reading the Signs: A Peirce-Based Text Semiotics*.

Graham, Joseph F. (ed., intro., and trans.) (1985). *Difference in Translation*. Ithaca: Cornell University Press.

Greenberg, Joseph H. (1971). Is language like a chess game? Dil (ed.) 1971:330-352.

Greenlee, Douglas (1973). *Peirce's Concept of Sign* (=Approaches to Semiotics, pbk ser. 5). The Hague: Mouton.

Greenlee, Douglas (1981). Translational meaning and articulational meaning. Ketner, Ransdell, Eisele, Fisch, and Hardwick (eds.) 1981:141-146.

Greimas, A.J., R. Jakobson, M.R. Mayenowa, *et alii* (eds.) (1970). *Sign - Lang uage - Culture* (=Janua Linguarum, ser. maior 1). The Hague and Paris: Mouton.

Greimas, Algirdas-Julien (1980). A propos du jeu. *Documents de Recherches EHEES-CNRS* 13:29-34.

Greimas, A[lgirdas]-J[ulien], and J[oseph] Courtés (1979). *Sémiotique: Dictionnaire raisonné de la théorie du langage* (=Langue linguistique communication). Paris: Hachette.

Greimas, A[lgirdas]-J[ulien], and J[oseph] Courtés (1982). *Semiotics and Language: An Analytical Dictionary* (=Advances in Semiotics). Trans. Larry Crist, Daniel Patte *et alii*. Bloomington, IN: Indiana University Press. (The original, *Sémiotique: Dictionnaire raisonné de la théorie du langage*, is from 1979)

Greimas, A[lgirdas]-J[ulien], and J[oseph] Courtés (1986). *Sémiotique: Dictionnaire raisonné de la théorie du langage II (Compléments, débats, propositions)* (=Langue linguistique communication). Paris: Hachette.

de Groot, Adrianus D. (1965). *Thought and Choice in Chess* (=Psychological Studies 4). Rev. ed. The Hague: Mouton.

Grzybek, Peter (ed.) (1991). *Cultural Semiotics: Facts und Facets* [Fakten und Facetten der Kultursemiotik] (=Bochumer Beiträge zur Semiotik 26). Bochum: Norbert Brockmeyer.

Güttgemans, Erhardt (1980). Ferdinand de Saussure: der redende Mensch als unbewusster Schachspieler. *Linguistica Biblica: Interdisziplinäre Zeitschrift für Theologie und Linguistik* 47:93-130.

Güttgemans, Erhardt (1982). Semiotik und Theologie: Thesen zu Geschichte und Funktion der Semiotik in der Theologie. *Zeitschrift für Semiotik* 4:151-168.

Hancher, Michael (1979). The classification of cooperative illocutionary acts. *Language in Society* 8:1-14.

Hardwick, Charles S. (1979). Peirce's influence on some British philosophers: A guess at the riddle. Ketner and Ransdell (eds.) 1979:25-30.

Harris, Roy (1987). *The Language Machine*. Ithaca, NY: Cornell University Press.

Hatim, Basil, and Ian Mason (1990). *Discourse and the Translator* (=Language in Social Life). London and New York: Longman.

Hawkes, Terence (1977). *Structuralism and Semiotics*. London: Methuen.

Hermans, Theo (1985a). Introduction: Translation studies and a new paradigm. Hermans (ed.) 1985b:7-15.

Hermans, Theo (ed.) (1985b). *The Manipulation of Literature: Studies in Literary Translation.* London and Sydney: Croom Helm.

Hilpinen, Risto (1982). On C. S. Peirce's theory of the proposition: Peirce as a precursor of game-theoretical semantics. *The Monist* 65-2:182-188.

Hintikka, Jaakko (1969). Quantification and the picture theory of language. *The Monist* 53:204-229.

Hintikka, Jaakko (1973). *Logic, Language-Games, and Information.* Oxford: Clarendon Press.

Hintikka, Merrill B., and Jaakko Hintikka (1986). *Investigating Wittgenstein.* Oxford: Basil Blackwell.

Hjelmslev, Louis ([1943]1969). *Prolegomena to a Theory of Language.* Madison: Univeristy of Wisconsin Press.

Holenstein, Elmar (1976). *Roman Jakobson's Approach to Language: Phenomenological Structuralism.* Trans. Catherine Schelbert and Tarcisius Schelbert. Bloomington and London: Indiana University Press.

Holmes, James S., José Lambert, and Raymond van den Broeck (eds.) (1978). *Literature and Translation: New Perspectives in Literary Studies.* Leuven: Acco.

Holmes, James S[tratton] (1988). *Translated! Papers on Literary Translation and Translation Studies* (=Approaches to Translation Studies 7). Raymond van den Broeck (intro.). Amsterdam: Rodopi.

Houle, Martha M. (1987). Play at work in semiotic theory. Deely and Evans (eds.) 1987:370-375.

Huizinga, Johan (1964). *Homo Ludens: A Study of the Play Element in Culture.* Boston: Beacon Press.

Hunter, J. F. M. (1980). Wittgenstein on Language and Games. *Philosophy* 55:293-302.

Innis, Robert E. (ed.) (1985). *Semiotics: An Introductory Anthology* (=Advances in Semiotics). Bloomington, IN: Indiana University Press.

Ivanov, Vjaceslav V. (1992). La traduction: Regard linguistique et sémiotique. *Meta* 37-1:9-17.

Jackson, Bernard S. (1992). Pour un modèle sémiotique de l'analogie du jeu en théorie du droit. *Revue Internationale de Sémiotique Juridique/International Journal for the Semiotics of Law* 5/13:55-90.

Jakobson, Roman ([1958]1971). Typological studies and their contribution to historical comparative linguistics. Jakobson 1971a:523-532.

Jakobson, Roman (1959). On linguistic aspects of translation. Brower (ed.) 1959:232-239.

Jakobson, Roman (1960). Concluding statement: Linguistics and poetics. Sebeok (ed.) 1960:350-377.

Jakobson, Roman (1961a). Linguistics and communication theory. Jakobson (ed.) 1961b:245-252.

Jakobson, Roman (ed.) (1961b). *Structure of Language and Its Mathematical Aspects* (=Proceedings of Symposia in Applied Mathematics 12). Providence, Rhode Island: American Mathematical Society.

Jakobson, Roman (1963). Parts and wholes in language. Lerner (ed.) 1963:157-162.

Jakobson, Roman (1967). *To Honor Roman Jakobson: Essays on the Occasion of his 70th Birthday*. 2 vols. The Hague: Mouton.

Jakobson, Roman (1971a). *Selected Writings I.* The Hague and Paris: Mouton.

Jakobson, Roman (1971b). *Selected Writings II.* The Hague and Paris: Mouton.

Jakobson, Roman (1977). A few remarks on Peirce, pathfinder in the science of language. *Modern Language Notes* 92:1026-1032.

Jakobson, Roman (1987). *Language in Literature*, Krystyna Pomorska, and Stephen Rudy (eds.). Cambridge,MA and London: Belknap Press of Harvard University Press.

Jakobson, Roman, and Linda Waugh (1979). *The Sound Shape of Language*. Bloomington: Indiana University Press.

Johansen, Jørgen Dines (1988). What is a text? Semiosis and textuality, a Peircian perspective. *Livstegn* 5:7-32.

Johansen, Jørgen Dines (1993). *Dialogic Semiosis: An Essay on Signs and Meaning* (=Advances in Semiotics). Bloomington: Indiana University Press. (Manuscript provided by the author)

Kaemmerling, Ekkehard (1980). Dramenübersetzung und semiotische Übersetzungsanalyse. *Va et vient*, Samuel Becketts Eigenübersetzung von *Come and Go* (1966) in einer den semantisch funktionalen Zuschauerbezug bedenkenden Analyse. Eschbach and Rader (eds.) (1980):2:55-85.

Kent, Beverley (1987). *Charles S. Peirce: Logic and the Classification of the Sciences*. Kingston and Montreal: McGill-Queen's University Press.

van Kesteren, Aloysius (1978). Equivalence relationships between source text and target text: Towards a typology on the basis of semiotics. Holmes, Lambert, and van den Broeck (eds.) 1978:48-68.

Ketner, Kenneth L., and Joseph M. Ransdell (eds.) (1979). Studies in Peirce's Semiotic: A Symposium by Members of the Institute for Studies in Pragmaticism (=Peirce Studies 1). Lubbock, TX: Institute for Studies in Pragmaticism.

Ketner, Kenneth L., Joseph M. Ransdell, Carolyn Eisele, Max H, Fisch, and Charles S. Hardwick (eds.) (1981). *Proceedings of the C. S. Peirce Bicentennial International Congress* (=Graduate Studies 23). Lubbock, TX: Texas Tech University.

Kevelson, Roberta (1977). Language-games as systematic metaphors. *Semiotica* 19-1/2:29-58.

Kevelson, Roberta (1985). Riddles, legal decisions, and Peirce's Existential Graphs. *Semiotica* 57-3/4:197-223.

Kevelson, Roberta (1988). *The Law as a System of Signs* (=Topics in Contemporary Semiotics). New York and London: Plenum.

Koller, Werner (1972). *Grundprobleme der Übersetzungstheorie, unter besonderer Berücksichtigung schwedisch-deutscher Übersetzungsfälle*. Bern and Munich: Francke Verlag.

Koller, Werner (1992). *Einführung in die Übersetzungswissenschaft* (=Uni-Taschenbücher 819). 4th, wholly revised ed. Heidelberg/Wiesbaden: Quelle & Meyer.

Krampen, Martin, Klaus Oehler, Roland Posner, Thomas A. Sebeok, and Thure von Uexküll (eds.) (1987). *Classics of Semiotics* (=Topics in Contemporary Semiotics). New York: Plenum.

Kristeva, Julia (1974). *La révolution du langage poétique. L'avant-garde à la fin du XIXème siècle: Lautréamont et Mallarmé*. Paris: Seuil.

Kurzon, Dennis (1986). *It Is Hereby Performed ... : Explorations in Legal Speech Acts* (=Pragmatics & Beyond). Amsterdam and Philadelphia: John Benjamins.

Ladmiral, Jean René (1979). *Traduire: théorèmes sur la traduction* (=Petite Bibliothèque Payot 366). Paris: Payot.

Lawendowski, Boguslaw P. (1978). On semiotic aspect[s] of translation. Sebeok (ed.) 1978:264-282.

Lefevere, André (1975). *Translating Poetry: Seven Strategies and a Blueprint* (=Approaches to Translation Studies 3). Assen: Van Gorcum.

Lerner, Daniel (ed.) (1963). *Parts and Wholes*. New York: The Free Press of Glencoe *and* London: MacMillan.

Lévi-Strauss, Claude (1958). *Anthropologie structurale*. Paris: Plon.

Lévi-Strauss, Claude (1960). On manipulated sociological models. *Bijdragen tot de Taal-, Land- en Volkenkunde* 116:45-54.

Levy, Jiri (1967). Translation as a decision process. Jakobson 1967:2:1171-1182.

Levy, Jiri (1969). *Die literarische Übersetzung. Theorie einer Kunstgattung*. Trans. Walter Schamschula. Frankfurt a.M./Bonn: Athenäum Verlag. (The original, *Umení prekladu*, is from 1963)

Levy, Jiri (1970). Generative poetics. Greimas, Jakobson, Mayenowa, *et alii* (eds.) 1970:548-557.

Liszka, James Jakób (1981). Peirce and Jakobson: Towards a structuralist reconstruction of Peirce. *Transactions of the Charles S. Peirce Society* 17:41-61.

Liszka, James Jakób (1990). Peirce's interpretant. *Transactions of the Charles S. Peirce Society* 26-1:17-62.

Lotman, Juri M. (1972). *Die Struktur literarischer Texte*. Trans. Rolf-Dietrich Keil. Munich: Wilhelm Fink.

Lotman, Juri M. (1990). *Universe of the Mind: A Semiotic Theory of Culture*. Trans. Ann Shukman. Intro. Umberto Eco. Bloomington and Indianapolis, IN: Indiana University Press.

Lotman, Juri M. (1992). Le phénomène de la culture. *Meta* 37-1:18-28.

Luce, R. Duncan and Raiffa, Howard (1967). *Games and Decisions: Introduction and Critical Survey*. New York: John Wiley.

Lucid, Daniel P. (ed.) (1988). *Soviet Semiotics: An Anthology*. 2nd ed. With a new foreword by Thomas A. Sebeok. Baltimore and London: Johns Hopkins University Press.

Ludskanov, Alexander (1975). A semiotic approach to the theory of translation. *Language Sciences* 35 (April):5-8.

van Luxemburg-Albers, Anneke (1990). Vertaalwetenschap en het konijn van Willard Van Orman Quine. *Linguistica Antverpiensia* 24:201-215.

MacCannell, Dean, and Juliet Flower MacCannell (1982). *The Time of the Sign: A Semiotic Interpretation of Modern Culture* (=Advances in Semiotics). Bloomington,IN: Indiana University Press.

Mahony, Patrick (1982). Towards an understanding of translation in psychoanalysis. *Meta* 27-1:63-71.

de Man, Paul (1979). *Allegories of Reading: Figural Language in Rousseau, Nietzsche, Rilke, and Proust*. New Haven and London: Yale University Press.

de Man, Paul (1985). Conclusions: Walter Benjamin's "The task of the translator". *Yale French Studies* 69:25-46.

Marcus, Solomon (1975). Eight types of translation in the scientific language. *Revue Roumaine de Linguistique* 20-4:375-376.

Martinet, Hanne (1985). Why do we know how to translate what? *Semiotica* 55-1/2:19-42.

Matthews, Robert J. (1985). What did Archimedes mean by 'χρυσός'? Graham (ed.) 1985:149-164.

Menninghaus, Winfried (1980). *Walter Benjamins Theorie der Sprachmagie*. Frankfurt am Main: Suhrkamp.

Merrell, Floyd (1982). *Semiotic Foundations: Steps Toward an Epistemology of Written Texts* (=Advances in Semiotics). Bloomington, IN: Indiana University Press.

Merrell, Floyd (1991). *Signs Becoming Signs: Our Perfusive, Pervasive Universe* (=Advances in Semiotics). Bloomington and Indianapolis, IN: Indiana University Press.

Morgenstern, Oskar (1968). Game theory: Theoretical aspects. Sills (ed.) 1968-1979:6:62-69.

Morris, Charles W. (1938). Foundations of the theory of signs. *Foundations of the Unity of Science*, vol.1, nr.2:1-14. Chicago, IL: University of Chicago Press.

Morris, Charles W. (1971). *Writings on the General Theory of Signs*. The Hague: Mouton.

Murphey, Murray G. (1961). *The Development of Peirce's Philosophy*. Cambridge, MA: Harvard University Press.

Nabokov, Vladimir (1941). The art of translation. *The New Republic* 105 (August 4):160-162.

Nagel, Ernest (1963). Wholes, sums, and organic unities. Lerner (ed.) 1963:135-155.

von Neumann, John, and Oskar Morgenstern ([1944]1964). *Theory of Games and Economic Behavior*. Princeton, NJ: Princeton University Press.

Nida, Eugene A. (1964). *Toward a Science of Translating: With Special Reference to Principles and Procedures Involved in Bible Translating*. Leiden: Brill.

Niklas, Ursula (1988). On the practical and the theoretical in Charles S. Peirce. *Versus: Quaderni di Studi Semiotici* 49:31-38.

Nöth, Winfried (1990). *Handbook of Semiotics* (=Advances in Semiotics). Bloomington and Indianapolis, IN: Indiana University Press.

de Oliveira, Ana Claudia, and Lucia Santaella (eds.) (1987). *Semiótica da cultura, arte e arquitetura* (=Cadernos PUC 29). Sao Paulo: Educ.

Pazukhin, Roscislaw (1985). An innocent amusement with signs, tools, and models. *Semiotica* 55-3/4:265-273.

Peirce, Charles Sanders (1931-1966). *Collected Papers of Charles Sanders Peirce*, Charles Hartshorne, Paul Weiss, and Arthur W. Burks (eds.). 8 vols. Cambridge, MA: Belknap Press, Harvard University Press. (In-text references are to *CP*, followed by volume and paragraph numbers)

Peirce, Charles Sanders (1953). *Charles S. Peirce's Letters to Lady Welby*, Irwin C. Lieb (ed.). New Haven: Whitlock.

Peirce, Charles Sanders (1955). *Philosophical Writings of Peirce*, Justus Buchler (ed.). New York: Dover.

Peirce, Charles Sanders ([1958]1966). *Charles S. Peirce: Selected Writings*, Philip P. Wiener (ed.). New York: Dover. (Republication of the 1958 original edition, *Values in a Universe of Chance*) (In-text references are to *SW*, followed by page number)

Peirce, Charles Sanders (1977). *Semiotic and Significs: The Correspondence between Charles S. Peirce and Victoria Lady Welby*, Charles S. Hardwick (ed.). Bloomington and London: Indiana University Press. (In-text references are to *PW*, followed by page number)

Peirce, Charles Sanders (1979). *The New Elements of Mathematics by Charles S. Peirce*, Carolyn Eisele (ed.). 4 vols. The Hague and Paris: Mouton/Atlantic Highlands, NJ: Humanities Press. (In-text references are to *NEM*, followed by volume and page numbers)

Peirce, Charles Sanders (1982-1989). *Writings of Charles S. Peirce: A Chronological Edition*, Max Fisch, Edward C. Moore, Christian J. W. Kloesel, *et alii* (eds.). 4 vols. Bloomington, IN: Indiana University Press. (In-text references are to *W*, followed by volume number and page number)

Peirce, Charles Sanders. Unpublished manuscripts. Peirce Edition Project. Indiana University-Purdue University at Indianapolis. (In-text references are to *MS*, followed by manuscript number and page number)

Pelc, Jerzy, Thomas A. Sebeok, Edward Stankiewicz, and Thomas G. Winner (eds.) (1984). *Sign, System and Function* (=Approaches to Semiotics 67). Berlin, New York, and Amsterdam: Mouton.

Pencak, William (1991). Charles Sanders Peirce, historian and semiotician. *Semiotica* 83-3/4:311-332.

Petöfi, János S. (1983a). Verbal-Semiotik, Texttheorie, Übersetzungstheorie. Petöfi (ed.) 1983b:295-309.

Petöfi, János S. (ed.) (1983b). *Texte und Sachverhalte: Aspekte der Wort- und Textbedeutung* (=Papiere zur Textlinguistik / Papers in Textlinguistics 42). Hamburg: Helmut Buske.

Pharies, David A. (1985). *Charles S. Peirce and the Linguistic Sign* (=Foundations of Semiotics 9). Amsterdam: John Benjamins.

Plaza, Julio (1981). Reflections of and on theories of translation. *Dispositio* 6-17/18:45-91.

Plaza, Julio (1985). *Sobre traducao intersemiótica* (Doctoral Thesis, Catholic University of Sao Paulo, 1985).

Plaza, Julio (1987a). *Traducao intersemiótica* (=Estudos 93). Sao Paulo: Perspectiva.

Plaza, Julio (1987b). A arte da traducao intersemiótica. Oliveira and Santaella (eds.) 1987:161-167.

Popovic, Anton (c.1975). *Dictionary for the Analysis of Literary Translation.* Edmonton, Alta.: Department of Comparative Literature, University of Alberta.

Prewitt, Terry, John Deely, and Karen Haworth (eds.) (1988). *Semiotics 1988.* Lanham, New York, and London: University Press of America.

Propp, Vladimir (1958). *Morphology of the Folktale.* Bloomington, IN: Indiana University Research Center.

Quéré, Henri (1988). Sur le fragment. Cesarini, Bravo, Pugliatti, and Quéré 1988:44-56.

Quine, William Van Orman (1960). *Word and Object.* Cambridge, MA: M.I.T. Press.

Raffel, Burton (1988). *The Art of Translating Poetry.* University Park, PA: Pennsylvania State University Press.

Ransdell, Joseph (1976). *The Pursuit of Wisdom: A History of Philosophy.* Santa Barbara, CA: Intelman Books.

Ransdell, Joseph (1980). Semiotics and linguistics. Rauch and Carr (eds.) 1980:135-185.

Ransdell, Joseph (1981). Semiotic causation: A partial explication. Ketner, Ransdell, Eisele, Fisch, and Hardwick (eds.) 1981:201-206.

Ransdell, Joseph (1986a). Semiotic objectivity. Deely, Williams, and Kruse (eds.) 1986:236-254.

Ransdell, Joseph (1986b). Charles Sanders Peirce. Sebeok (gen. ed.) 1986:2:673-695.

Rapoport, Anatol (1961). *Fights, Games, and Debates.* 2nd. prt. Ann Arbor: Michigan University Press.

Rauch, Irmengard, and Gerald F. Carr (eds.) (1980). *The Signifying Animal: The Grammar of Language and Experience* (=Advances in Semiotics). Bloomington, IN: Indiana University Press.

Rauch, Irmengard (1986). Semiotics and linguistics. Sebeok (gen. ed.) 1986:2:912-920.

Rethoré, Joelle (1988). *La Sémiotique linguistique de C. S. Peirce: Propositions pour une grammaire phanéroscopique.* A.N.R.T., Université de Lille III (Doctoral Thesis, University of Perpignan, 1988).

Robin, Richard S. (1967). *Annotated Catalogue of the Papers of Charles S. Peirce.* Amherst: University of Massachusetts Press.

Robinson, Douglas (1991). *The Translator's Turn* (=Parallax: Re-visions of Culture and Society). Baltimore and London: Johns Hopkins University Press.

Rorty, Richard (1961). Pragmatism, categories, and language. *Philosophical Review* (April):197-223.

Rosensohn, William L. (1974). *The Phenomenology of Charles S. Peirce: From the Doctrine of Categories to Phaneroscopy* (=Philosophical Currents 10). Amsterdam: Grüner.

Saarinen, Esa (ed.) (1979). *Game-Theoretical Semantics*. Dordrecht: Reidel.

Sanders, Gary (1970). Peirce's sixty-six signs? *Transactions of the Charles S. Peirce Society* 6-1:3-16.

Santaella Braga, Lucia (1991). Instinct, logic, or the logic of instinct. *Semiotica* 83-1/2:123-141.

Saumjan, Sebastian K. (1970). Semiotics and the theory of generative grammars. Greimas, Jakobson, Mayenowa, *et alii* (eds.) 1970:244-255.

de Saussure, Ferdinand (1966). *Course in General Linguistics*, Charles Bally and Albert Sechehaye (eds.). Trans., intro., and notes by Wade Baskin. New York: McGraw-Hill. (The original, *Cours de linguistique générale*, is from 1916)

Savan, David (1983). Toward a refutation of semiotic idealism. *Recherches Sémiotiques/Semiotic Inquiry* 3(1):1-8.

Savan, David (1987-1988). *An Introduction to C. S. Peirce's Full System of Semeiotic* (=Monograph Series of the Toronto Semiotic Circle 1). Toronto: Victoria College of the University of Toronto.

Schmitter, Peter, *et alii* (1986). Humboldt, Wilhelm von. Sebeok (gen. ed.) 1986:317-323.

Schwayder, D. S. (1969). Wittgenstein on mathematics. Winch (ed.) 1969:66-116.

Searle, John R. (1969). *Speech Acts: An Essay in the Philosophy of Language*. Cambridge: Cambridge University Press.

Searle, John R. (1976). A classification of illocutionary acts. *Language in Society* 5:1-23.

Sebeok, Thomas A. (ed.) (1960). *Style in Language*. Cambridge, MA: MIT Press.

Sebeok, Thomas A. (1975). Six species of signs: Some propositions and strictures. *Semiotica* 13-3:233-260.

Sebeok, Thomas A. (ed.) (1978). *Sight, Sound, and Sense* (=Advances in Semiotics). Bloomington and London: Indiana University Press.

Sebeok, Thomas A. (1981). *The Play of Musement* (=Advances in Semiotics). Bloomington, IN: Indiana University Press.

Sebeok, Thomas A. (1984). Signs of life. *International Semiotic Spectrum* 2:1-2.

Sebeok, Thomas A. (1985a). Zoosemiotic components of human communication. Innis (ed.) 1985:292-324.

Sebeok, Thomas A. (1985b). *Contributions to the Doctrine of Signs* (=Sources in Semiotics 4). Lanham, New York, and London: University Press of America.

Sebeok, Thomas A. (gen. ed.) (1986). *Encyclopedic Dictionary of Semiotics* (=Approaches to Semiotics 73). 3 vols. Berlin: Mouton de Gruyter.

Sebeok, Thomas A. (1991). *Semiotics in the United States* (=Advances in Semiotics). Bloomington and Indianapolis, IN: Indiana University Press.

Sebeok, Thomas A., and Jean Umiker-Sebeok (eds.) (1991). *The Semiotic Web 1990: Recent Developments in Theory and History* (=Approaches to Semiotics 100). Berlin and New York: Mouton de Gruyter.

Shannon, Claude E., and Warren Weaver (1949). *The Mathematical Theory of Communication*. Urbana, IL: University of Illinois Press.

Shapiro, Michael (1980). Poetry and language, "considered as semeiotic." *Transactions of the Charles S. Peirce Society* 16:97-117.

Shapiro, Michael (1983). *The Sense of Grammar: Language as Semeiotic*. Bloomington, IN: Indiana University Press.

Sheriff, John K. (1981). Charles S. Peirce and the semiotics of literature. De George (ed.) 1981:51-74.

Sheriff, John K. (1989). *The Fate of Meaning: Charles Peirce, Structuralism, and Literature*. Princeton, NJ: Princeton University Press.

Short, Thomas L. (1986a). What they said in Amsterdam: Peirce's semiotic today. *Semiotica* 60-1/2:103-128.

Short, Thomas L. (1986b). Life among the legisigns. Deely, Williams, and Kruse (eds.) 1986:105-119.

Short, Thomas L. (1988). Why we prefer Peirce to Saussure. Prewitt, Deely, and Haworth (eds.) 1988:124-130.

Sills, David L. (ed.) (1968-1979). *International Encyclopedia of the Social Sciences*. 18 vols. New York: MacMillan and Free Press.

Siskin, Jay (1987). A medieval semiotics of translation. *Semiotica* 63-1/2:129-142.

Sonesson, Göran (1989). *Pictorial Concepts: Inquiries into the Semiotic Heritage and Its Relevance for the Analysis of the Visual World* (=Aris Nova Series 4). Lund: Lund University Press.

Spinks, C. W. (1991). Diagrammatic thinking and the portraiture of thought. Anderson and Merrell (eds.) 1991:441-481.

Stanosz, Barbara (1990). Radical translation, actual translation, and the problem of meaning. *Semiotica* 80-1/2:81-88.

Steiner, George (1975). *After Babel: Aspects of Language and Translation*. Oxford and London: Oxford University Press.

Sturrock, John (1991). On Jakobson on translation. Sebeok and Umiker-Sebeok (eds.) 1991:307-321.

Tarasti, Eero (ed.) (1992). *Center and Periphery in Representations and Institutions* (=Acta Semiotica Fennica 1; Publications of the International Semiotics Institute 2). Imatra: International Semiotics Institute.

Taylor, Donald W. (1968). Problem solving. Sills (ed.) 1968-1979:12:505-511.

Toury, Gideon (1978). The nature and role of norms in literary translation. Holmes, Lambert, and van den Broeck (eds.) 1978:83-99.

Toury, Gideon (1980a). *In Search of a Theory of Translation.* Tel Aviv: The Porter Institute for Poetics and Semiotics, Tel Aviv University.

Toury, Gideon (1980b). Communication in translated texts: A semiotic approach. Wilss (ed.) 1980:99-109.

Toury, Gideon (1986). Translation: A cultural-semiotic perspective. Sebeok (gen. ed.) 1986:2:1111-1124.

Toury, Gideon (ed.) (1987). *Translation Across Cultures.* New Delhi: Bahri Publications Private Limited.

Trabant, Jürgen (1986). *Apeliotes oder Der Sinn der Sprache. Wilhelm von Humboldts Sprach-Bild* (=Supplemente 8). Munich: Wilhelm Fink.

Verburg, P. A. (1961). Het schaakspel-model bij Ferdinand de Saussure en bij Wittgenstein. *Wijsgerig perspectief op maatschappij en wetenschap* 1-5:227-234.

Vernadsky, V. I. (1926). *Biosfera.* Leningrad.

Waugh, Linda R. (1984). Some remarks on the nature of the linguistic sign. Pelc, Sebeok, Stankiewicz, and Winner (eds.) 1984:389-438.

Weiss, Paul, and Arthur Burks (1945). Peirce's sixty-six signs. *The Journal of Philosophy* 42-14:383-388.

Wilss, Wolfram (1977). *Übersetzungswissenschaft: Probleme und Methoden.* Stuttgart: Ernst Klett.

Wilss, Wolfram (ed.) (1980). *Semiotik und Übersetzen* (=Kodikas/Code;suppl.4). Tübingen: Günther Narr.

Wilss, Wolfram (1988). *Kognition und Übersetzen. Zu Theorie und Praxis der menschlichen und der maschinellen Übersetzung* (=Konzepte der Sprach- und Literaturwissenschaft 41). Tübingen: Max Niemeyer Verlag.

Winch, Peter (ed.) (1969). *Studies in the Philosophy of Wittgenstein* (=International Library of Philosophy and Scientific Method). London: Routledge & Kegan Paul.

Wincor, Richard (1970). *The Law of Contract* (=Legal Almanac Series 36). Dobs Ferry, NY: Oceana Publications.

Wittgenstein, Ludwig (1931). *Typescript 211.* Unpublished Cornell MS211 (Typed version of MS111).

Wittgenstein, Ludwig ([1922]1960). *Tractatus Logico-Philosophicus* (=International Library of Psychology, Philosophy and Scientific Method). Trans. C. K. Ogden. 8th reprt. London: Routledge and Kegan Paul. (In-text references are to *TLP*, followed by paragraph numbers)

Wittgenstein, Ludwig ([1953]1968). *Philosophische Untersuchungen - Philosophical Investigations*, G. E. M. Anscombe and R. Rhees (eds.). Trans. G. E. M. Anscombe. Rprt. Oxford: Basil Blackwell. (In-text references are to *PI*, followed by 1 --Part I-- and paragraph number, or 2 --Part II-- and page number)

Wittgenstein, Ludwig ([1958]1960). *The Blue and Brown Books (Preliminary Studies for the "Philosophical Investigations", Generally Known as The Blue and Brown Books)*, Rush Rhees (ed.). Rprt. Oxford: Basil Blackwell. (In-text references are to *BBB*, followed by page number)

Wittgenstein, Ludwig (1967). *Zettel*, G. E. M. Anscombe and G. H. von Wright (eds.). Trans. G. E. M. Anscombe. Oxford: Basil Blackwell. (In-text references are to Z, followed by paragraph number)

Wittgenstein, Ludwig (1969). *Über Gewissheit - On Certainty*, G. E. M. Anscombe and G. H. von Wright (eds.). Trans. Denis Paul and G. E. M. Anscombe. Oxford: Basil Blackwell.

Wittgenstein, Ludwig (1980a). *Remarks on the Philosophy of Psychology*, I, G. E. M. Anscombe and G. H. von Wright (eds.). Trans. G. E. M. Anscombe. Oxford: Basil Blackwell. (In-text references are to *RPP:1*, followed by paragraph number)

Wittgenstein, Ludwig (1980b). *Remarks on the Philosophy of Psychology*, II, G. H. von Wright and Heikki Nyman (eds.). Trans. C. G. Luckhardt and M. A. E. Aue. Oxford: Basil Blackwell. (In-text references are to *RPP:2*, followed by paragraph number)

Wittgenstein, Ludwig (1980c). *Culture and Value*, G. H. von Wright and Heikki Nyman (eds.). Trans. Peter Winch. Oxford: Basil Blackwell.

Wollin, Lars, and Hans Linquist (ed.) (1986). *Translation Studies in Scandinavia: Proceedings from the Scandinavian Symposium on Translation Theory (SSOTT) II* (=Lund Studies in English 75). Lund: Gleerup.

13. INDEX OF NAMES